Contents

Data abstraction and program design
From object-based to object-oriented programming

Second edition

Rod Ellis
University of Westminster

UCL
PRESS

First published 1991 by Pitman Publishing.

Second edition 1996 by UCL Press.

UCL Press Limited
University College London
Gower Street
London WC1E 6BT

and
1900 Frost Road, Suite 101
Bristol
Pennsylvania 19007-1598

The name of University College London (UCL) is a registered
trade mark used by UCL Press with the consent of the owner.

British Library Cataloguing in Publication Data
A catalogue record for this book is available from the British Library.

ISBN: 1-85728-570-0 PB

Typeset in Palatino.
Printed and bound by Bookcraft (Bath) Ltd.

Preface to the first edition

The term *object-based* is used to denote a common conceptual region shared by modern "conventional" languages, such as Modula-2 and Ada, and the object-oriented languages Smalltalk, C++, Eiffel, etc. This region not only encompasses specifically linguistic concepts, of which data abstraction possesses a significance suggested by its prominence in the title of this book, but also an approach to software design without which these concepts lose much of their significance. In other words, these languages are not neutral in respect of the methods of software design with which they are utilized. Their features can be understood, and exploited successfully, only in the light of the design philosophy, in its various versions, that informed their development.

This book provides an introduction to object-based techniques of software construction. Its intended readership falls into two categories:

1. Software engineering students in higher education who have completed their initial programming courses, probably in a language such as Pascal. The text introduces them to the concepts of "programming in the large" and develops these along an object-based trajectory. As such the book will form a useful basis for an academic course suitable for the second year of a software engineering degree programme.

2. Experienced software engineers who have come across references to object-based techniques in the computer press, or by word of mouth, and who wish to update their knowledge in this area. The treatment in relation to this readership should enable the acquisition of a useful level of competence in some or all of the techniques dealt with, in conjunction with further reading selected from the bibliographic notes.

In writing a book with this objective two possible alternative approaches suggest themselves. The first, more radical approach, assumes no prior knowledge on the part of the reader and discusses object-based concepts without reference to other, more familiar techniques. The second accepts that very few readers are likely to approach the subject with a mind innocent of programming experience and knowledge, and accordingly attempts to modify the "mind-set" of its intended readership, by working from the reasonably familiar to the unknown in a gradual development.

This latter approach has been adopted for this book, in recognition of its intended readership. Thus the issues are developed through a progression from a Pascal context, through recognizable developments of Pascal, to the fairly remote areas of algebraic specification and object-oriented programming languages and techniques. The central, unifying theme of data abstraction is particularly useful in this context in providing a bridge from conventional to object-based techniques.

Part of the motivation underlying its writing was the recognition of the difficulty that the average student (and the above-average student for that matter) has in coming to terms with the concept of "programming in the large", or "architectural" software design. This difficulty, which is endemic to the technology, is often exacerbated by the typical programming methodology course which, with its emphasis on "programming in the small", or the detailed implementation of algorithms, provides a set of skills largely different from that involved in high-level, structural design. This emphasis induces a fascination with imperative detail that is extremely difficult to displace. The function of Chapter 1 is, accordingly, to get the reader to think in terms of "programming in the large", or high-level design, to encourage an appreciation of the importance of defining software components in terms of their behaviour rather than their implementation, and to view success in this high-level design activity in terms of its outcome in supporting apparently mundane qualities such as modifiability and maintainability.

Readers who are experienced in software production may well find that Chapter 1 is preaching to the converted, and prefer to skip to Chapter 2. This interprets the criteria of good design identified in Chapter 1 in a more specifically software orientated context, articulated in terms of the vocabulary of modular software design. These ideas are not new, although their recognition in many works on software design seems fairly scanty.

Chapter 3 considers the support provided for the achievement of good modular design by conventional programming languages, for which Pascal is taken as the model. An examination of the deficiencies that this discussion reveals leads to an appreciation of the need for a new program structure – the data abstraction – the ubiquity of which, to program design, forms a core theme of the book.

Chapters 4 and 5 continue the discussion of language design issues by introducing two descendants of Pascal, Modula-2 and Ada, from the particular standpoint of their support for the data abstraction. The aim of these chapters is to convey the essential features of these languages while, particularly in the case of Ada, avoiding becoming enmeshed in detailed complexity.

The first five chapters approach software design from an analytic viewpoint – *what* constitutes good design and how it can be reinforced by linguistic features. The next two chapters consider design as a synthetic issue

– *how* design is carried out as an activity so as to achieve the goals defined earlier, using the tool of the data abstraction.

Chapter 6 is a case study based on a well-known paper by Parnas, showing how the criteria introduced in earlier chapters can be used to evaluate alternative approaches to design; and how information hiding, a quality closely related to the use of data abstraction, can be "designed into" a system. Chapter 7 develops this idea but from a different standpoint – a consideration of the application and implementation domains – leading to an exposition of object-oriented design.

A subsidiary theme is developed strongly in the second half of the book: software reuse, and its implications for design. The qualities of integrity and encapsulation conferred by the data abstraction provide the necessary syntactical support for reusable software components, but are not in themselves sufficient to ensure reusability. The nature of the requirements for reuse are discussed in Chapter 8 in a mainly Ada context, but leading to ideas going beyond Ada.

Chapter 8 can be seen as a bridge to two different facets of reuse. The first arises from the obligation of the writer or supplier of a software component to define clearly the semantics of its use. It is precisely those qualities of information hiding, of separation of interface from implementation detail, that make the communication of the semantics of these interfaces a critical issue – it is neither desirable nor, often, possible for the user of such a component to determine its correct usage by inspecting the code that realizes its implementation. In Chapter 9 the necessity for formal, or mathematical, semantic specification techniques is discussed, as a precursor to an introduction to a particular formal technique – algebraic specification – that has found favour as the most appropriate for specifying components based on the data abstraction.

The second of these facets involves the deployment of a new programming paradigm – object-oriented programming – that combines data abstraction and reuse in a way that both contrasts with and parallels the Modula-2/Ada approach. Chapter 10 presents the major features of the object-oriented paradigm while Chapter 11 contains a comparison of the characteristics of a representative selection of object-oriented programming languages.

Finally, Chapter 12 reviews the contribution made by the data abstraction to modern approaches to software design and considers the tendency for convergence between the two models of exploitation within which the concept is found – a tendency that suggests a considerable unexploited potential.

Acknowledgements

The author would like to thank his colleagues for their forbearance during the gestation of this book, and particularly Mark Priestley for comments on Chapter 9. Thanks are also due for the helpful suggestions of the reviewers of the draft, particularly Gordon Blair of the University of Lancaster, and to John Cushion of Pitman for his patience and convivial encouragement.

Preface to the second edition

Since the publication of the first edition of this book in 1991 there have been several relevant developments:

- the emergence of C++ as the *de facto* standard object-oriented programming language;
- the production of an updated version of the Ada programming language, Ada 95, which includes support for the oject-oriented paradigm;
- the elaboration and enrichment of object-oriented design methodology;
- the recognition of the object-oriented paradigm, particularly in the central elements of inheritance and polymorphism, as being a powerful vehicle for abstraction.

In this second edition all these have been addressed and, it is hoped, fitted coherently into the developmental structure of the original.

The treatment of C++ has been considerably expanded, with separate chapters on its support for data abstraction (6) and the object-oriented paradigm (13). The fact that C++ is a "hybrid" language, and can be used as an object-based or as an object-oriented language, permits this separation of issues and eases the cognitive load on the reader.

The same applies to Ada, where, again, support for the object-oriented paradigm in the new revision is provided as an optional facility, allowing this divided approach. The Ada revision also has relevance to the first edition apart from its object-oriented features, in that it confirms the tendency suggested in the final chapter, for the language to move to a more liberal approach to reuse, allowing encapsulation to be compromised in the interests of extensibility – "programming-by-difference".

As this removes much of the point of the original final chapter, it has been replaced by a treatment of a new subject – the use of inheritance, and its associated version of polymorphism, as a tool for abstraction realized in a number of archetypal "design patterns".

These major changes have been accompanied by numerous detailed corrections and amendments, of which the most significant is the inclusion of new material relating to object-oriented design, following developments of the original Abbott/Booch methodology.

PART I

Object-based programming

CHAPTER 1

Programming in the large

1.1 Large systems and complexity

In this book we are concerned with the construction of significant software systems. "Significant" is a fairly vague term – it is intended to convey both the ideas of large and important, in the sense of involving a considerable investment to ensure a long and useful operational life. In other words, the kind of system on which industry, commerce and indeed society at large is ever more increasingly dependent.

In this context, a large software system comprises something of the order of several hundred thousand to a million lines of source code. Even a slight experience of programming will have convinced the reader of the fact that the ease of understanding of a program or program fragment is adversely affected, in an all too dramatic way, by its size. Moreover, this effect is noticeable in numbers of statements counted in tens, rather than tens of thousands, with an all important threshold occurring, as noted by Brooks (1975), after *one page*. The difficulty involved in comprehending several hundred thousand statements, and more importantly, in guiding the generation of several hundred thousand statements so as to realize a design, can easily be imagined therefore. So the question arises, how can the all too finite human mind cope with this kind of complexity? The answer is not a new one: it is by *abstraction* – in other words, by the removal of inessential detail, by the removal of the trees obscuring the wood.

1.2 Abstraction and design

The technique of abstraction is well established in other, more mature branches of engineering. An aircraft wing, for example, is a highly complex structure. When viewed in the context of the predicted performance of the aircraft at the design stage, however, this complexity can be reduced to a few quantitative values: two constants that enable the calculation of the lift and drag of the wing over the range of speeds for which the aircraft is designed, and its weight and major dimensions, particularly including

2

its volume (which normally determines the fuel capacity). Provided the designer of the wing manages, in "fleshing out" its detailed design, to remain within the framework defined by these few values then the validity of the original predictions will be preserved. Another way of saying this is that, at the *level of abstraction appropriate* to performance calculations, the wing can be considered to *be* this rather small collection of values. Questions as to the aerofoil section of the wing, its construction, control surfaces and so on are irrelevant *in this context* and need not be considered at the initial, high-level stages of design.

Abstraction is even more strongly established in electronic engineering with a theoretical basis that allows for any arbitrarily complex system component – an amplifier, say – to be replaced, for the purposes of the analysis of the complete system, by an *equivalent circuit*. An equivalent circuit consists of one each of the primitive circuit components: resistance, capacitance and inductance, together possibly with a current or potential source. All specific details of the components in question are *abstracted away* as far as the rest of the system is concerned.

There are two notions involved in these examples of abstraction:

- the splitting up, or *partitioning*, of the design into discrete parts or components;
- the ability to treat these components individually in terms of their effects on the rest of the system, whilst ignoring their internal structure. In these examples these effects can be captured by a small set of values.

1.2.1 Partitioning

When we consider design in these other areas of engineering the process of partitioning is a very natural one. An aircraft or a car can naturally be seen as a collection of components – integrated in the sense that the components fit and work together so as to enable the machine to achieve its designers' objectives. Moreover, the major components of a car such as the engine, the body, the transmission and so on, can be treated as single, monolithic objects at a high level of abstraction, or they may alternatively be viewed as being themselves composed of components populating a lower level of abstraction. For example, the engine is composed of the cylinder block, crankcase, crankshaft, connecting rods and pistons, cylinder head and valve gear, and so on. By choosing an appropriate level of abstraction we can reduce the complexity of the unstructured mass of basic, in the sense of "having no components", components, that actually results from dismantling the car until no further dismantling is possible.

The process of design naturally follows a path from a high level of abstraction to lower levels. The car designer initially considers very high level "broad-brush" factors such as the size and major features of the body, the position of the engine and so on. Once these major, high-level features have been determined then the filling out of the next level of detail may be undertaken. Then this process may be continued successively until (literally) the nuts and bolts level is reached.

Common sense suggests that there is something wrong if the designer commences the task of designing a car by a detailed analysis of the instrument panel or the radiator grill. Not only does this offend against commonly held views on "getting bogged down in detail" but it also offends against the idea that over-attention to one part of the design may well lead to an unbalanced final result.

Conventional engineering design techniques, then, suggest that success in the comprehension or design of large or complex systems is very dependent on the ability to consider these systems as comprising components at various levels of abstraction.

1.3 Partitioning in software systems

Turning back to the consideration of software systems, with which we are concerned, it is clear that an important distinction between software and other forms of engineering is that the partitioning of a system into components is far less obvious. There are very few "standard structural models" to be found generally in software systems, particularly at a high level of abstraction. It is true that many batch systems exhibit an input and an output component, but the rest is both application specific and dependent on the inspiration of the production team involved. Perhaps more significant is the fact that in the one example where there *is* a generally-recognized standard partitioning, namely compilers, which generally comprise components that perform *lexical analysis, syntax analysis, semantic analysis* and *code generation,* there is considerable doubt about whether this partitioning is a good one.

The software designer, then, does not work within the framework of a high-level structure of standard components. In the typical case a software system might be realized by *many different alternative* sets of components, any one of which would "work", and it is the task of high-level design to determine the best partitioning from these alternatives.

1.4 Programming in the large

The discussion above suggests that the major problem to be overcome in the design of large-scale software systems is that of devising strategies for breaking down the design into a hierarchy of components. Also from the foregoing discussion it can be seen that the critical phase of this process is likely to be the initial one: the defining of the major components of the system at the topmost level of the hierarchy that form the *architectural* description of the system.

This high-level activity has become known as *programming in the large*, as contrasted with *programming in the small*, by which is meant the activity generally associated with the term *programming* – the translation of well defined algorithms into some form of program structure expressed using a programming language. The term *programming* in the phrase *programming in the large* represents a deliberate attempt to get away from the idea that programming *means* "writing source code".

Computer science students and, perhaps more surprisingly, professional programmers are often puzzled at the lack of appreciation or importance given to "programming skills" by software managers and the like. They are even more disheartened to learn that the writing of "clever bits of code" is positively frowned upon in the gritty reality of the software industry. In other words, value is placed on programming in the large rather than programming in the small. This simply a reflection of the fact that it is the large-scale structure of a system (any kind of system) that is important – *it is the function of the high-level design to ensure that this is so* – to ensure that the internal details of individual components are relatively unimportant as compared with the architecture, the major high-level structure.

This guiding principle to design is known under various pseudonyms. The term *black box* is well known in the world of electronics and has been borrowed by software engineers. It conveys the idea of components whose internal workings are hidden, and so inaccessible, with the complementary notion that what is important about such a component are the ways in which it interacts with other components over some well defined interface: its *behaviour*. Recently, the term *mortar before the bricks* has been employed in respect of software systems to get over this idea that what is important is how the components fit together, rather than how each performs its particular function. The underlying theme is that the most important characteristic that a component may possess – given the satisfaction of minimal performance constraints – is that it may be replaced by an alternative version with no effect on the rest of the system. This reflects the inevitability of constant change throughout the operational life of any significant piece of software.

1.5 Evaluating design

How then do we go about the high-level design of a software system? The normal starting point is the agreed requirements specification that defines how the system will behave when it is used by its prospective users. But then, as we have seen, we are faced with many alternative designs that could satisfy the requirements, and apparently few guidelines as to howto choose between them – a blank sheet of paper (or VDU screen) in fact. Obviously, we want to choose "the best" design – a possibility that depends on the existence of an objective basis for comparison between different designs.

The first question to be answered, then, is "how can we tell a good high-level design from a bad one?" The easy "answer" is to wait and see how the subsequent life of the design progresses – through detailed design, implementation and maintained use. But of course this is really no answer at all. What is required is to be able to evaluate a high-level design *before* it is too late to do anything about its shortcomings. Proving software puddings by eating them is a very expensive procedure. However, the "wait and see" approach does suggest that it is possible to identify problems that are caused by failures in the high-level design of a software system when they occur during subsequent stages of its life. A consideration of these problems can lead to a characterization of design faults whose absence can be regarded as indicative of good design. The following sections, therefore, describe characteristic problems arising from bad high-level design at the various stages in the life of a software system.

1.5.1 In detailed design and implementation

The immediate objective of high-level design, programming in the large, is to be able to produce a "mind-sized" model of the final system: to break it down into a manageable number of components. This model is then elaborated during the successive, detailed design phases. However, the success of these detailed design phases is dependent not just on partitioning into components. It is dependent on partitioning that produces components that can be treated as simple units, because their effects on the rest of the system are limited and may be captured by a small collection of information comprising a *behavioural* description.

If the high-level design fails to produce components with these characteristics then subsequent design tasks are hindered rather than helped by it. The inability to isolate components conceptually, and to have a clear view of the interactions between them, makes a proper understanding of the design impossible.

This effect will become more noticeable as the detailed design progresses, as inconsistencies and omissions are overlooked in the general confusion. The designer of a software component is far more likely to do a good job if he or she has a clear idea of precisely what the component is supposed to do. This may seem so obvious as to be hardly worth stating; it is the case, however, that very many software systems contain "ragbag" components that have accumulated a large and unrelated set of functions that they perform. Often this is the result of design changes being made "on the fly" during the implementation phase in conjunction with a bad structural design. It is also the case that these ragbag units frequently give rise to a quite disproportionate number of errors and consequent trouble during maintenance.

Distributivity
A different set of problems may also arise from bad high-level design. These are concerned with the practical realities of the software production process and in particular with the fact that, probably during the design, and absolutely certainly during the implementation ("programming") phases, the work will have to be distributed to several designers/programmers. It is simply impossible for one person to produce the volume of program code characteristic of large systems within the time that is normally acceptable, and thus it is inevitable that the work will be divided up between a production team, typically of anything from five to fifty members.

If work is to be progressed in parallel by a number of people then, making the reasonable assumption that each component is the responsibility of one person, it is clear that the components must possess a degree of independence so as to allow their separate development. If the structure is a bad one in which the components are insufficiently independent then each team member will constantly need to check up on what everybody else is doing, and be obliged to rewrite constantly to compensate for detailed changes made by others.

Testing
Testing, both of individual components and of larger assemblies up to full system test, is hindered by bad structural design resulting in components with a confused or badly-understood functionality. Both the devising of test data and the construction of test harnesses are affected, and the identification of bugs made difficult. Furthermore, a structure that fails to preserve adequate component independence will allow the modifications made to correct bugs when they are detected to proliferate to other components, causing new errors in consequence.

1.5.2 In operational life

Reliability
An unreliable software system continually throws up new bugs throughout its operational life. The cause of unreliability is a combination of inadequate testing, resulting from the kind of problems mentioned above, and a lack of independence between system components. This allows errors to migrate into regions remote from their original sites, often remaining undetected until a new combination of input data or usage reveals them. Both of these causes stem originally from bad high-level design.

Performance aspects

So far nothing has been said about the likely effects of shortcomings in high-level design on the performance of the software system in question, including such aspects as speed and memory occupancy, and less tangible measures such as user friendliness. The short answer to the question as to the extent to which these are affected by high-level design is "not at all". This is, perhaps, an over-simplification. But it has been well established that attempts to base *high-level* design on the achievement of specific performance levels have invariably produced poor designs. In most kinds of software system unsatisfactory performance can be remedied by the "tuning" of critical components. But the possibility of tuning is dependent on the ability to modify individual components without disrupting other parts of the system, which is dependent, in turn, on good high-level design. Given a good structure the achievement of specific performance levels is generally possible, but a bad structure can never be remedied.

Maintenance

The maintenance activity consists of the modification of an existing software system: either to cure errors ("bug-fixing") or to incorporate improvements ("enhancements"). The activity is traditionally bedevilled by the interdependence of the system components arising from the inadequacy of high-level design. This interdependence is often poorly documented and apparently carefully hidden from the unsuspecting maintenance programmer, who all-too-often after a time-consuming search for a bug finds it and incorporates a modification to cure it, only to find that the "cure" causes bugs to appear in some other part of the system. Similar problems occur when modifications are made in the course of the evolution of the functionality of the system, for change is endemic in any piece of software.

It is not unknown for this kind of problem to be so deep-seated in a badly-designed system as to make maintenance effectively impossible and to necessitate a complete "ground-up" rewriting.

1.5.3 Reuse

Mention of the enforced need for the rewriting of a software system may generate a distant ideal that is its opposite – the *reuse* of a software component – that is its incorporation in a system other than the one in which it was originally implemented. Reusable software has been used for many years in the form of "compiler-planted" code such as input/output packages, intrinsic functions etc., and also a small but well supported set of subroutine libraries, often concerned with computer graphics. The reuse of higher-level, application-oriented software components, however, is still in its infancy.

The motivation underlying this idea is not difficult to understand: software is legendarily expensive; if the investment in the production of a software component can be amortized over several systems that use it then the economics of software production begin to look somewhat more encouraging. The problem is that the functionality of a software component is normally heavily dependent on the environment in which it was designed, as the result, once again, of poor high-level design leading to a lack of independence.

It is also the case that software components are likely to be candidates for reuse only if they perform some well defined function that is sufficiently general in its application so as to be relevant to many different contexts. Perhaps more importantly, only components that perform *well defined* functions are likely to find application within a different environment if that function is *free-standing*: the kind of idea that is conveyed in other technologies by the phrase *plug-in* – a self-contained, integrated functional unit that performs a commonly-needed service. Again, these characteristics are critically dependent on high-level design.

1.6 Good high-level design

We were led into this discussion of what characterizes good high-level design by a realization of the amorphousness, or plasticity, of software: virtually any partitioning into components can be made to work. It turns out that, except in a few very specialized applications, what constitutes good high-level design has little to do with the primary aim of satisfying the requirements specification, and everything to do with what might, in other areas of engineering, be considered secondary factors such as modifiability, maintainability, reliability, and so on. The justification for this view is based on the ever-changing nature of software. To talk of "the" requirements specification is unrealistic. Requirements change constantly in response to user aspirations and experience, the effects of competitive products, new technologies and many other factors. The behaviour of a system at any particular point in its life can be seen as a cross-section across an evolutionary process of responding to these changing requirements. Thus the most important quality that a software design can possess is the ability to evolve systematically in a trouble-free way.

The discussion above leads to the conclusion that good high-level design results in a partitioning into components that exhibit two not entirely distinct characteristics. One of these is concerned with each component considered individually. The other is concerned with the relationships between components. These characteristics are:
- the possession of a well defined, unified functionality. The touchstone of this quality is that such a functionality can be defined as the

9

"behaviour" that the component exhibits externally, without recourse to knowledge of its internal structure: *what* it does rather than *how* it does it, in other words.

• a high degree of independence between the components. It is of course impossible for components to be completely independent, otherwise they would no longer constitute a system! What is required is the highest level of independence consistent with the satisfactory functioning of the system as a whole.

As noted above, these characteristics are related. A component is unlikely to have an adequate level of independence if its functionality can be defined only in terms of its internal structure (because the designers of components that interact with it will be obliged to use their knowledge of this structure in the design of *their* components). Again, a component that is intimately (that is, structurally) dependent on other components is unlikely to exhibit a well defined, unified functionality. Although they are related, it is useful to continue the discussion in terms of two separate characteristics, for reasons that will be clarified in the next chapter.

1.7 Summary

In this chapter we have set the scene for an exploration of the principles of design relevant to large software systems. The universal engineering principle of abstraction has been related to software engineering, and the uniquely flexible nature of software has been found to necessitate a high-level design activity – programming in the large – concerned with devising architectural structure, a partitioning into components. The far-reaching effects of high-level design decisions have been considered and found to suggest criteria for evaluating programming in the large. These may be expressed in terms of the achievement of partitions into well defined, independent components.

So far the discussion has not addressed itself to the actual techniques that will produce designs meeting these criteria. Indeed it will be several chapters before these techniques are discussed. For the moment we are concerned with *what* characterizes good design rather than *how* it may be achieved. Perhaps surprisingly, an analysis of the former will provide a pathway to the discovery of the latter.

Following this analytical approach, the next chapter relates the characteristics recently identified as being intrinsic to good high-level design more specifically to the realities of software construction – considering questions such as, for example, what does it mean for software components to be independent?

1.8 Further reading

The classical, and readable, work on the traumas and tribulations of software development is still F. P. Brooks, *The mythical man-month: essays on software engineering* (Reading, Mass.: Addison-Wesley, 1975). A more conventional text-book treatment may be found in D. A. Lamb, *Software engineering: planning for change* (Englewood Cliffs, New Jersey: Prentice-Hall, 1988), or H. van Vliet, *Software engineering: principles and practice* (Chichester: John Wiley, 1993).

CHAPTER 2

Concepts of modularity

In the last chapter a discussion of high-level design, or programming in the large as it is known in the software context, led to the conclusion that good high-level design results in a partitioning into components that exhibit:
- the maximum level of independence;
- a well defined, integrated functionality.

In this chapter these criteria are interpreted in terms of modular software design, so that they may be more readily applied to the realities of software construction using conventional programming techniques and languages.

2.1 The nature of modules

The term *component* that has been borrowed from other areas of engineering is actually of only fairly recent use in software engineering. The established term, whose meaning roughly corresponds to that of component, is *module*. Before looking further at how we can decide whether the breakdown of a software system design is a good one, or to put it in a slightly less clumsy form, whether the *modular structure* is a good one, we need to clarify our ideas about the kind of entities that modules must be.

The important considerations here are the practical ones noted previously concerned with the parallel development of a system by different members of the development team. If this is to happen in an acceptably efficient way then each team member must be able to test his or her own module(s). In turn this means that modules must be individually compilable. The alternative, which would require the shuffling around of bits of source program between programmers, is too horrible to contemplate – although this does not mean that it has not happened! There are some quite far-reaching implications to be drawn here:
- Modules must be well formed syntactic units according to the rules of the programming language being used, and they should be capable of being compiled independently. (This is obviously a requirement imposed by the compilation system for the language.)

- The nature of the communication between modules, which obviously affects the degree of interdependence, is determined by the language used and, particularly, the structures used to implement modules.

Two concepts have become associated with the idea of modules, which correspond closely with the design criteria enumerated in the opening paragraph. They are:

- *module coupling*, which corresponds to the criterion of independence – or rather to the reverse notion of *interdependence*;
- *module cohesion*, which corresponds to the criterion of possessing a well defined, integrated functionality.

They were first explored as such by Myers (1975), on which a good deal of the discussion of them in the next two sections is based.

2.2 Module coupling

Module coupling is a measure of the extent to which modules are dependent upon each other in the sense of one module being affected by the *internal structure* of another. One way of illustrating this idea in action is to consider the extent to which the *designer* of a module would have to know about the internal structure of another module, in order to be able to design the new module so that it would work correctly with the other.

2.2.1 Content coupling

The highest level of coupling can be seen when direct branches are made into and out of the code of another module. Clearly our designer would need to have a complete knowledge of the way in which the target module works, including the labels of the points to which control is to be transferred. He or she would also presumably have to plant the return jump back from the target module.

This level of coupling is so tight that the modules involved can hardly be considered to be independent in any real sense. A change to one, particularly the target, module will almost inevitably necessitate changes to the other – giving exactly the kind of pathological maintenance problems mentioned in the last chapter. Again, the parallel development of modules linked in this way would require the constant consulting of the two programmers involved. The result would really be one large, messy module produced by two people, rather than two individual modules.

Fortunately, very few high-level programming languages in current use will support branches, or jumps, between the kind of constructs that might be used as modules. So this kind of direct branch coupling, called *content coupling* by Myers, possesses significance only in so far as it stands as the extreme limit in the range of degrees of coupling, perhaps as a reminder of why modern programming languages prevent it.

Although content coupling is normally ruled out by the language used, a more diluted, and slightly more sanitized, version is still commonly to be found as what will be referred to as *control coupling*. Before considering control coupling in detail it would be appropriate to consider another dimension of coupling, that formed by the two possibilities of intermodule communication: shared variable and parameter.

2.2.2 Parametric and global coupling

In conventional imperative languages, such as Pascal or C, communication between the modules of a program (note the assumption that modules are sub-program structures) is achieved by means of either shared variables or parameters.

Global coupling

Shared variables are typically declared as *global* to the program units utilized as modules in a block-structured language such as Pascal or are defined in COMMON areas in languages such as FORTRAN. Communication via shared variables is accomplished by the result of an assignment to such a variable made within one module being accessible to all the other modules that share it. All the modules that share such a variable may either read from or, more importantly, write to it in a completely uncontrolled way.

When viewed in the context of module coupling it is clear that shared variable communication represents a high level of coupling. Each module that participates in the sharing of COMMON or global areas must be aware of how all the other participating modules use them and, as was noted above, there is no possibility of any kind of discipline, like "read-only" access, being imposed. In the late 1960s it was very common to find program designs based on a large "spine" of common areas, along which the subroutines were arranged in a way analogous to the way the components in a computer are arranged along a bus. This was particularly so in systems written in FORTRAN and also assemblers, which often provided a FORTRAN-like COMMON facility. The GINO-F graphics package, which achieved quite a significant level of popularity in the UK and was still in use in 1990, was an example of such a design.

This superficially pleasing arrangement was frequently the cause of disaster. In those long-departed days it was not uncommon for programs to become short of memory (when 12K was a big machine), and programmers were imbued with the idea of saving space. One way of making your own module apparently smaller was by utilizing some of the common area to hold local data – there were always "unused" locations, or ones that "wouldn't be used until the output phase". The result was that eventually, during enhancement or whatever, these "unused" common areas would be used, and of course promptly corrupted by the "private" use made by some space-conscious programmer.

This kind of bug is extremely difficult to find, particularly in the absence both of the miscreant who perpetrated it, who had probably left by then, and the kind of software tools that are taken for granted now. This difficulty arises from the documentary problem with common or global data items: references to them in the program text – in assignment statements, say – give no clue as to their special status, except in the *very* unusual case of the highly disciplined programmer who comments every such reference. Consequently, the task of searching through a few thousand lines of program listing for references to globals is both time-consuming and boring, with a low success rate as a result. The task is made even worse by languages such as FORTRAN because it is not necessary for the variables in a FORTRAN COMMON block to be consistently named in each instance of the block.

To summarize: the use of global or common data items represents a high level of coupling, essentially because the intermodule communication that they support is too free, too uncontrolled and thus requires too much discipline and mutual awareness on the part of the communicating modules.

Parametric coupling
Communication via parameters is, by contrast, a much more constrained affair, particularly in the more "structured" languages. Parameterization is associated with the *calling* operation, which is applied to program units commonly named *subroutines, subprograms, procedures, functions* and so on; we will use the term *subprogram* in this discussion. Subprogram declarations may incorporate *formal parameters*, which typically occupy a distinguished position at the head of the declaration, and which both act as local variables from the point of view of the subprogram and support *parameter substitution* – the transmission of values into and/or out of the subprogram from its external, calling environment.

By contrast with the use of global variables, parameterization provides the *potential* for very low, or loose, coupling. This is particularly the case when *value* or *read-only* mode parameters are used, where the called subprogram receives only *copies* of the actual parameter values, and thus any modification to the formal parameters is localized within the called subprogram – there is no possibility of changes being propagated to the external, calling module. Clearly, read-only mode parameters can be used only when it is not required to export results from a procedural module, in which case input/output or read/write mode parameters must be used (or the result returned as the value of a function). This is still a much more controlled arrangement, however. The formal parameters of a subprogram are modifiable only by the subprogram during its call or invocation. They form a well defined and distinguished collection of variables whose

15

purpose is quite clearly involved with the communication of data into or out of the subprogram. Furthermore, this communication is normally synchronized with the *call* or *return from call* actions. To put it another way: the designer of a module consisting of a subprogram that calls another, existing subprogram knows exactly the extent to which his or her module is affected by the call(s) to the other subprogram, provided that communication is restricted to parameter passing: only the actual parameters can be affected, and only those substituting for input/output or output mode formal parameters. This provides a powerful contrast with subprograms linked by a large set of global variables – any of which could be changed by a subprogram with the appropriate visibility.

Consideration of the shared-variable/parameters axis shows, therefore, that the use of parameterization is a necessary condition for achieving low coupling. It is not a sufficient condition, however. It is quite possible to use parameterization in such a way as to require a high "interface commitment": in other words, to be dependent on a particular complex interface format, which is still indicative of high coupling.

2.2.3 Interface commitment

A high level of interface commitment may arise from one of two causes:
- the use of *control* parameters;
- the use of *data structure* parameters.

Control parameters
It was suggested previously that the tightest form of intermodule coupling is exhibited by direct branch, or content, coupling and also that a slightly diluted and sanitized version exists. This version involves the use of *control parameters*, i.e. one or more parameters whose values are not used as data to be transformed in some way but as selectors determining the sequence of execution that the called module is to perform. The typical structure of a module that possesses a control parameter is that of a large case statement of the kind found in Pascal – the values of the control parameter corresponding to the various cases, each of which selects a sequence of statements (blocked into a compound statement in the case of Pascal). Such a module consists, in fact, of a collection of separate modules corresponding to the set of cases; this point will be returned to shortly.

The coupling involved in the use of control parameters is high because of the requirement that they place on external modules, or rather their designers, to understand the internal structure through which the paths of control selected by the control variable values are traced. It may be objected that this is merely a matter of documentation. The interface definition of the module should simply include the range of values for the control variable, together with a description of the function corresponding to each value. Complexity almost invariably arises, however, because it is very rare for the multiple functions discriminated by the control variable to need the same set of data parameters.

Let us consider an example, namely a *queue*. Queues are widely used in software systems, in operating systems for example; they are lists that impose a first-in first-out discipline. A queue has four essential operations associated with it:

1. *initialize* the queue, that is, set it or reset it to an empty state;
2. *enqueue* an item, that is, enter it into the queue;
3. *dequeue* an item, that is, remove the item from the queue that has been there for the longest time and make it available externally;
4. *test for empty* a Boolean (true/false) value made available externally. Alternatively, a count operation may give the number of items currently in the queue.

A module that implements a queue with these operations will require four parameters, as follows:

1. `control` – an integer valued (see below) input parameter with values, say 0 . . . 3 corresponding to initialize, enqueue, dequeue and empty?
2. `input` – an input (value) mode parameter with the type of the queue items, to supply the item for the enqueue operation;
3. `output` – an output (variable) mode parameter with the type of the queue items, to make available the item exported by the dequeue operation;
4. `is_empty` – an output parameter of Boolean type, to make available the result of the empty test operation.

It may be objected that two item parameters are unnecessary: one parameter would suffice for both the enqueue and the dequeue operations; this is true but represents bad programming practice and is, in fact, illustrative of the dubious nature of control coupling.

The use of control parameters, because they require the remainder of the parameter set to accommodate *all* the operations, inevitably causes complexity in the use of the parameters. Some will be unused in any particular operation, such as the Boolean parameter in the two item transfer operations; no parameters are used in conjunction with the initialization operation. At the same time dummy actual parameters must be supplied for the sake of the syntactic correctness of the calls. At the risk perhaps of overstressing this point it is worthwhile showing a typical calling sequence to a module – a Pascal procedure called **queue** – implementing a queue in this way

```
queue(2,in_item,out_item,is_empty);
(* test for empty Q *)
if not is_empty
then (* get item in out_item *)
        queue(1,in_item,out_item,is_empty);
```

17

As can be seen, this kind of arrangement falls somewhat short of the ideal of low coupling. Both parties to a module interaction are committed to a reasonably complex interface, which is made intelligible only by comments, with a correspondingly increased possibility of error. This is exacerbated by the common use of integer values for those of control variables – it is fairly difficult to remember that "0 means initialize" while "1 means enqueue" and so on, particularly while checking code rather than actually writing it.

At this point the experienced Pascal programmer may well be saying "yes but in a civilized language we have enumeration types so that the control values can be given meaningful names and the calls become self-documenting". Unfortunately the use of an enumeration type in this way will increase the coupling of the relevant module to its environment, because the scope rules of Pascal and similar languages dictate that the declaration of the enumeration type must be global to both the module and the external calls made to it. The effect would be to require the module to trail a detached declaration around with it, destroying its status as an independent, integrated unit and doing considerable violence to the whole idea of a module.

This raises the question of the types of the parameters that constitute module interfaces. As we have seen there are strong objections to the use of user-defined types, in strongly typed languages like Pascal at least, because of the necessity for the type declarations to be external to the module – so that both the formal and actual parameters can themselves be declared. In fact this restriction is fortuitous because there are other good reasons for avoiding the use of user-defined, particularly structured, types.

Structured type parameters
It has been common practice, particularly in the operating system world, to use module interfaces with large, structured parameters. The typical example is the *file header block* (FHB), which is often passed back and forth between operating system services and user programs. When the user program requests the creation of a file, for example, the operating system will pass back a FHB containing details of the file just created. In Pascal terms these structures are records – consisting of a number of fields of differing types: integer block numbers, character string names, and so on.

Normally, however, the language used is not Pascal, but a less strongly-typed language that permits different record structures to be supplied as the actual parameter corresponding to an unchanged formal parameter, the fields in such a structure being identified by their offset from the base address of the whole. This arrangement has proved to be a fruitful source of errors over the years. Inevitably the format of the FHB structure is changed in successive releases of the system and, equally inevitably, the custodians of the modules using the structure fail to notice or are not informed of the changes. The user modules, which "unpack" the structure using the (out of date) offset information, then wrongly interpret the data, and the system "falls over", to use the colourful term.

It is also the case that a read/write parameter effectively constitutes a global location as far as the calling and called modules are concerned. In languages that are unable to impose a read-only discipline on a large data structure parameter, or indeed in any language environment where a field of such a parameter, and therefore the whole data structure, is required to be read/write, there is no protection against the possibility that a user module may corrupt the "global" data structure.

The moral is that the use of data structure parameters implies a high level of coupling both because of the "sub-global" coupling that they entail, and because of the need of the user module (designer) to know their formats. It may be objected that the use of a strongly typed language would prevent this kind of problem, because the module calls would no longer compile if the format, and therefore the type, of the structure was changed. This ignores the fact that type checking is often, as in C or Pascal, restricted to compile time. Normally modules are independently compiled, and so the matching of formal and actual parameters goes by the board – structures that occupy the same space can be passed haphazardly.

Pointer-connected structure parameters
Another possibility for the passing of complex data structures is the use of dynamic, pointer-connected structures rather than static structures such as arrays or records. Typical examples are lists and trees. Superficially the parametric interface commitment for such a structure is very simple: a pointer value that is the "header" or "anchor" of the data structure. This is passed as a parameter and then can be used as the "keyhole" through which the traversal of the whole structure may be initiated.

In fact the underlying commitment is equivalent to that for the record structure which defines the format for each node in the structure, so that the calling module can access the "next node" pointer(s). This leads to exactly the same kind of problems as have been described in the context of static, record structure parameters. A further problem with dynamic structures is the requirement to mark the limits of the structure – to terminate a list, for example. Conventionally this is done by "nil" value fields – but, of course, there are many alternative possibilities, whose existence represents yet more information that the user of a module with this kind of parameter must respect.

Unstructured parameters
We are led inexorably to the conclusion that low coupling implies the use of parameters with "simple", unstructured types of the kind that are

generally available – that is pre-defined or declared by default – such as integers or ASCII characters. The relevant point about these types is that their formats are, to all intents, fixed. Their use requires no *specialized* or *application specific* knowledge on the part of users because they are universal and unchanging: no bug correction or enhancement is going to change the ASCII character set, for example.

In addition to the types of the parameters we can also see that coupling, in the usual sense of the measure of how much the user needs to know, is also dependent simply on the number of parameters – the fewer, the lower the coupling. Finally, the ultimate in low coupling is provided, in languages that support the feature, by read-only or *value-mode* parameters. Here the reduction in coupling is more a matter of physical isolation, because a read-only parameter cannot cause the propagation of any effects, particularly erroneous ones, outside the module for which it is defined.

The reader may well be feeling by now that the discussion has entered a somewhat unreal stage. It is obvious that a module interface comprising a few read-only integer parameters exhibits a low level of coupling – but surely any attempt to design systems in which all interfaces are like this is quite impractical! Operating system designers did not invent file header blocks out of some wilful desire to produce unmaintainable systems after all – they exist because it is useful and indeed necessary to group information relating to entities such as files together – and how can this be done without using structures that provide this grouping? The answer to this question will be provided in the next chapter.

2.3 Module cohesion

The second criterion that was previously identified was a measure of the extent to which the function that a module carries out is a unified, integrated, well defined one. The terminology that has become established to denote this idea is *module strength* or *cohesion*. The advantages of high module strength both complement and, to a certain degree, are interdependent with those of low coupling.

The replaceability of a module, which is the key to avoiding problems both in parallel development and maintenance, is obviously highly compromised if it performs several unrelated activities. Modification will invariably be intended to affect a subset, typically of one, of these activities, yet all will be potentially involved if the module is replaced. By contrast, a well defined "single-function" module can be "unplugged" and replaced with the minimum of disturbance to the rest of the system: provided, of course, that this cohesion is supported by a low level of coupling between the module and its environment.

Again, the implementor of a module is far more likely to perform the task well if he or she understands fully the intentions of the designer, and these are obviously much clearer if the functionality is well defined and unified in some way. A further benefit of high module cohesion is that of improved error locating; if there is a clear relation between the overall functions of the system and the modules that comprise it then the pinpointing of the source of a failure of functionality is made much easier. The contrast, i.e. systems in which modules have little cohesion, provide nightmares for maintenance staff who are obliged to spend large amounts of time searching through source files trying to find "where it does . . ."

Myers uses the term *strength* rather than *cohesion*: the author prefers the latter but it is, of course, a matter of taste. Myers gives a classification of module strengths, with names that in some cases seem rather less than obvious, but which provides a useful framework for discussing the concept. Briefly, Myers' classification is as follows:

1. *Coincidental* is the lowest strength classification and is possessed by what have been inelegantly termed "ragbag" modules previously in this text. In other words, modules whose components, or elements to use Myers' term, have no relationships other than their common home. Coincidental strength is often the result of the "modularizing" of an existing program whose design is simply incapable of being split into a good structure. Or, as has been suggested previously, the result of redesigning during the implementation process.

2. *Logical* strength is possessed by modules whose elements have relationships that are derived from the application – in other words a module that contains "all the XXXXX operations" where XXXXX is a feature of the application. Myers gives the examples of a module that performs all the input/output operations for a program and one that does all the editing of data. Logical strength, in practice, is low on the strength scale because the relationships derived from the application are not necessarily visible at the program level, and attempts to package them up invariably result in "tricky code" that is difficult to understand and modify. Perhaps *superficial* strength would be a more illuminating term.

3. *Classical* strength, apart from representing the pinnacle of Myers' inspiration in the way of names, is logical strength with the additional constraint that the components are related in time. The characteristic examples of classical strength modules are the "program initialization, open all files . . ." or "system shutdown, clean up, close files . . .". Classical strength is close to logical strength, but, according to Myers, classical strength modules "are higher on the scale since they tend to be simpler". Myers also makes the point that classical strength modules are often unavoidable – most programs have a module whose functions are "when an error condition occurs diagnose the

error, correct it if possible and continue execution". Such a module inevitably has classical strength.

4. *Procedural* strength is the analogue of logical strength at the implementation level. In other words, a module with procedural strength has components that are related by the structure of the program's procedural sequence. Conceptually, and indeed practically on occasion, procedural strength modules correspond to a box or a connected set of boxes from the program flowchart.

   Myers places procedural strength above classical strength in his scale, but at a position that is still well below the ideal, which is described below. Interestingly, design methodologies based on the use of "structure charts" would appear inevitably to generate procedural strength modules, and thus, according to this classification, to fall short of ideal modular design. As we shall see in a later chapter, this suspicion is actually borne out in practice.

5. *Communicational* strength is possessed by a module with procedural strength, but with the added constraint that the module's elements share or communicate a common set of data between themselves. Obviously the effect of this common set of data is to bind together the elements in terms of their functions, and so communicational strength is placed higher on the scale than procedural strength. Also, it can be seen in the light of the previous discussion that communicational strength may possess complementary effects on module coupling, depending on whether the common set of data is isolated from access by other modules.

6. *Functional* strength is the ideal of maximum module strength, derived from the idea of the mathematical function. Informally this may be described as an object that produces a single, unified output value for every call, the output being a well defined transformation of the input parameters, or arguments, to use the conventional mathematical terminology. Importantly, the results of calling a function are restricted completely to the value that it returns, the arguments being unchanged. Its elements, therefore, are totally integrated into the internal algorithm that produces the output value and are irrelevant to the outside world, so long as the output value represents the correct transformation.

   Like mathematical functions, modules with functional strength may have no arguments. Unlike mathematical functions, functional strength modules may return no value – thus having no effect at all on the program in which they exist. Myers gives the following examples of modules with functional strength:

   • *Compute square root* which closely resembles the model of a mathematical function, producing an output value for each value of its single input parameter.

- *Obtain random number* (presumably by some such method as timing an unpredictable hardware process) is given as an example of a module that produces an output with no input arguments.
- *Write record to output file* is an example of a functional strength module with no output value – the file is external to the program and so no effect is visible within the program.

Once again the reader may be struck by a sense of unreality. It is fairly easy to see that modules that are like mathematical functions will be well defined in a way that has been identified as desirable. But surely it is quite impractical to think of basing an entire system on modules of this type. Apart from any other considerations there is the problem that, by their nature, functional strength modules cannot possess *memory*; in other words, a module that behaves like a mathematical function will always produce a specific output value every time it is called with a particular set of argument values – its behaviour cannot be modified by the sequence of calls that it has undergone. In turn this means there are very considerable difficulties in implementing something like the queue, which is defined in terms of the way its behaviour is dependent on its history.

Myers recognizes that functional strength represents a largely unattainable ideal and introduces a classification related to it but lower on the scale. *Informational* strength, to use Myers' definition, is possessed by a module that "performs multiple functions where the functions, represented by entry points in the module, deal *with a single data structure*. In other words, this module represents the physical packaging together (into one module) of two or more modules having functional strength".

Myers gives the example of a module with two entry points corresponding to two functions, respectively "insert symbol into symbol table" and "search for symbol in symbol table". The two entry points deal with a single data structure, the symbol table, and each is equivalent to a functional strength module. Informational strength thus seems to have the advantages of functional and communicational strength and might be thought to be higher on the scale, at least in view of its practicality, than functional strength. Myers rejects this view, although perhaps not without some reluctance, because of the added complexity implied by the "packaging-up" characteristic of this kind of module. Inevitably, this will provide the opportunity to "intertwine", to use Myers' term, the code for each entry point, with the corresponding tendency to complexity and errors.

The reader may well be puzzled by the term *entry point*. Although its meaning is perhaps intuitively reasonably obvious it is not, after all, a term associated with modern programming languages and indeed the concept denoted is not a feature of Pascal, say. At the risk of leaving things slightly up in the air, it is proposed to delay a definition of the term until the next chapter where the facilities of programming languages will be considered from the perspective of the criteria for modular design introduced here.

2.4 The principle and the benefits

In the discussion of these two criteria, module coupling and module cohesion, it has been transparently clear which end of the scale is desirable in each case. At the risk of stating the obvious, the criteria can be used to express the principle of good modular design, thus: *in a good modular design all the modules should exhibit* **low coupling** *and* **high cohesion**.

The benefits that flow from adherence to this principle are many, but may be characterized under the following headings:

1. *distributivity* – the independence and lack of interface commitment displayed by the modules allows for their separate development by members of the development team.
2. *clarity* – the effect of high cohesion and lack of interdependencies is to clarify the specific role of every module in the system, with corresponding benefits in terms of the achievement of the system requirements and low error content.
3. *localization of errors* – the clean nature of the interfaces, and the control over data flow that parameterization provides, tends to prevent the propagation of errors outside the modules in which they occur. This is important not only to the integrity of the system during its operational life but also to the location of errors as they occur.
4. *modifiability* – the ideal of the "plug-in" module with black-box characteristics can be most closely achieved in this way. The hiding of the internal implementation of such a module means that it may be modified, or completely replaced, with minimal effect on the rest of the system.
5. *maintainability* – the combination of clarity, localization and modifiability provides powerful support for the maintenance activity. This is obviously a benefit derived from the other characteristics, but because maintenance is so frequently a large-scale absorber of resources it is worthwhile emphasizing this aspect of good modular design.

2.5 Summary

In this chapter we have continued the analysis of the characteristics of good high-level design, discussed in terms of the concepts of *module coupling* and *module cohesion*, concluding with the general prescription that a good modular design exhibits low module coupling and high module cohesion.

As has been remarked, these concepts are not unrelated, but they differ significantly in their nature. Coupling is essentially a *syntactic* concept, which can be measured objectively by a consideration of program structure. An appropriate metric would determine the existence of global data, the number and nature of parameters, and so on. The process could be automated quite satisfactorily. Cohesion, on the other hand, is largely a *semantic* concept – it can be determined only in the light of an understanding of the *meaning* of the module in question. As such it is much less amenable to automatic measurement, and is an altogether less tractable idea. Perhaps surprisingly, a concentration on aspects of coupling will also produce useful insights into cohesion, and it is the consideration of language characteristics in this context to which to we turn in the next chapter.

2.6 Further reading

G. J. Myers', *Reliable software through composite design* (New York: Petrocelli-Charter, 1975), from which much of the material of this chapter is derived remains a useful, if slightly dated, text. Myers' categorizations of coupling and cohesion are frequently mentioned, without acknowledgement, for example in Steward, *Software engineering with systems analysis and design* (Monterey, California: Brooks/Cole, 1987).

CHAPTER 3

Language structures and modularity

3.1 Introduction

In this chapter we initially investigate the extent to which it is possible to achieve the ideals of low module coupling and high module cohesion in programs written in a conventional programming language. The language used as the vehicle for this investigation is Pascal, mainly because of its wide popularity as a first programming language, and also because it provides a representative model for a large class of languages.

The investigation will be based on the use of a particular program data structure – the *push-down stack* or, more simply, the *stack*. The author makes no apology for the very considerable lack of innovation displayed by the use of the stack – it has the advantage of being a real structure, albeit with few applications as compared with, say, the queue, but which may be implemented in a manner simple enough to avoid obscuring more important matters. It is also the case that the stack has attained a unique position in the literature surrounding data abstraction. Once having been introduced to it in this context, the reader will experience a feeling of warm familiarity at each new instance in more advanced works.

3.1.1 The stack

The stack, or *last-in first-out list*, is a structure that may be imagined to be the program analogue of a tube containing a spring. Objects may be pushed into the tube, against the pressure of the spring, and prevented from being expelled by a catch at the mouth of the tube. The catch may be released momentarily so that one object, the object at the end of the tube, pops out.

In program terms, the stack is a data structure with two characteristic *associated operations*. The operations are known as *push* and *pop*, following the operations of the tube analogue, and respectively allow data items to be inserted into, and removed from, the data structure. The *stack discipline* imposed by the structure ensures that the item that is "popped" is always the one that has remained for the *least* time of all the items that are in the structure. The stack may be seen, therefore, as in some sense the "opposite" or complement of the queue. Stacks are used in algorithms for parsing nested structures such as bracketed expressions – the well known "Dijkstra's marshalling yard", for example, uses two.

In addition to the characteristic push and pop operations the stack also needs to be initialized, i.e. cleared to an empty state. This produces in turn the need for an operation to test for the empty stack. Obviously a pop operation on an empty stack cannot be expected to produce a useful result.

The stack would appear to be an ideal candidate for implementing as a module – it is a self-contained, well defined component. It might be expected therefore to provide a useful benchmark against which to measure the support given to modularity by a language.

3.2 Pascal implementations of the stack

3.2.1 Support for modularity

The initial problem that we are faced with in devising Pascal implementations of a stack module is the fact that few Pascal systems support independent compilation, and thus it is impossible to have modules in any real sense at all. Many Pascal systems provide an "include file" facility, which allows the source of a program to be drawn from several source files. These are not compiled independently, however, but merged together before compilation. For the moment, however, we shall ignore this drawback.

3.2.3 A multiple subprogram implementation

The "single-ended" nature of the stack – both push and pop operations affect the same end of the tube model – means that a reasonable approach to a Pascal implementation is to use a one-dimensional array as the basic data structure. As items are pushed into the stack they are stored in successive elements starting from the left-hand end of the array. When an item is popped it is taken from the rightmost of the occupied elements, which is then made available for overwriting by a subsequent push operation.

The only additional data structure required is a variable to hold the index of the "last occupied element" in the array, a value conventionally called the *top of stack pointer*, abbreviated to TOS. TOS is incremented by the push operation and decremented by the pop operation. TOS is set to the value of the predecessor of the lowest array index by the initialization operation, thereby indicating a non-existent last occupied element and thus an empty stack. This value is used in the test for empty stack. The value of TOS is used also in the supplementary test for full stack operation, which is necessitated by the fact that the underlying array must be of a fixed size.

As an aside we may notice the fact that the operations of the stack are quite unaffected by the nature of the items manipulated by it, although a Pascal implementation is obliged to respect the strong typing of the language in the declaration of the underlying array. In other words, a Pascal stack must be a stack of objects of some specific type.

The straightforward approach is to implement each of the stack operations as a separate subprogram that accesses the common data structure. An implementation adopting this approach is shown in Figure 3.1. It is assumed that the stack forms part of a larger program called **stack_user** that contains numerous calls to its operations.

3.2.3 Coupling

If we apply the criterion of module coupling to the implementation we see immediately that the stack is tightly coupled to the rest of the program because of the global declaration of the data structure – the array **stack** and the stack pointer **TOS**. It is quite clear that these declarations must be global to the subprograms that implement the operations. If they were located within, say, the **initialize** procedure, the scope rules of Pascal would prevent any access being made to the data structure from any of the other operation subprograms.

A further reason for the necessity of the global declaration is that local data in Pascal subprograms exists only for the duration of the invocation during which it is established: local data items do not survive between calls. This means a locally declared data structure would have to be passed, in its entirety, via parameters with each call to any of the operation subprograms – a distinctly cumbersome arrangement with a relatively high interface commitment and thus high level of coupling.

The dangers inherent in the implementation may perhaps be illuminated by imagining a slightly unreal scenario, but one with its roots quite firmly embedded in reality. The reader is invited to imagine that he or she is a member of a programming team and has been asked to provide a stack module for incorporation into the system under development. The project leader, a man given to dramatic gestures, has asked that an absolute guarantee (signed in blood) is given that the stack will work correctly – after all, it's a simple enough bit of code isn't it?

The reader has produced the obvious implementation, not unlike the version shown in Figure 3.1. But of course the reader would be extremely foolish to give any guarantee about the working of the stack, because he or she *simply does not have enough control over the way that it is used.*

We are not here talking about errors in using the defined interface, such as popping an empty stack, that are part of the behaviour of a stack. What cannot be prevented is the circumvention of the means that the implementation provides for the manipulation of the stack – the operation

```pascal
program stack_user(input,output);

(*************** stack data structure ****************)

const   stack_size      = (* some suitable number *)

type    stack_range     = 1 .. stack_size;
        TOS_range       = 0 .. stack_size;(* allow for
                                           empty stack *)
        item            = (* the type of the items to be
                                              stacked *)
var     stack           : array [stack_range] of item;
        TOS             : TOS_range;

(*********** stack operations **************)

        procedure initialise_stack;
        begin
                TOS := 0
        end;

        procedure push (I : item);
        begin
                TOS := TOS + 1;
            stack[TOS] := I
        end;

        function pop : item;
        begin
                pop := stack[TOS];
                TOS := TOS - 1
        end;

        function stack_empty : boolean;
        begin
            stack_empty := TOS = 0
        end;

        function stack_full : boolean;
        begin
            stack_full := TOS = stack_size
        end;
(******** end of stack operations **********)
```

Figure 3.1 Pascal stack implementation – multiple subprograms.

subprograms. The global declaration of the data structure means that direct assignments may be made to it from any point in the program. So that, for example, the **TOS** could be decremented directly, rather than as the result of **pop** operations. This would destroy the discipline of the structure – the next item popped would not then be the item that had remained within the stack for the least duration.

The moral of the story is that the designer of a module should allow him or herself to be committed to its correct working only to the extent that users are made to use the module via the intended interface. Furthermore, the obvious Pascal implementation does not so constrain users of the stack, because of its tight global coupling.

3.2.4 A single subprogram implementation

If we attempt to find a solution within the Pascal context it is clear that we need to isolate, or *encapsulate* to introduce a resonant term, the declaration of the data structure so that it is protected from the rest of the program. In other words, to restrict the scope of the declaration so that attempts to include assignments to the data structure in other parts of the program will be rejected by the compiler.

The only way that Pascal provides for this is to make the declaration local to a single subprogram. Now, as we have seen, this raises the problem of the ephemeral nature of local data; for the purposes of this discussion, however, we will assume the use of a Pascal variant, such as VAX Pascal, which provides a *static* qualifier for local declarations. The effect of this is to make the contents of any variable so qualified survive the exit of control from the subprogram to which the declaration is local. This feature is somewhat far from the spirit of Pascal but it will allow the implementation of the stack as a single procedure. The implementation, in the form of a procedure called **stack**, is shown in Figure 3.2.

The incorporation of all the operations within a single procedure means that the implementation is obliged to provide a *control parameter*, called **s_func** in the figure, in order to select from the five operations that characterize the stack. But as we have seen already in Chapter 2, the use of control coupling tends to produce both an unclean interface, with the requirement for dummy actual parameters, and an over-complicated internal structure with low cohesion. These characteristics are quite in evidence even in something as simple as the stack.

The messy interface is illustrated by a selection of calls to it shown in Figure 3.3, along with the corresponding calls of the earlier implementation. The directness and simplicity of the original implementation of the operations as individual subprograms, each displaying a high level of cohesion, is lost.

```
program stack_user(input,output);
type    item    = (* the type of the items to be stacked *)

        procedure stack(s_func: integer; in_val : item;
        var out_val : item; var ok : boolean);
          (******* stack data structure *******)
        const   stack_size      = (* some suitable number *)

        type    stack_range     = 1 .. stack_size;
                TOS_range       = 0 .. stack_size;(* allow for
                                                    empty stack *)
        var     stack           : [static] array [stack_range]
                                                    of item;
                TOS             : [static] TOS_range;

        begin (*** stack ***)
                case s_func of
                0 : (* initialise stack *)
                        TOS    := 0
                1 : (* push *)
                        begin
                            TOS        := TOS + 1;
                            stack[TOS] := in_val
                        end;
                2 : (* pop *)
                        begin
                            out_val := stack[TOS];
                            TOS     := TOS - 1
                        end;
                3 : (* stack empty? *)
                        ok:= TOS <> 0
                4 : (* stack full? *)
                        ok:= TOS < stack_size
                end
        end; (* of stack *)
```

Figure 3.2   Pascal stack implementation – multi-function subprogram.

```
if token in op
then
        if not stack_full
        then push(token)
        else
                begin
                        writeln ('stack overflow');
                        . . . . .

if token in op
then
        begin
                stack(4,dummy,dummy,not_full);
                if not_full
                then
                        stack(1,token,dummy,dont_care)
                else
                        begin
                                writeln('stack overflow');
                                . . . . .
```

Figure 3.3 Comparison of the two implementations.

3.2.5 Pascal's deficiencies

It can be seen then that the possibilities provided by Pascal for the implementation of the stack, as represented by the two candidates shown, both possess unfortunate characteristics that make them less than ideal from the point of view of modular design. The multiple subprogram version possesses a clean interface, but one which can be circumvented because of the tight coupling resulting from the global data structure that it requires. The single subprogram, multiple-function implementation necessitates control coupling with its inevitably ugly interface and is, in any case, dependent on a non-standard Pascal feature. We are left with the conclusion that, in this respect at least, Pascal is deficient. What is perhaps of more interest is to consider how the language might be extended so as to support the concepts of modular design that we have discussed.

3.2.6 Encapsulation – a syntactic wall

If we return to the point of the discussion that led to the investigation of the single procedure implementation we recall that the requirement was to restrict, or encapsulate, the scope of the declaration of the data structure on which the implementation depends. Pascal provides only two scope-defining structures: program blocks and subprograms. The first is clearly too large for this purpose; the second too small, because the several operations that need to have access to the data structure are each implemented as subprograms. What is needed is a scope-defining structure smaller than a program block but bigger than a subprogram – a *syntactic wall* that can be placed around the data structure *and* the subprograms that implement its associated operations. This syntactic wall would need to provide encapsulation in such a way that the data structure is visible only to the operation subprograms, whilst the subprograms themselves remain callable from the rest of the program. This idea is that the *signatures* of the subprograms – their names and parameter lists, the information necessary to allow them to be called – "shine through" the encapsulating wall while the code of the subprograms and the data structure that they share is hidden. Given this arrangement the only external access provided to the data structure would be *via the operation subprograms* – and so the designer of the structure could control completely the way in which external users use the structure because of this indirection.

The qualification implied by the word *syntactic* means that the encapsulation is a source program feature, enforced by the compiler, which will simply refuse to compile inappropriate accesses to the data structure. There are no "walls" visible in the object program.

3.3 The data abstraction

This notion – an encapsulated data structure that can be accessed only by means of associated operations – is known as the *data abstraction*, and it forms the basis of many advances in software engineering techniques over the last fifteen years or so.

It should be pointed out that there is a fair amount of variation in the use of the term. Quite often it is used as a verb phrase, as though derived from the verb "to data abstract", denoting a process or activity *of* data abstraction. Abstraction in general, as we have seen, means the removal of inessential detail. In the context of (the) data abstraction this inessential detail is that concerned with the actual implementation of the underlying data structure and we may regard the term as denoting either the result of this abstracting away, or the process itself, with little danger of ambiguity. In this book the term is used generally in its noun-phrase version, following the definition in Liskov & Zilles (1975), and so appears in the form of its introduction above as *the* data abstraction.

3.3.1 Informational strength

The introduction of the data abstraction permits us finally to tie up the ends that were left loose in the last chapter in relation to *informational strength*. The reader may recall that informational strength, according to Myers' definition, is possessed by a module that contains a data structure shared by a number of "entry points", each corresponding to a functional strength module.

At the time that this concept was introduced it was remarked that the term "entry point" is something of an anachronism. We can now see that the operation subprograms of a data abstraction act as its entry points, and that, with suitable implementations, they will possess functional strength and the data abstraction as a whole will possess informational strength. Furthermore, the encapsulating qualities of the data abstraction mean that the data structure that is accessed by the entry points, i.e. the operation subprograms, is isolated from direct access by external modules and so avoids the tight coupling that a global data structure normally implies.

3.3.2 Kinds of operation

The data abstraction has been defined as an encapsulated data structure that may be accessed only via the operations associated with it. As we have seen, this arrangement enables the designer of such a structure to control the way in which its external users are permitted to access it. There is a corresponding responsibility placed on the designer to ensure that the interface supported by a data abstraction – the collection of operations that are externally accessible – is adequate to enable the users to realize its complete functionality. To return to our example: a stack data abstraction that omitted the `is_empty` operation would be functionally incomplete, and therefore useless, because a user would be unable to detect the empty condition and so would not know whether a subsequent `pop` operation would be valid or not.

The design of data abstraction interfaces is a comparatively new activity and is one that has received surprisingly little attention in the literature. The objective is a fairly clear one: to present the user with an adequate and convenient language of operations that is complete and consistent but which allows no more access than is necessary. There are, as we shall see, different styles of interface design, but there are also some basic principles and categorizations that it will be useful to introduce at this point.

Constructors and observers
Returning, yet again, to the stack, we can see an obvious difference between on the one hand the characteristic `push` and `pop` operations, which actually change the encapsulated data structure, and on the other hand operations like `is_empty`, which simply report on some state of the data structure without actually changing it. Following Liskov & Zilles, we will adopt the terms *constructors* to apply to the former kind of operation, and *observers* to the latter. Obviously constructors require special care on the

part of the designer (and user), but also, as the example of the `is_empty` operation shows, observers are equally important from the point of view of completeness.

A very significant and general constructor, which tends to be over-looked by programmers used to more conventional techniques is the *initialize* operation. Data abstractions invariably require the ability to reset, or return to an empty state, the underlying data structure to provide a well defined "baseline" in the sequence of operations.

Selector operations

A common, if somewhat unexciting, data abstraction, is a simple repository of data, consisting essentially of a record structure containing a number of fields, normally of different types (the reader may recall the file header block structure referred to in Ch. 2). The interface to such a data abstraction will consist of a collection of pairs of operations, one constructor and one observer per pair, with basically one pair per field.

The constructor item of each pair enables the setting of the related field to a particular value, and hence is often named a *set* operation; the corresponding observer operation allows the current value of the field to be read. An observer operation that is associated with a particular field or component of the data structure in this way is known as a *selector* operation and often given a name including *get*. Typically, set operations are implemented as procedures, with a read-only parameter containing the new value for the field, while get operations are implemented as functions, returning the current field value. A naming convention that associates each set/get pair with its related field, e.g. `set_start_block, get_start_block`, can provide useful self documentation in user modules.

As a slight diversion, the reader may be wondering quite what the point of such a data abstraction is. Its significance is that it provides the answer to the question posed in Chapter 2 in relation to data structure parameters: how is it possible to communicate grouped data, of the kind of which the file header block is a typical example, without using such parameters? This answer is – by encapsulating the structure in a data abstraction and making its various fields accessible as the result of operations. The indirect access to the underlying data structure means that, for example, the set operations may include checks on the values submitted, in terms of both their individual values and their consistency with other values. Such checks would, of course, be impossible to associate *with the data structure* in the case of a conventional global record.

Again, although ultimately set operations must be provided for every field, applications that require read access only to some or all of the fields can be accommodated by providing them with a second data abstraction that "encloses" the first, while making available only those set operations that are required.

Finally, the underlying structure may be changed, but the external interface maintained, by modifying the internally hidden details of the set and get operations.

It might also be remarked that a database is essentially a data abstraction of this type, albeit normally with a somewhat more elaborate external interface.

Operations for repetitive structures

The use of constructor/selector, or set/get, pairs is natural for a data structure of the record or **struct** kind, with a relatively small fixed number of fields. It is not so appropriate for data structures with a potentially variable number of fields, of which examples abound in software – trees, lists, sequences, strings and so on.

A typical component found in a file header block structure is a character string containing the alphanumeric filename. Character strings provide a miniature paradigm of the applications of the data abstraction. Conventional imperative languages, certainly including Pascal, invariably have trouble with character strings. The problem is the essentially indefinite length of a character string – "how long is a piece of (character) string?" – which is difficult to map onto the fixed-size character array: the obvious data structure available for realizing character strings in such languages. There are inevitable problems with different conventions for representing the length of a string, for example by some terminator character, or by a length value stored in a record structure with the array containing the string sequence.

The existence of a "difficult" data structure, with what are really coupling problems because of the requirement for users to know about format details, suggests an appropriate application for the data abstraction. The question then arises as to the nature of the interface, the set of subprogram signatures visible through the encapsulation, that is to be provided. Obvious candidates for inclusion are, inevitably, **initialize** and also **length_of_string** – an observer that returns the length of the string.

Perhaps less obvious is, or are, the constructors. The constructor operations perform the insertion of the sequence of characters that forms the content of the string into the data abstraction. One possibility would be to adopt a numerical index approach. In other words, to provide a **set_character_at** operation that takes two parameters:

1. the character to be inserted;
2. the position in the string at which the character is to be inserted.

This is certainly a workable solution indeed it is used in a slightly developed form in a very well known case-study in techniques of data abstraction (see Ch. 6). The only quibble with it is that it provides an *over-specified* abstraction, with too powerful a functionality. The point is that character strings are sequences that derive their meaning from the predecessor–successor relationships between successive characters. The index mechanism provides effectively a random access to the string structure. There is nothing, for example, to prevent a succession of operations like:

```
set_character_at(4,'X');
set_character_at(5,'Y');
set_character_at(4,'A');
```

where the string is being used essentially as an array. There is nothing particularly harmful with this, except that it involves an additional complication, the index parameter, which might well be used in a "tricky" way that is difficult to understand and which is really unnecessary. Also, the index mechanism inevitably suggests an array-based implementation, which may or may not reflect the real underlying structure.

If we consider a typical use of a string data abstraction provided with an indexed interface, we can imagine that characters will be transferred into it by a piece of code something like the following:

```
pos := 1;
(* get first character in next_ch *)
set_character_at(pos, next_ch);
pos := pos + 1;
while (* some characters left *)
do
        begin
            (* get next character in next_ch *)
                set_character_at(pos, next_ch);
                pos := pos + 1
        end;
```

The variable **pos**, which is used to index the characters, is simply incremented for each character, so that the sequence of the input is maintained. It is, in fact, just being used to indicate "the next character position" – a function that does not require the generality of an integer variable and that could be accommodated perfectly easily within the data abstraction itself.

Auto-incrementing

What is required is largely covered by a constructor that automatically increments the character position every time it is called, say **set_next_char_to**. The qualification "largely" is necessary because of the need to initialize the process, i.e. to indicate that the next character should be placed in the first position. This could be done either by a standard **initialize** operation, or by a more specific constructor that is used for the first character only – say **set_first_character_to**. This is a matter of taste, as is the decision to provide an explicit termination operation, or to leave open the possibility of extending a string at some future point simply by more calls to `set_next_character_to`. The latter choice has a slightly unsatisfactory air about it and so we might decide on the following set of constructors, showing only their signatures as, of course, their implementation is irrelevant:

```
procedure set_first_character_to(C: char);
procedure set_next_character_to(C: char);
procedure terminate; (* calls to set_next_character_to
will be ignored until after next set_first_character_to
*)
```

The revised piece of code would then look like the following:

```
(* get first character in next_ch *)
 set_first_character_to(next_ch);
 while (* some characters left *)
 do
         begin
     (* get next character in next_ch *)
                 set_next_character_to(next_ch)
         end;
 terminate;
```

This is clearer than the earlier version and illustrates the idea that complexity can be reduced by providing an appropriate set of operations that can considerably improve the self-documentation of the program.

Iterators

Turning to the observer operations that enable the extraction of a string, we can see that a straightforward reversal of the constructors will provide an appropriate interface. The main observer will return the value of the "next character" in the sequence of the string, a function called `get_next_character` or perhaps `next_character`. (The reader may find this agonizing over names rather trivial, but the use of well chosen names can illuminate the interface of a data abstraction in a very significant way.)

The `next_character` operation, like its constructor counterpart, requires complementary operations both to start the read-out at the beginning of the string, say `get_first_character` or `first_character`, and also to allow the user to terminate the process. Again, there is a range of possibilities – the data abstraction may provide a `length_of_string` function that returns the number of characters in the string. The user is then obliged to set up a count in the loop that performs the extraction – the counterpart of the `pos` variable in the first example above. In view of the "next character" approach adopted for the main observer this seems slightly inappropriate. A more consistent design would support a Boolean operation that allows the user to test for the exhaustion of the string, say **string_exhausted** or **no_more_characters_left**. The complete observer interface might be, therefore:

```
function first_character : char;
function next_character : char;
function string_exhausted : boolean;
```

A set of observer operations like this, which is designed to allow for the systematic read-out of the items in the encapsulated data structure of a data abstraction, is known as an *iterator*. The general structure of the application of an iterator is shown below:

```
    next_ch := first_character;
(* do something with next_ch *)
    while not string_exhausted do
    begin
          next_ch := next_character;
       (* do something with next_ch *)
    end;
```

The significant point about an iterator such as this is that the internal format of the string is hidden – abstracted away to an interface that allows the user to deal with strings in their simplest form: a sequence of characters with a beginning, an end, and a successor relation. All strings must possess these characteristics and so no modifications to the underlying implementation can affect them. It should also be noted that all parameters are read-only and either characters or Boolean.

It might also be remarked that a **length_of** operation, although stylistically undesirable as an iterator component, provides a very convenient functionality, for example in applications where the string is to be read into an array that requires dimensioning. There is no problem in providing this functionality, even though it overlaps with the iterator, other than the requirement placed on the implementor to ensure that consistency between the operations is maintained. (That is to say the **string_exhausted** operation returns **true** after **length_of** characters have been extracted, and **false** before.) The complete interface for the string data abstraction is shown in Figure 3.4.

This is obviously a very basic string data abstraction. The knowledgeable reader may query the lack of features such as substring handling, and also the way in which limit problems, both empty strings and over-sized strings, have been ignored. The addition of these sophistications does not require alteration to the basic pattern shown, and has been avoided at this stage to retain the clarity of the main concepts.

The last caveat to mention is that, of course, the data abstraction is not supported by Pascal in its standard version(s), and so, again, we must end

39

```
procedure set_first_character_to(C: char);
procedure set_next_character_to(C: char);
procedure terminate; (* calls to set_next_char_to will be
            ignored until after next set_first_char_to *)

function first_character : char;
function next_character  : char;
function string_exhausted : boolean;

function length_of_string : integer;
```

Figure 3.4   Interface for character string data.

the chapter in a somewhat indeterminate state. We will look at some languages that do provide support for the data abstraction in the following chapters.

3.4 Summary

In this chapter we have investigated the extent to which the precepts of good modular design are supported by a conventional language such as Pascal. The investigation has revealed serious shortcomings, but also led to the suggestion of a new program structure, the data abstraction, which, if it was actually available, would contribute powerfully to the ability of the software designer to achieve the objectives of modular programming.

The data abstraction has been defined as an encapsulated data structure accessible only via operations associated with it, which form its externally visible interface. The syntactic information necessary to allow for the use of this interface may be given by the signatures of the operations: their names and parameter lists. The roles of these operations – the nature of the access they afford to the encapsulated data structure – can be usefully categorized in terms of constructors and observers, the latter with subcategories of selectors and iterators.

3.5 Further reading

The terminology introduced in this chapter is taken from B. H. Liskov & S. N. Zilles, "Specification techniques for data abstractions", *IEEE Transactions on Software Engineering*, **SE-1**, 7–19, 1975. This article is mainly concerned to compare a number of formal specification techniques, but also provides a useful overview of the data abstraction.

CHAPTER 4

Languages and data abstraction – 1

4.1 Introduction

In this and the next chapters we consider developments in the design of programming languages that have been introduced to support data abstraction.

We have seen already that Pascal provides little in the way of support for data abstraction. It is rather unfair to expect that it would provide such support in view of the fact that the design of Pascal, at least in its first version, predated the widespread recognition of the power and usefulness of the data abstraction, although at least one language of the sixties (SIMULA 67) had incorporated it in a modified form.

The developing interest in the data abstraction in the early to mid-1970s coincided with a major growth in the popularity of Pascal, particularly in the United States, where UCSD Pascal became the standard language for 8-bit microprocessor software. It is no surprise, therefore, to find that many Pascal extensions produced in this period, including UCSD Pascal itself, provided support for the data abstraction; Concurrent Pascal and Pascal Plus are notable examples.

In this and the next chapter we discuss two Pascal extensions, representing two points in a roughly linear progression from the parent language – the first representing a comparatively minor, though significant, advance, the second a much more radical one, to such an extent that the phrase "Pascal extension" is probably hardly appropriate. These two points are identified respectively with the languages Modula-2 and Ada. This chapter is devoted to the relevant aspects of Modula-2, Chapter 5 to those of Ada.

4.2 Modula-2

The first Pascal extension that we shall consider is one devised by the original designer of Pascal, Nicklaus Wirth. This is his second essay in this area and is accordingly named Modula-2.

Modula-2 has become perhaps the best-established of all the Pascal extensions, with a significant usage and the imprimatur of the British Standards Institute. Modula-2 differs from Pascal in two major aspects that are immediately relevant to this book; these are both additional features, with no corresponding Pascal equivalents, and are:
- support for the separate compilation of modules;
- item support for the data abstraction.

As can be seen, these additional features compensate for precisely those weaknesses in Pascal, in the context of modular design, that were identified in the last chapter.

4.3 Modules

The construct that provides the basis for both these features is called, appropriately enough, the *module*. Syntactically, the module possesses much the same structure as the Pascal scope-defining units: program, procedure and function blocks. It consists of a *statement part*, enclosed by the reserved words BEGIN and END, which is preceded by a *declarative part* in which constants, types, variables and program units may be declared. Like the Pascal blocks, a module is headed by by a distinguishing reserved word, in fact MODULE, which is followed by an identifier that serves to name the whole construct. One rather pleasing improvement in Modula-2 is the requirement for the name of a module, and indeed of a subprogram, to follow the final END, thus providing an often much-needed documentary strengthening of the conventional text indentation. The basic form of a module is shown in Figure 4.1.

The module construct provides the equivalent of the *program* block in Pascal. Or, to put it rather more precisely: there is no *program* construct in Modula-2 because the language is intended to be used for writing software components that will be assembled to form program systems. In this context there is no requirement for an enclosing "envelope" construct within which various subordinate units are collected, which is the Pascal program

```
MODULE  identifier_1;

        (* declarations *)

BEGIN

        (* statements *)

END  identifier_1.
```

Figure 4.1   Basic form of a module.

block model. The collecting, or assembling, of software components is a function of the dedicated linker, which is effectively a secondary part of the compilation process, taking semi-compiled units from a library and integrating them into the operational system. So, for any particular program system there will be a "master" or *program* module, which is essentially distinguished by the fact that it is used by no other program unit. The relationship of the program module to the other program units in the system is, however, that of a user, a "first amongst equals", rather than a higher-level "super unit".

This distinction between the Modula-2 module and the Pascal program block can be seen also in the fact that a module may itself contain modules, in line with the fact that modules do not necessarily act as the outermost enclosing structure of a program system. It is the case, however, that compilation units – the text items expected by the Modula-2 compiler – are modules.

4.3.1 Local modules

As noted above, a module may be nested within another. Such a module is known as a *local* module, in much the same way that variables and procedures are referred to as being local in Pascal when they are declared within an enclosing procedure. There is a major difference between modules and procedures, however, in that modules are not *called*.

The question then arises as to the role of the statement part in a local module – when is it executed? The answer is: at the start of execution of the program, in fact *before* the start of execution of the module in which it is declared. If modules are nested to a depth of several levels, which is perfectly in accordance with the grammar of the language, the statement parts will be executed "from the innermost out" until the statement part of the outermost, or program module – *the* program in conventional terms – is executed. The nature of this arrangement effectively dictates that the statement parts of local modules are brief, and invariably devoted to initializing the values of variables; for this reason they are known as *initialization sections*. The existence of initialization sections both compensates for a notable deficiency in Pascal, at least in its later versions, and they also, in their "once per program run" mode of execution, point to another important difference between modules and procedures – the variables declared local to a module exist for the duration of the whole program. Modules are not called and not exited from, so their variables enjoy the same permanence as those of a main program.

As described so far, local modules would appear to have a rather minimal usefulness, limited to enclosing some declarations and a, possibly null, initialization section. Their full significance can be seen only in the light of the regions of scope they introduce into program structures.

43

```
MODULE Outer

(* some outer declarations *)

    MODULE Inner;

    VAR     IntVar : INTEGER;

    BEGIN

        (* statements *)

    END Inner;

BEGIN (* Outer statement part *)

    (* statements *)

    IntVar := 0;

END Outer;
```

Figure 4.2 Nested modules – IntVar in an illegal assignment

Scopes and local modules

In the schematic program layout in Figure 4.2, the local module Inner contains the declaration of an integer variable IntVar. (Modula-2's improvements over Pascal do not extend as far as dispensing with the "words" CONST and VAR to introduce, respectively, constant and variable declarations. The schematic also exhibits perhaps the least lovable of Modula-2's characteristics – its case sensitivity, and the rule that reserved words are always upper case.)

The scope rules of Modula-2 follow closely those of Pascal, or indeed any other statically block-structured language, and dictate that the scope of a variable like IntVar in Figure 4.2 extends as far as the END of the structure that most closely encloses its declaration. In this case, the scope of IntVar extends to the END of Inner, which in accordance with the commendable rule is labelled "Inner". This, of course, means that the assignment to IntVar contained in the initialization section of module Outer is outside the scope of IntVar and will therefore give rise to a compiler error (assuming that the declarative part of Outer does not contain a declaration of an IntVar also).

EXPORT clauses

Clearly, the usefulness of a scope region entirely isolated from its environment is, again, limited, particularly as the "uncalled" nature of modules precludes any parameter passing, which might have provided a basis for external communication. In the next schematic, shown in Figure 4.3, we include a new feature immediately following the heading line of module **Inner**. This is the addition of what is called an *EXPORT clause*, and it has the effect of extending the scope of any identifier included in it to the END of the next outer enclosing module: in this case **Outer**. The incorporation of the EXPORT clause in the above has the effect, therefore, of making the assignment to **IntVar** syntactically correct. The general use of the export mechanism is to provide a means of *selectively* making the items declared in a local module available to enclosing modules.

```
MODULE Outer
              MODULE Inner;
                     EXPORT IntVar;
              VAR     IntVar : INTEGER;
              BEGIN
                         (* statements *)
              END Inner;
       BEGIN (* Outer statement part *)
              (* statements *)
                 IntVar := 0;
       END Outer;
```

Figure 4.3 Nested modules with an EXPORT clause.

The effect of an EXPORT clause in a local module is restricted to one level of nesting, so that the introduction of an intermediate level, as shown in the schematic in Figure 4.4, will have the effect of constraining **IntVar**'s scope to the END of the new module **middle**, and yet again render the assignment illegal. Once again an export clause can be used to pierce the encapsulation of an enclosing unit, this time in the **middle** module, as shown in Figure 4.5.

Figure 4.5 illustrates the fact that an EXPORT clause may include an identifier that is not declared at the same lexical level – all that is required is that the scope of the identifier, which may have been extended by another EXPORT clause, includes the EXPORT clause. We may also note the fact that in Modula-2, unlike Pascal, the scope of a declaration extends over the whole of the most closely enclosing declarative part, including the region *before* the declaration. If this was not the case, EXPORT clauses would not work because they are always placed just after the module heading line and thus before any declarations – including the declarations of the EXPORTed identifiers.

```
MODULE Outer

    (* some outer declarations *)

    MODULE Middle;

        MODULE Inner;

            EXPORT IntVar;

            VAR    IntVar : INTEGER;

            BEGIN

                (* statements *)

            END Inner;
        BEGIN
        END Middle;
    BEGIN (* Outer statement part *)

        (* statements *)

        IntVar := 0;

END Outer;
```

Figure 4.4   An intermediate level of nesting.

We also take the opportunity, by including the schematic declaration of procedure **Proc** in module **Inner**, to emphasize that subprogram identifiers are subject to precisely the same rules as those of variables. This means that the call to **Proc** in the statement part of module **Outer** requires the pair of export clauses to make it legal.

IMPORT clauses
So far we have considered the expanding of scopes from local modules over enclosing modules, but the rules of Modula-2 require also that scopes be explicitly "filled in" where they extend from enclosing modules over local modules. In the schematic program shown in Figure 4.6, the scope of the variable **IntVar** *does not* extend over module **Inner**. There is in fact a "hole" in the scopes of any identifiers declared in the declarative region of **Outer** corresponding to the extent of **Inner**, and once again the assignment to **IntVar** is incorrect.

This can be corrected by the inclusion of an *IMPORT clause* in module **Inner**, which has the effect of extending the scopes of identifiers men-

```
MODULE Outer
   (* some outer declarations *)
   MODULE Middle;
         EXPORT IntVar, Proc;

         MODULE Inner;

               EXPORT IntVar, Proc;

         VAR     IntVar : INTEGER;
                 PROCEDURE Proc;
                 (* declarations *)
                 BEGIN
                       (* statements *)
                 END Proc;

         BEGIN

               (* statements *)

         END Inner;
   BEGIN
   END Middle;
BEGIN (* Outer statement part *)

         (* statements *)

      IntVar := 0;
      Proc;

END Outer;
```

Figure 4.5 Exporting through two levels of
nesting.

tioned by it from the enclosing module over the whole of the module in
which it occurs. Like the EXPORT clause, an IMPORT clause is placed at
the beginning of a module, immediately after the heading line. Where both
IMPORT and EXPORT clauses occur in the same module the IMPORT is
placed first. The corrected version of the schematic is shown in Figure 4.7.

4.3.2 Modules and the data abstraction

The reader may well have recognized, in the above references to "extending scopes" and "piercing encapsulation", more than a hint of the flavour

```
MODULE Outer

VAR     IntVar  :  INTEGER;

        MODULE Inner;          (*              / \           *)
                               (*               |            *)
        BEGIN                  (* hole in IntVar's scope *)
             IntVar := 0; (*                 |            *)
        END Inner;             (*              \ /           *)
BEGIN


END Outer;
```

Figure 4.6   Fragmented scope of the global variable IntVar.

```
        MODULE Outer

        VAR     IntVar  :  INTEGER;

                MODULE Inner;

                     IMPORT IntVar;

                BEGIN
                          IntVar  := 0;

                END Inner;
                BEGIN


                END Outer;
```

Figure 4.7   IntVar's scope
extended by and Import clause.

of the data abstraction, and indeed the simple structure of the module and the associated mechanism of the export clause is quite sufficient to support the concept. The encapsulation required by the data structure underlying a data abstraction is provided, by default, by enclosing it in a local module. The visibility of the applicable operations of the data abstraction is provided by including their identifiers in an export clause.

Without more ado, we may now return to our old friend the stack and show how the model that was sketched in the last chapter may be achieved using Modula-2. In so doing it is perhaps appropriate to say a little more about the sub-module structure of Modula-2:

```
MODULE Stack;

EXPORT Init, Push, Pop, IsEmpty, IsFull;

(*** beginning of encapsulated structure ***)

CONST
        StackSize     =    100;
TYPE
        StackRange    =    [1..StackSize];
        TOSRange      =    [0..StackSize];
VAR
        StackArray    : ARRAY StackRange OF INTEGER;
        TOS           : TOSRange;

(***** end of encapsulated structure ******)

PROCEDURE Init;
BEGIN
        TOS    := 0
END Init;

PROCEDURE Push (IntVal : INTEGER);
BEGIN
        TOS    := TOS + 1;
        StackArray[TOS] := IntVal
END Push;

PROCEDURE Pop () : INTEGER;
BEGIN
        TOS    := TOS - 1;
        RETURN StackArray[TOS + 1]
END Pop;

PROCEDURE IsEmpty () : BOOLEAN;
BEGIN
        RETURN TOS = 0
END IsEmpty;

PROCEDURE IsFull () : BOOLEAN;
BEGIN
        RETURN TOS = StackSize
END IsFull;
END Stack;
```

Figure 4.8   Modula-2 realization of the stack abstraction.

- *Procedures* differ very little from their Pascal counterparts.
- *Functions* in Modula-2 are referred to as "FUNCTION PROCE-DURES" and are distinguished syntactically from procedures only by the return type, which terminates the heading line, prefixed by a colon, and the use of RETURN statements to cause both the evaluation of the returned expression and the actual exit from the function. The declaration of a FUNCTION PROCEDURE without parameters must still include the (empty) parentheses that contain the empty formal parameter list.
- *Subrange* type definitions rather than array type definitions are associated with square brackets; this means that, once a subrange type has been declared, its name may be used in an array type declaration without the adornment of square brackets.

The Modula-2 realization of the stack data abstraction is shown in Figure 4.8.

4.4 Library modules

The features of Modula-2 that have been discussed above, specifically local modules and export clauses, provide a comprehensive support for the data abstraction but are incapable of standing alone – they must be textually incorporated within another program module. In order to be of *practical* use in the creation of modules with low coupling and high cohesion these features, or some similar, must be combined with the facility of independent compilation, in such a way that their attributes are not lost.

4.4.3 Separate compilation

Modula-2 does this by providing for *separate compilation*, which includes all the facilities of independent compilation – the ability to compose a software system from a collection of compiled components held in one or more *component libraries* – but with the additional feature that strong typing and encapsulation are maintained over the separately compiled components. This additional feature has considerable implications for the properties of the libraries and the linker. In conventional, independent compilation systems, e.g. such as the standard Unix library system, type information and "syntactic walls" disappear after the compilation phase – they are simply not present in the library-resident versions of the components and so the compiler is quite incapable of checking, say, parameter type matching against a library procedure.

The ability to check these attributes over separately compiled units, therefore, requires a library format capable of storing relevant type and other syntactic information. This will be specific to the language involved, and so the library will be dedicated, in this case to units compiled from Modula-2. The advantages of separate compilation, then, carry the penalty of losing the flexibility and generality of independent compilation. Additionally, the linker is required to be driven by information contained within source modules rather than the conventional language-independent parameters, and so it also must be a language-specific tool. The upshot is that a language like Modula-2, a *secure* language in the current terminology, requires more than a compiler in order to be practically useful. The term *language processor* has been coined to denote the necessary combination of compiler, dedicated library (with library maintenance tools) and linker.

4.4.4 External and internal views

The Modula-2 program unit corresponding to a library component is the module: in a different form, however, from the *program* and *local* modules that we have met so far and called, logically enough, *library* modules. This version possesses a form that reflects the two views of a module, particularly one that realizes a data abstraction:

- the *user's view* – defining the interface presented to an external user – *what the module does;*
- the *implementor's view* – *how it does it.*

A library module is syntactically split into two components corresponding to these two views, called respectively the DEFINITION MODULE and the IMPLEMENTATION MODULE. The definition and implementation modules of a library module are distinct as source language entities only. When compiled into the library they form a single unified component.

Of the two the definition module is the most important from the point of view of programming in the large – it provides the external users with the interface details that enable the use of the module, and its design determines the quality of the interaction with other modules in terms of functionality and level of coupling. Syntactically, definition modules contain only declarations, which may be any of the usual range of constants, types, variables and procedures. Procedure declarations in definition modules have a special form, however, which defines the interface presented by the procedure: its name and parameter list, and result type if a function procedure, and nothing else. Effectively, procedure declarations are given as the "heading line" of a conventional procedure: the signature, to use the term introduced in the last chapter. The declarations local to the procedure and its statement part are not shown because these are implementation details that are, or should be, of no concern to a user and are accordingly hidden within the implementation module.

The definition module contains all the entities that the underlying module needs to export to permit its use by an external module. For this reason,

51

definition modules, in later versions of Modula-2 at any rate, do not contain export clauses: there is no reason for including an item within a definition module if it is not to be exported and so an implicit export clause may be considered to include every item. (Earlier versions of the language did require export clauses in definition modules, an illogicality that has been removed.)

The definition module for a library module providing a stack data abstraction is shown in Figure 4.9.

```
DEFINITION MODULE Stack;

  PROCEDURE Init;

  PROCEDURE Push (IntVal : INTEGER);

  PROCEDURE Pop () : INTEGER;

  PROCEDURE IsEmpty () : BOOLEAN;

  PROCEDURE IsFull () : BOOLEAN;
END Stack;
```

Figure 4.9 Definition module for a stack data abstraction.

Implementation modules possess the same format as the program and local modules that have been described previously, with the difference that the heading line is introduced by the reserved words IMPLEMENTATION MODULE. An implementation module must include full declarations for any items that are incompletely declared in the corresponding DEFINITION MODULE – all the procedures declared there, for example.

4.4.5 Importing library modules

How does one module avail itself of an existing library module? The answer is by including the name of the library module in an *import clause*, which appears immediately after the module heading line. The effect of the import clause is analogous to that of an import clause in a local module – it extends the scopes of the identifiers that it includes, over the module that contains it. This means that the types, procedures and any other imported objects whose identifiers appear in the import clause may be used in the module that includes it, as though they were declared at the module's outermost lexical level.

Obviously the dedicated linker, which forms part of the language processor, uses import clauses in order to scan the libraries in the environment to find the nominated library modules and link them into the final executable image.

4.4.6 Name space management

An apparently banal, but nonetheless significant, problem that occurs when several programmers work together on a software system is that of avoiding name clashes – the inadvertant use of the same name for two or more distinct objects.

The hierarchical file system supported by many program development-orientated operating systems provides, by means of the extended name (the "path-name") that identifies each file uniquely within the system, a way of overcoming this problem. As long as each programmer keeps his or her files within a separate directory then each individual need worry about avoiding name clashes in this directory only, as every file name is prefixed automatically with the path of directories leading from the root of the file system to the one in which the file is held – which must be unique.

When a secure language processor for a language such as Modula-2 is used the employment of large numbers of library components provides the potential for an exacerbation of the name-clash problem. Clashes may arise in the names of the operations exported by library modules. There is obviously a strong chance of duplication (or multiplication) of names like **initialize** or **is_empty** in a number of modules realizing data abstractions. Equally obviously, it would be a tedious imposition if the designer of such a module had to scan through all the other modules in the library to avoid such name clashes.

The use of the extended filename is not appropriate in this context because the names by which modules reference each other must be syntactically correct in the language being used, rather than to the operating system command interpreter. Modula-2, for example, would not be happy with "/usr/res/progs/JSmith". It is also the case that in many language processors the names of files containing source modules are not required to reflect the names of the modules contained within them, and in any case are not retained within the library into which they are compiled.

Instead, in line with the incorporation of library facilities actually in the language, rather than being supported by the operating system environment, Modula-2 provides for extended names in the form of *qualified identifiers* or "qualidents". A qualified identifier consists of the identifier that names an object: type, variable, procedure or whatever, exported from a library module prefixed by the identifier that names the exporting module, the two identifiers being separated by a full stop. So if operations named **is_empty** are exported by two modules **Stack** and **Queue**, they may be differentiated by using their qualified identifiers, of the form **Stack.is_empty** and **Queue.is_empty**, in a module that uses both.

The existence of the qualident has led to the elaboration of the IMPORT clause to allow for variations in whether or not the full qualified identifier is used or not. If the IMPORT clause takes the form:

IMPORT *module name*

then any object imported from the nominated library module must be qualified with the module name. On the other hand, the module name (and full stop) may be omitted, if an IMPORT clause of the form:

FROM *module name* **IMPORT** *identifier list*

is used, from the identifiers included in the list. It is generally recommended that the shortened (i.e. unqualified) form is **not** used except in the case of very commonly used library modules. This is because the value of the self-documenting properties of the qualident far outweighs the inconvenience involved and, even though the IMPORT clause will always enable the source of an identifier to be discovered, it is better to avoid the need constantly to be turning back to the beginning of the listing. This is a good example of an application of the principle that *a program is read many more times than it is written*.

4.5 Abstract data types

The quite extended discussion of the data abstraction and its realization in Modula-2 that has occupied most of this book so far has tended to identify individual data abstractions with specific instances of the construct – the module that provides the syntactic wall encapsulating the underlying data structure. In other words, we have assumed one data abstraction per module.

If this were to be the general case then some practical problems would become apparent fairly rapidly. Many applications require several copies of a data abstraction – even our paradigm case, the ubiquitous stack, is needed in pairs for Dijkstra's algorithm. The character string abstraction might well be required in thousands in a text processing application. If a separate module was required for each character string then clearly requirements of memory size alone would rule out this approach.

The solution to this problem represents a step beyond the concept of the data abstraction as it has been discussed so far. The idea is to break the one-to-one relationship between module and data abstraction, replacing it by a one-to-many relationship. This is done in Modula-2 by the means of *hidden* or *opaque* types.

4.5.1 Opaque types

An opaque type, as its name so aptly captures, is one whose implementation is hidden from its users. It is exported from a module and may be used to declare objects such as variables, array elements and record fields, in modules that import it. But because the implementation of such a type is hidden, the only manipulations that can be carried out on these objects, within an importing module, are those provided by the *applicable operations* of the type. Applicable operations are exported from the same module as the opaque type, and are procedures with one or more parameters of the opaque type, through which objects of the type may be manipulated.

An opaque type is declared in a DEFINITION MODULE simply by the appearance of its name after the TYPE heading, with the usual adornment of a semi-colon, and commas if more than one appears, but without any definition of how the type is implemented. The full declaration is then given in the corresponding IMPLEMENTATION MODULE, and is therefore unavailable to an external user.

The use of an opaque type to permit the stack module to export an indefinite number of stacks is shown in Figure 4.10. As can be seen we have adopted the slightly dubious Modula-2 style by distinguishing the new module from the old one, and also from the **stack** type, by making its name all upper case. Otherwise, the important changes are the declaration of the opaque **stack** type, and the use that is then made of this type to declare the formal parameters of the applicable operations.

An external user may then declare any number – perhaps an array or linked list, of **stack**s, but these may be used only as actual parameters in calls to the operations exported by **STACK**.

The important point to note is that every externally declared object of type **stack** is as protected from its users as if it had been the single data

```
DEFINITION MODULE STACK;

    TYPE    Stack;  (* Opaque Type *)

    PROCEDURE Init(VAR S : Stack);

    PROCEDURE Push (VAR S : Stack; IntVal : INTEGER);

    PROCEDURE Pop (S : Stack) : INTEGER;

    PROCEDURE IsEmpty (S : Stack) : BOOLEAN;

    PROCEDURE IsFull (S :   Stack) : BOOLEAN;
END STACK;
```

Figure 4.10 Definition module for a stack abstract data type.

abstraction realized by the original **stack** module. The only way in which their underlying data structures can be manipulated is via the operations exported from the module, in this case **STACK**. In other words, every object of type **stack** is a stack data abstraction.

From now on we will use the term *abstract data type* to refer to types, such as may be realized by opaque in Modula-2, that permit the declaration of external data abstractions in the way just described. This usage is a slight distortion of the normal meaning of the term: conventionally "abstract data type" and "data abstraction" are synonymous. Terminology in this area is far from standardized, however, so that the introduction of a useful distinction would seem to be quite justifiable.

4.5.2 Data abstraction *versus* abstract data type

This introduction of a useful but rather artificial distinction should be followed by a careful review of what actually is involved. The data abstraction has been (frequently) defined as an encapsulated data structure accessible only via its applicable operations. The definition of an abstract data type extends this concept to the generality characteristic of a type – essentially a schema or pattern for defining many objects, thus producing a higher level of abstraction. As defined, the relationship between the two is that of the particular to the general: a data abstraction may be seen as the only instance of an unnamed abstract data type. Typical applications require both unique data abstraction objects and also abstract data types that may be used to declare many replicated objects – a payroll program, for example, recognizes the existence of both **a** payroll and **many** employees.

4.5.3 Implementing abstract data types

The fact that the full declaration of an opaque type is given in the relevant IMPLEMENTATION MODULE, and not in the corresponding DEFINITION MODULE, raises the question of how the compiler can compile the DEFINITION MODULE separately, which is the normal way in which Modula-2 language processors handle the compilation of library modules. The point is that the compiler is required to allocate storage for the parameters of the applicable operations that are of the opaque type, and yet it must do this in ignorance of its full declaration.

This problem has been overcome by requiring that all opaque types are actually pointer types, declared to provide an indirect access to the "real" data structure. As all pointers occupy a fixed memory size – invariably one word of storage – the compiler is enabled to allocate appropriate amounts of memory for the parameters concerned. External modules that import the opaque type may also be compiled because the nature of opaque types,

```
IMPLEMENTATION MODULE STACK;

CONST
    StackSize   =   100;
TYPE
    StackRange  =   [1..StackSize];
    TOSRange    =   [0..StackSize];
    StackArray  =   ARRAY StackRange OF INTEGER;
    (**************************************************)
        Stack       =  POINTER TO StackStruct;
        StackStruct =  RECORD
                          StackItems : StackArray;
                          TOS        : TOSRange
                       END;
    (**************************************************)
```

Figure 4.11 Hidden declaration of opaque type stack.

particularly the fact that no "internal" manipulation can be performed on them by an external user, means that opaque type objects can be treated as one-word "black-box" areas. In practice this would mean that the IMPLE-MENTATION MODULE for **stack** would begin with the declarations shown in Figure 4.11 (*Note:* some necessary IMPORT items have been excluded for the sake of clarity). Modula-2 replaces the Pascal caret by the rather more meaningful phrase POINTER TO, and so type **stack** is actually declared as a pointer type, the objects of which are pointers to, or addresses, in some sense, of objects of the RECORD type **StackStruct**. Each **StackStruct** object is, of course, the data structure necessary to record the state of a stack. The use of a RECORD type here is effectively mandatory as only RECORD types permit the declaration of heterogeneously typed components, which are typically a feature of the kind of data structures that underlie data abstractions.

When **stack** objects are declared they are uninitialized pointers – the creation of the necessary data structures must be explicitly programmed, a fact that makes the **Initialize** procedure particularly important. **Initialize** must execute the NEW procedure (or the lower level equivalent Modula-2 provides) to allocate memory for the new data structure. Each of the operation procedures must therefore take account of the fact that access to the data structure is via this pointer link. Code for the **Initialize** and **Push** operations is shown in Figure 4.12, revealing that the caret still retains its Pascal role as the dereferencing operator in Modula-2.

The requirement that opaque types should be pointer types would appear to be somewhat of an imposition, at least in so far as it necessitates additional complexity in the form of referencing and dereferencing. It is a

```
PROCEDURE Initialise (VAR S : Stack);
BEGIN
        NEW (S);
        S^.TOS := 0
END Initialise;


PROCEDURE Push (VAR S : Stack; IntVar : INTEGER);
BEGIN
        S^.TOS := S^TOS + 1;
        S^.StackItems[S^.TOS] := IntVar
END Push;
```

Figure 4.12   Implementation of stack operations.

fact, however, that abstract data types are very frequently implemented as pointer-connected data structures because of the representational power and flexibility that they possess. Given this it is quite natural to implement opaque types as pointer types.

4.6 Review of Modula-2

Modula-2 represents a considerable advance over Pascal, particularly in those areas relating to programming in the large that we are interested in. That it does so by introducing a comparatively economical set of additional features might be seen either as an indication of the fertility of the original design of Pascal, or of the ingenuity of the design of Modula-2. Either way, a tribute to the designer of both languages is appropriate, before turning to a language that represents, in its provenance at least, a very different approach.

4.7 Summary

In this chapter we have discussed a language, Modula-2, that builds on Pascal by providing support for data abstraction and, thus, for enabling the construction of programs that satisfy the criteria for good modular design identified in earlier chapters. We have seen how Modula-2 makes explicit the distinction between the external interface of a data abstraction and its implementation, when realized as a library module. We have also seen how the concept of the data abstraction is generalized to allow the definition of classes of objects, each possessing the characteristics of an exclusively operational external interface and hidden implementation details, rather than just single objects possessing these qualities, in the notion of the abstract data type.

In the next chapter we move on to the more complex reworking of these ideas found in the Ada programming language.

4.9 Further reading

There are numerous books on Modula-2, many of which can be recommended, for example A. H. Sale, *MODULA-2 discipline and design* (Reading, Mass.: Addison-Wesley, 1986). N. Wirth's own book is rather terse for an introductory work, although his updated *Algorithms and data structures* (Englewood Cliffs, New Jersey: Prentice-Hall, 1986), which uses Modula-2 as its illustrative language, is a very useful book.

CHAPTER 5

Languages and data abstraction – 2

5.1 Ada

The Ada programming language represents perhaps the ultimate, and final, stage in the evolutionary family of strongly-typed, imperative languages that descended from Algol 60 and includes Pascal and its immediate offspring, Modula-2. This is not the place to relate the history of Ada. Suffice it say that it is a large and complex language that, perhaps as a result of its association with the military and its general "establishment" aura, has attracted a rather mixed press, including some occasionally somewhat intemperate criticism.

Ada's importance in the context of this book lies in the fact that it was designed specifically to support the ideas of "programming in the large" that have been discussed in earlier chapters. Essentially, it covers the same objectives that inspired Wirth in the design of Modula-2, but without the latter's rather "minimalist" approach. Modula-2 provides sufficient extensions to Pascal to support the data abstraction, and component software. Many of the features of Pascal, including some of the less desirable such as the lack of facilities for variable initialization, are still visible unchanged in Modula-2.

By contrast Ada, although still recognizably a descendant of Pascal, represents a much more radical revision of the parent language. The fascinating aspect of Ada is its orthogonality – the way in which virtually every point in the "space" defined by the axes of types, program and control structures is well defined. In other words, the designers of the language did a very thorough job of thinking through the implications of including various features: strong typing, data abstraction, separate compilation, concurrency and so on, and particularly in their interaction. It is precisely because of this thoroughness that the language is complex. Ada has recently been updated – the first revision since the original language specification was finalized in 1983. The new version, Ada 95, incorporates extensive modifications, many of which are concerned with object-oriented programming and are covered in relevant chapters later in this book. As might be anticipated, the revision of the language has been done in such a way as to provide almost complete compatibility between the two standards. In this chapter there is virtually no need to distinguish between the two.

In this book we will not attempt to provide anything approaching a comprehensive treatment of Ada. At this point the aim is to impart an appreciation of the major features that support data abstraction and, thus, good modular design. To provide, in other words, a top-down view with the emphasis firmly on the wood rather than the trees. It should be noted that this is more than an exercise in programming language dilettantism – Ada was designed to provide a vehicle for program design and a firm grasp of its relevant characteristics is perhaps the most important requirement for successful use of the language.

5.2 Data abstraction in Ada

5.2.1 Ada program units

Ada provides a number of program units, i.e. constructs that are self-contained in some way and define named components for the construction of program systems, as follows:

- *Subprograms* – both procedure and function subprograms exist in Ada, corresponding quite closely to their Pascal equivalents.
- *Tasks* are program units designed to run concurrently, and are thus identified both with static collections of code and with processes.
- *Packages* are the constructs that support data abstraction and object-based programming in Ada.

Like Modula-2 (a phrase that will recur fairly frequently in this section) Ada does not have a "program" construct, and for the same reason: the language is intended to be used for writing secure software components for reuse in many applications, not for monolithic programs. Ada differs, however, in that the role of "main program" is invariably assumed by a procedure. This is because the package is purely a *passive* syntactic construct that cannot be "executed" as such, unlike the Modula-2 module, which supports both the roles of active and passive program components.

5.2.2 The package

The name "package" is perhaps less appropriate than "module". It has overtones of the "subroutine package", which was (is?) a major feature of the FORTRAN programmer's world, with examples such as GINO-F and other graphics libraries, and the NAG library. This connotation certainly conveys the idea of a set of components collected together for the convenience of external users. But it fails to capture the idea of encapsulation, which is the key to data abstraction and which is in fact comprehensively supported by the Ada package.

Format

The duality of views of the data abstraction, those of the external user and the implementor, was noted in connection with the syntactically separate DEFINITION and IMPLEMENTATION modules of Modula-2. Ada similarly splits the logically unified package into two syntactically separate constructs: the package *specification* and, perhaps rather less meaningfully, the package *body*. The contents of the package specification are very similar to those of the DEFINITION MODULE – declarations of various kinds of entity, but particularly subprograms defining the operational interface to the encapsulated data structure. The body corresponds to the IMPLE-MENTATION MODULE and is exclusively the concern of the implementor. The body provides the syntactic wall that encapsulates the data items declared within it, and also any subprograms or packages whose specifications do not appear in the corresponding specification. Package bodies possess much the same format as IMPLEMENTATION MODULEs, including an initialization section.

An impression of the flavour of the Ada package can be obtained from the realization of the familiar stack in Figure 5.1. The structure is reasonably self explanatory. The specification of a package is distinguished by the heading **package** rather than **package body**. As in Modula-2 the identifier that names a unit is repeated after the final **end**; in Ada this highly desirable practice is optional, however. Ada comments are introduced by contiguous pairs of dashes and terminated by line ends. The specifications of

```
package stack;
--
-- a package that provides the semantics of a push-
-- down stack data abstraction with integer items
--
    procedure init;

    procedure push (int_val : integer);

    function pop return  integer;

    function is_empty return  boolean;

    function is_full return  boolean;

end stack;
```

Figure 5.1   Ada package specification for a stack data abstraction.

the interfaces of the subprograms – procedures and functions – are given as signatures in a manner very similar to Modula-2. The result type of a function appears after the reserved word **return**, rather than the Pascal/ Modula-2 "**:**", mimicking the **RETURN** statement that fulfills a similar role to its Modula-2 (or C) counterpart. Ada permits the use of the underscore character to provide identifiers with simulated "spaces", which leads to a recognizable Ada style.

Implementation
For completeness, and again to give a flavour of the language, the package body for the **stack** package is shown in Figure 5.2. Two points are worth noting:

- Ada has finally done away with the unlovely non-words, **CONST**, etc. to introduce the various kinds of declaration. Variable, constant and type (also subtype – see below) declarations are sufficiently distinguished by key words such as **constant** and **type**.
- The subtype concept is a new feature of Ada and was introduced to support some of the applications of types, without incurring the full rigour of strong typing – which, in Ada, is *very* strong. The examples given in Figure 5.2, **stack_range** and **TOS_range**, provide the kind of properties that subrange types provide in Pascal and Modula-2. That is, they provide well defined ranges of equally-spaced, exact values for applications such as array indexing.

Packages and library units
Like modules in Modula-2, Ada packages may be nested – declared within other program units. Unlike Modula-2 there is not a different format as for local modules: packages have only the single two-component format. The declaration of a package within the specification part of another package may include only the specification; the body must be placed within the body of the enclosing package.

There are no equivalents of EXPORT clauses in Ada. When a package is nested within another unit the scopes of any identifiers declared within the *public part* of the package specification are extended to the end of the enclosing unit. In packages, such as the **stack** example, that do not export *private types*, which will be described shortly, the public part comprises the whole of the specification. Unlike the case in Modula-2, nested packages do not create a "hole" in the scopes of globally declared identifiers and so there is no need for the equivalent of an IMPORT clause to make them available within the enclosing package.

Ada is designed above all for the writing of libraries of secure software components. The package is the main unit for the creation of components but, perhaps surprisingly, procedures and functions, and also *generic units* (Ch. 9), may be compiled into an Ada library. The requirement to allow

```
package body stack is

--
--    encapsulated data structure
--
      stack_limit : constant integer := 100;
      subtype stack_range is integer
              range 1 .. stack_limit;
      subtype TOS_range is integer
                    range 0 .. stack_limit;
      --
      stack_array : array ( stack_range )
                          of integer;
              TOS : TOS_range;
      --
      procedure init is
      begin
              TOS := 0;
      end init;

      procedure push (int_val : integer) is
      begin
              TOS := TOS + 1;
              stack_array(TOS) := Int_val;
      end push;

      function pop return  integer is
      begin
              TOS := TOS - 1;
              return stack_array(tos + 1);
      end pop;

      function is_empty return  boolean is
      begin
              return TOS = 0;
      end is_empty;

      function is_full return  boolean is
      begin
              return TOS = stack_size;
      end is_full;
end stack;
```

Figure 5.2   Ada implementation of the stack.

procedures to be compiled into and called from libraries is necessary anyway, apart from its conformance with the general "subroutine library" idea. This is because any successful Ada compilation results in the creation of one or more library units. In other words, there is no way in which the "main program unit" can exist outside a library – the only distinction from an ordinary library unit is that a main program unit, normally a procedure, is invoked by the operating system rather than another library unit.

The great majority of library units, however, can be expected to be packages. The requirements for reusability, obviously the most important attribute for a library unit, in effect dictate that data abstractions should be employed (this topic will be discussed in more detail in a later chapter), and so the package is the natural choice.

Context clauses

The way in which one Ada program unit avails itself of a library unit is by means of a *context clause*, which must be placed at the beginning of the compilation unit that contains it – presumably to help the compiler to find the dependencies as quickly as possible. The context clause consists of the reserved word **with**, followed by one or more library unit names, separated by commas if there are several, the whole clause being terminated by a semi-colon. The effect of a context clause is much the same as an IMPORT clause in Modula-2: it causes the scopes of the identifiers exported from the "with-ed" library unit to be extended over the whole of the compilation unit that it introduces.

A procedure that wishes to use the **stack** package must therefore be submitted as a compilation unit with the first line:

```
with stack;
```

The name clash problem that was discussed in relation to Modula-2 is confronted by Ada in a similar manner. The identifiers exported by a package are combined with the name of the package, separated by a full-stop, to form *extended names* that are the Ada equivalents of qualified identifiers. The stack-using procedure would therefore invoke the stack operations as, for example, **stack.init** or **stack.push**.

Also like Modula-2, Ada provides a means of missing out the package name (and its attendant full-stop), the *use clause*. This has the same format as the context clause except that the reserved word **use** replaces **with**. A use clause may appear anywhere in a declarative part and has a scope like a conventional declaration. Within the scope of a use clause any package name included in the clause may be omitted from a name exported from the package. There is little doubt, however, that the use clause is a **bad thing**. The arguments for using extended names in Ada are similar to those for the corresponding use of qualified identifiers in Modula-2, but are strengthened by the fact that the Ada context clause does not list the individual identifiers imported from the nominated library unit, only the name of the unit itself. There is, therefore, no way of telling, other than by inspecting the specifications of all the packages mentioned in the context clause, from where an identifier has been imported if its source package name has been omitted by means of a use clause. This is by no means a trivial problem – a reasonable size Ada program may contain several dozen packages and it is not uncommon to find ten in the context clause of a high-level package.

5.2.3 Private types

We have discussed previously the additional power given to the concept of the data abstraction by the abstract data type. It is not surprising, therefore, to find that Ada provides very comprehensive support for abstract data types, in the form of *private* and *limited private* types.

Private types are Ada's equivalents of Modula-2's opaque types. As usual the Ada design team do not seem to have quite possessed Wirth's flair for suggestive terminology, but the basic notion of a type whose implementation details are hidden from its users is fully supported. In the Ada context we must be rather more precise about what is meant by "user", because the implementation details of a private type *may* be completely revealed to a *human* user. The additional features in the specification of a package that exports a private type are:

- the declaration, in the public part of the specification, of one or more private types. Each such declaration takes the form:

    type *identifier* **is private**

- a section following the reserved word **private** and terminated by the **end** at the end of the specification, in which the implementation details of the private type or types are declared.

A package derived from the **stack** package that permits the external declaration of many stacks is shown in Figure 5.3.

Before discussing the specific details concerned with the private type a few words of explanation are in order in respect of the changed operations. The **stack** type parameters are used to pass stack objects into the package where they are either modified, for example by the **push** operation, or simply read out in part, for example by the **is_empty** operation. In the former case read/write parameter modes are required: the Ada equivalent of the Pascal/Modula-2 VAR mode is the considerably more readable "in out", which appears with the type, rather than the inevitably forgotten position before the complete parameter declaration. In the latter case, read-only parameter modes are appropriate; in Ada the mode is specified, quite meaningfully as "in". In mode is the default for procedure parameters, and is not normally specified explicitly. More importantly, the parameter

```
Package Stacks;
--
-- a package that exports an abstract data type
-- that provides the semantics of a  push-down
-- stack data abstraction with integer items
--
        type STACK is private;

        Procedure Init(S : in out STACK);

        Procedure Push (S : in out STACK; Int_val : integer);

        Procedure Pop (S : in out STACK);

        Function Top (S : STACK) return  integer;

        Function Is_empty (S : STACK) return  boolean;

        Function Is_full (S : STACK) return  boolean;

private
        --
        --      full declarations for type STACK
        --
                stack_limit : constant := 100;
                subtype stack_range is integer
                                      range 1 .. stack_limit;
                subtype TOS_range is integer
                                      range 0 .. stack_limit;
                --
                type STACK is
                  record
                      stack_array : array ( stack_range )
                                                   of integer;
                      TOS : TOS_range;
                  end record;
end stacks;
```

Figure 5.3 Specification of an Ada package exporting a stack abstract data type.

modes for functions may *only* be specified as "in". In other words, Ada functions, in a way that makes them closer to their mathematical equivalents than, say, the Pascal version, *may not modify their parameters*. This is the reason for the introduction of the additional function **top**, which returns the value held at the top of the stack, the **pop** operation being unable both to provide this value and truncate the stack.

Turning now to the private type: as can be seen, the data structure for each stack type object is defined in full, as a record type, in the private part of the specification. Ada places no restriction on the implementation of private types. The important point here, though, is that these implementation details are quite invisible to *another program unit* – i.e. a non-human "user". Any attempt to compile a direct assignment to one of the components, `stack_array` or `TOS`, of a variable declared as being of type `stack` in an external unit will cause an error. In other words, the syntactic wall that provides the encapsulating properties of the package is pushed out into the specification, up to the `private` heading. Note that not only the immediate details of the `STACK` type are hidden – the auxiliary subtypes `stack_range` and `TOS_range` are also encapsulated.

The reader may well be wondering for what purpose this visibility of the implementation of a private type is required. The answer is concerned with the need for the compiler to inform itself of these implementation details so that it can compile the specification. However, the (human) user of such a private type may well find the implementation details of interest, but would be quite wrong to base the design of any external unit on them. Their visibility can be seen only as a kind of temptation. More seriously, the incorporation of implementation details into a specification compromises its role as essentially an interface definition that can be defined and, often, finalized during the design phase. The implementation detail should be decided at a later stage in the project – in fact at *the latest possible stage* in line with the well established software engineering principle of *decision deferment* – a reinterpretation of the biblical tenet "sufficient unto the day is the evil thereof".

The reader may suggest that the value of Ada as a design language need not be affected by this because there is no need to compile a design language and so the requirement to provide the implementation details of private types can simply be ignored until the actual implementation phase is reached. In fact, the ability to compile individual package specifications into a library provides the powerful checks on consistency and visibility characteristic of automatic translation and is an important support tool for Ada, one that considerably increases its viability for this application.

There is also a more practical reason for questioning this arrangement, which derives from the dependency rules of Ada.

Dependency

Part of the design aims of Ada were concerned with providing support for *configuration management* – the control of the production of a software system composed of many separate components, each of which has its own development pathway, along which its compatibility with the other components of the system will vary. As a contribution to the control of program development in this kind of environment an Ada system is required to impose an order on the sequence in which units are compiled, and recompiled. This order is determined by the *dependency* between units, the essential rule being that if unit A is dependent on unit B, then A cannot be compiled before B is compiled, and if B is recompiled then A must be recompiled. The dependency rules that are relevant to this discussion are:

1. A unit that nominates a package in its context clause is dependent on the *specification* of the package, *and not its body*.
2. A package body is dependent on its specification.

The significance of these rules is that a change to a package specification will necessitate the recompilation of all units that **with** it, together with its body. In this context, a change to the declarations following the **PRIVATE** heading are just as visible from the point of view of recompilation as those made to the public objects in the specification.

Access private types

The recommended practice of compiling package specifications during the design phase, with the consequential requirement to provide implementation details for private types, would therefore seem to raise two awkward problems:

1. the need to arrive at detailed implementation decisions during the design phase;
2. the need frequently to recompile the units (including other package specifications) that depend on a specification as these implementation details, inevitably, are changed.

The solution to these problems lies in the use of pointers, following closely the earlier Modula-2 practice of requiring opaque types to be pointer types, and continuing the association of pointers and abstract data types.

Ada's version of pointer types are known as *access* types, perhaps suggesting that, as in the current context, they have uses other than in the construction of pointer-connected data structures. Access types resemble pointer types in Pascal and Modula-2, with some relatively minor modifications intended to do away with some of the known drawbacks of the earlier version: notably the "dangling-pointer problem". Like Pascal pointers, values of an Ada access type are addresses of objects of one specified type – known as the *designated type*; there is no possibility of a pointer value being allowed to point to arbitrary objects.

The form of an access type declaration is:

```
type a_t_identifer is access d_t_identifer
```

Typically, for quite logical reasons, the designated type of an access type is a record type and, again typically in the construction of data structures, the record type in question is required to contain one or more fields of the access type, i.e. pointers to its own type. This recursive arrangement then allows the setting up of pointer connections between nodes of the record type. It also causes a problem because the mutually recursive definitions of the two types, access and designated (record) types, cannot be specified without some form of forward reference. In Pascal and Modula-2 this is done simply by allowing a forward reference in this one special case. In Ada, the problem is solved in a rather more elegant manner by the device of an *incomplete declaration*, which introduces the name of the designated type without giving any further details. For the moment this is all the compiler needs to know, on the understanding that the full declaration will be given at a point later in the program text.

The declaration of a typical access/designated type pair is shown below:

```
type NODE; -- incomplete declaration
type NODE_PTR is access NODE;
type NODE is record -- complete declaration
                data : data_type;
                NEXT : NODE_PTR;
            end record;
```

In the context of private types the important point is that the complete declaration need not appear in the specification of a package even though the incomplete declaration does. As long as the complete declaration appears within the package body the incomplete declaration is acceptable as a perfectly respectable declaration. In other words, the above set of interrelated declarations could be split over the specification/body boundary, as shown in Figure 5.4. This technique can be employed both to hide the implementation details of a private type and, initially, to avoid the need to arrive at decisions about the implementation. It thus solves both the problems identified previously, albeit at the cost of a slight increase in complexity in the implementation of the operations we have seen already in the Modula-2 context.

```
-- package specification for pack_1
private
    type NODE; -- incomplete declaration
    type NODE_PTR is access NODE;
end pack_1;

package body pack_1 is
    type NODE is  record  -- complete declaration
                    data : data_type;
                    NEXT : NODE_PTR;
                end record;
    --
-- remainder of body
    --
```

Figure 5.4 Declarations of NODE split over package components.

```
Package Stacks;
--
-- a package that exports an abstract data type
-- that provides the semantics of a push-down
-- stack data abstraction with integer items
--
    type STACK is private;

    Procedure Init(S : in out STACK);

    Procedure Push (S : in out STACK; Int_val : integer);

    Procedure Pop (S : in out STACK);

    Function Top (S : STACK) return  integer;

    Function Is_empty (S : STACK) return  boolean;

    Function Is_full (S : STACK) return  boolean;

private
        type STACK_STRUCT;
        type STACK is access STACK_STRUCT;
end stacks;
```

Figure 5.5 Type **STACK** declared as an access type.

Using this approach, the **stacks** package specification would then look as shown in Figure 5.5. The complete declaration of **STACK_STRUCT** would then be given in the package body as shown in Figure 5.6.

It seems then that what Ada appears to give in the way of freedom to use non-pointer types for the implementation of private types is a somewhat mixed blessing: the requirements of good software engineering practice invariably tend to militate against their use anyway. In fact Ada is rather more restrictive in this matter than Modula-2, as the result of the dependency rules of Ada. These permit the compilation of a complete package, specification and body, that depends on a package, of which only the specification has been compiled. The complete hiding of the implementation of a private type in the package body would mean that the compiler would have no clue as to memory allocation for private type objects in the dependent package. The use of an access type allows this allocation to be performed – albeit really by pushing the problem onto the run-time kernel, which handles dynamic memory allocation.

```
package body stacks is
--
--      definitions for type STACK_STRUCT
--
stack_limit : constant := 100;
subtype stack_range is integer range 1 .. stack_limit;
subtype TOS_range is integer range 0 .. stack_limit;
--
type STACK_STRUCT is record
                        stack_array : array ( stack_range )
                                            of integer;
                        TOS : TOS_range;
                    end record;
--
-- remainder of body
--
```

Figure 5.6   Implementation of the stack private type.

5.2.4 Limited private types

The ability to declare variables normally carries with it the ability to manipulate these variables by a number of standard operations. Typically these include assignment – the operation that allows the value of one variable to be overwritten by the value of another – and also an operation to test that the values of two variables are equal. These standard operations are available for objects of any private type, and so the complete set of operations for such objects is:

1. *applicable operations* – subprograms exported from the same package that exports the private type with at least one parameter, or the result type if a function, of the private type;
2. *assignment* – the operation that overwrites a variable with the value of an object;
3. *equality test* – a Boolean-valued function, which is pre-defined for all types and private types.

This last operation seems to be a very straightforward affair for variables with types such as integer or character. It becomes rather more complicated for more complex types, however: are two records carrying the same data in the same set of fields, but arranged in different orders, equal? These problems become more significant when abstract data types are considered, particularly when they are realized as private types implemented as access types.

The nature of the problem can be seen by imagining a (slightly unreal) requirement to test if two stacks, both declared as being of the type STACK exported from stacks, are equal. In order to see what is involved it will be useful to show the implementation of the init operation:

```
procedure init(S : in out STACK) is
begin
        S := new STACK_STRUCT;
        S.TOS := 0;
end init;
```

(As can be seen, Ada distinguishes a subprogram *body* from its specification, as given in a package specification, by the word **is** that follows the formal parameter part. Other points to note are that:

- The familiar word *new* in Ada denotes an *allocator* that is more visibly like the memory allocation system calls provided in the Unix–C environment. An allocator is functional in the sense of returning a value – the address of the newly created object – rather than procedural as in Pascal. The effect of the execution of an allocator is rather clearer than its Pascal equivalent, because the "operand" of the expression is the type of the object that is actually created, rather than the pointer to it.
- There is no dereferencing operator in Ada, because an expression such as **S.TOS** quite obviously refers to a field of the object that **S** is pointing at – the value of **S** itself is an address and has no fields. An ambiguity can arise when the whole of a "pointed-at" object is required, in which case the expression **.all** is appended to the access variable name.)

The two stack variables in question, after being initialized, will denote two distinct address values obtained by two distinct executions of the allocator. Of necessity these values will be different – something would be seriously wrong if this was not the case because it would mean that dynamically created objects would overwrite each other. The important point is that any attempt to compare these values for equality will *always* produce the answer **false**, no matter what the contents of their respective **STACK_ STRUCT** records happen to be.

Structure-specific equality

What equality between two stacks actually means is presumably something along the lines that each corresponding pair of items in the two are equal. A test to determine equality would have to examine the contents of the two **stack_array** fields, but only in their "used" parts, i.e. up to the elements indexed by the **TOS** value(s). It is quite clear that the application of the standard equality test to the address values does nothing approaching this, and so the requirement to test for equality can be satisfied only if it is possible to disable the standard test and replace it by one specific to stacks.

This, in fact, is (one half of) the significance of *limited* private types. Objects – variables or constants – declared as being of a limited private type have available *only* the applicable operations exported from the package in which the type is declared, for their manipulation. In particular, in the context of the preceding discussion, the standard equality test is disabled, and in the case of limited private type operands only, Ada permits the redefinition, or *overloading*, of the equality test operator : *"="*. This is done by declaring a function with a specification of the form:

```
function "=" (left,right : LPT) return boolean;
```

where **LPT** is some limited private type.[1] This feature allows for an operation specific to the data structure in question to be defined.

Structure-specific assignment
As implied above, the standard assignment operation also is disabled for limited private types. The reason for this follows that for the equality test – the assignment of one private type object, implemented as an access variable, to another will simply cause both to point to the same data structure. This can lead to unexpected, and unwelcome, effects, symbolized by the following:

```
x := y;
modify(x);
```

modify is assumed to be a procedure that changes in some way its parameter. If **x** and **y** are of ordinary types, say integer, then the value of **y** will remain unchanged after the execution of the two statements. By contrast, if **x** and **y** are pointers, then the call to **modify(x)** will affect **y**, or at least the structure that **y** points at; a result that may well catch the programmer napping. What is normally required is a copying operation that produces a new structure, a so-called *deep copy*, to be denoted by the left-hand side of the assignment. Once again the standard operation cannot perform this operation for generalized structures; instead, it must be disabled and replaced by a specific version. If assignment is required for a limited private type, the operation must be exported as an applicable operation – a procedure, because assignment essentially modifies its left-hand operand. Note that Ada does not regard := as an operator like = and it cannot be overloaded. A procedure named **assign** or some such must be used. The final version of the **stacks** package, with exported assignment and equality test operations is shown in Figure 5.7.

5.3 Parameterizing abstract data types – discriminants

In the earlier array-based version of the **STACK** type the size of the underlying array, determined by the integer constant **stack_limit**, was

---

1. One of the changes introduced into Ada 95 is to allow *"="* to be overloaded for *any* types.

```
Package Stacks;
--
-- a package that exports an abstract data type
-- that provides the semantics of a
-- push-down stack data abstraction
--
    type STACK is limited private;

    Procedure Init(S : in out STACK);

    Procedure Push (S : in out STACK; Int_val : integer);

    Procedure Pop (S : in out STACK);

    Function Top (S : STACK) return  integer;

    Function Is_empty (S : STACK) return  boolean;

    Function Is_full (S : STACK) return  boolean;

    Function "=" ( left,right : STACK)
                            return  boolean;

    Procedure assign ( left : in out STACK;
                                right:  STACK);

private
    type STACK_STRUCT;
    type STACK is access STACK_STRUCT;
end stacks;
```

Figure 5.7   Stack defined as a limited private type.

set somewhat arbitrarily to 100. There is nothing intrinsic to the type in this value – it could be changed to one of many different values without altering the viability of the type declaration. Obviously, questions as to the appropriate size for the array would depend on the application within which the package was to be used, and thus can be deferred until this use actually occurs. In other words, the size of the array could be *abstracted away*, provided that some means is provided to set it in an actual application of the package. Such a means is provided in Ada by a *discriminant* for the type concerned: effectively a parameter for the type. The inclusion of a discriminant is done, naturally enough, in a way that resembles a formal parameter attached to the type name in its declaration. It may then be used within the declaration, again like a formal parameter. An appropriate

```
      --
      type STACK(size : positive) is private;
      --

private
      --
      --    full declarations for type STACK
      --
      type stack_store is array (positive range <>) of integer;
      type stack(size : positive) is
             record
                  stack_array : stack_store(1..size);
                  TOS : natural;
             end record;
```

Figure 5.8   Use of a discriminant to parameterize type STACK.

modification to the **stack** declaration to include a size discriminant is shown in Figure 5.8.

Ada requires array components of a record type, such as **stack_array**, to be of a named type, i.e. it could not be declared as:

```
    stack_array : array(1..size) of integer;
```

Instead, we are obliged to use an *unconstrained* array type, which omits the bounds on its indexes, although giving their base type, as indicated by the expression **positive range <>** in the declaration of **stack_store**. (**Positive** is a pre-defined subtype with all the positive values of **integer** – an appropriate range for array bounds.) The bounds on **stack_array** are imposed by the *discriminant constraint* **(1..size)**, which includes the "parameter" **size**. Note that there is no way of using **size** to constrain the range of **TOS**. Instead we have used **natural** – another predefined subtype with the range of **positive**, plus 0, to allow for the "empty stack" index value.

In their role as parameters of types, discriminants can be seen as performing the initialization of the corresponding objects, e.g. a declaration such as:

```
    large_stack : stacks.stack(1000);
```

causes the creation of a **stack** object called **large_stack**, with an underlying array initialized to a size of 1000 elements. We shall return to the question of the initialization of data abstractions both in the next chapter and later.

5.4 Review of Ada

Despite its size and complexity Ada has become well established as a standard language, particularly in the field of defence applications. Much of the reason for this is precisely the standardization imposed on the language by its design authority – the US Department of Defense. This has meant that genuinely portable programs can be written on such diverse platforms as personal computers, workstations, mini and mainframe computers. It is also the case that the spur of competition provided by the restriction of much of the software commissioned by the DoD to the use of Ada has encouraged the manufacturers of compilers for the language to achieve prodigious feats of performance – both at compile time and run time.

In the context of this book, the importance of Ada lies in the fact that its design is centred about the use of data abstraction as a constructional technique for software systems. There have been a number of languages that have exhibited a similar orientation including Alphard, Clu and, of course, Modula-2, which we have already discussed. If the use of data abstraction were restricted to these languages, however, the technique would remain an interesting curiosity with a significant but small following, restricted largely to the academic world. The adoption of Ada by the DoD, with its huge financial muscle, has changed this picture substantially and placed data abstraction techniques in the centre stage of software production.

5.5 Summary

In this and the preceding chapter we have looked in some detail at the support for the data abstraction provided by two languages descended from Pascal: Modula-2 and Ada. The practical considerations of the use of the data abstraction, which have been recognized by the designers of both languages, have led to the incorporation of support for abstract data types – a generalization of the original concept, which provides a very powerful facility at the expense of a certain increase in complexity when the practicalities of compilation and also considerations such as equality are accommodated.

In the next chapter we turn to a different language "culture", with a correspondingly different approach to the support of data abstraction.

5.6 Further reading

Again, as might be expected, Ada has inspired a considerable volume of literature, of variable quality. For a straightforward introduction to the language, despite occasional lapses in structure, it is difficult to beat

Programming in Ada (Reading, Mass.: Addison-Wesley, 1984) by J. G. P. Barnes, who was one of Ada's designers. G. Booch, *Software engineering with Ada* (Menlo Park, California: Benjamin/Cummings, 1986), is a splendidly committed exposition, which attempts, with considerable success, to provide a "top-down" view of the language in which, inevitably, some of the detail is obscured. The final arbiter on the 1983 version of the language is the "LRM" – *Reference manual for the Ada programming language* (Tunbridge Wells, Kent: Castle House, 1983), which is an ANSI standard: MIL-STD-1815. As the definition of a large and complex language the LRM is a considerable achievement, and any serious Ada programmer should possess a copy – most Ada compilers produce error messages that refer to the relevant sections of the LRM.

CHAPTER 6

Languages and data abstraction – 3

6.1 Introduction – C and C++

So far the discussion of programming language support for data abstraction has been restricted to Pascal and its descendents, Modula-2 and Ada. In addition to their obvious family likenesses, these languages possess a shared reputation for "security" – one might almost say "respectability" – deriving from the original didactic aims enshrined in the design of Pascal, and realized in practice by the strong typing that is a major common characteristic.

By contrast, the C language has possessed a somewhat raffish reputation as a result of its "loose typing" and terse style, which have endeared it to computing students and hackers (not necessarily separate classes) alike in a way that the Pascal family has singularly failed to achieve.

Perhaps surprisingly, C derives its ancestry from the same Algol 60 roots as Pascal, but via a very specialized intermediary, the type*less* language BCPL. The designer of C, Dennis Ritchie, (strictly speaking we should mention Ken Thompson, the designer of "B", C's immediate predecessor) felt unable to follow BCPL in its total abandonment of the concept of type, but allowed very great flexibility in type conversions, which are often implicit. C, for example, finds no problem in the addition of an integer to an ASCII character. In this C possesses characteristics similar to those of assembly languages, reflecting accurately the intended use of the language as the implementation language of the Unix operating system.

The original role of C as a "high-level assembler" has been somewhat lost as the result of its adoption as the major *application* programming language in the MS-Dos/PC environment. Although not totally suitable for this kind of use, the very freedom that the language permits has led to the widespread adoption of programming conventions that attempt to impose good practice and "structuredness". Amongst these, again perhaps surprisingly, is a basic level support for data abstraction, albeit provided in a somewhat *ad hoc* way.

The limitations of C as a "secure" language led Bjarne Stroustrup to devise an extended version of the language, C++ (the name being a fairly obvious joke). C++ is generally known as an (or the) object-oriented language, in which guise it appears in Chapter 11. In many ways, however, it can be seen, and is certainly often used, as a "cleaned-up" C, with a much more systematic (if not exactly strict) approach to typing, and strong support for data abstraction. In this role C++ forms the material for the second part of this chapter, following a discussion of data abstraction in C.

6.2 Data abstraction in C

As we have seen, support for data abstraction depends generally on some form of "module" construct, which allows for the separation of an interface, defined in terms of operations, usually subprograms, from the underlying implementation hidden, or encapsulated, within it. In the examples discussed so far, Modula-2 and Ada, this separation is quite explicitly defined. They provide different constructs for the interface and implementation aspects of a data abstraction, the two being eventually united by the compilation system.

6.2.1 External definitions

The C language defines no module construct as such. Indeed, the only construct larger than a statement is the *function* – a subprogram construct with the conventional "functional" attribute that it returns a value, which, however, may be null or "void". Like Ada, C does not have an enveloping "program" construct – a C "program" simply consists of one or more source files containing functions and, unlike Ada, optionally, data items.

Although not defined in the language, the (source) file or "translation unit" possesses a "semi-official" status in C, for example in the way that data items may be declared within a file but outside any function. The scope of such "external" items extends over the entire file in which they are declared, and thus they are global to any functions within the file.

6.2.2 Header files

The possibility, mentioned above, of composing a program from several source files (that may be compiled at different times), requires allowing references between files to be specified, so that, for example, calls to functions contained in one file may be made in functions contained in another. At a minimal level this depends on the compiler being given sufficient information to allocate memory for the parameters to the functions in question.

The standard technique for achieving this is the use of *header* files, which depends on a feature of C permitting the interface of a function, i.e.

its return type, name and formal parameter list, or *prototype*, to be included any number of times as a separate item in a source program. C terminology distinguishes between the *definition* of a function, which includes its implementation-defining body, and its *declaration*, which constitutes its interface. The definition of a function may appear only once in the collection of files that make up a program, but its declaration may appear any number of times. The declaration of a function is enough to permit a call to it to be compiled. This means that a function may be called from a file other than the one in which its definition appears, provided its declaration is given in the file.

Header files conventionally contain only declarations, and it is recognized "good practice", when writing a set of C function definitions, to provide a separate header file containing the function declarations. This may be incorporated into another source file by using the **#include** mechanism,[1] so permitting calls to the "included" functions to be compiled. In the Unix environment header files are conventionally given a ".h" file extension to distinguish them from the ".c" C source file extension.

It will be seen that the header file technique is based on the separation of interface and implementation, in a manner that might well be utilized in the support of data abstraction. Figure 6.1 shows an attempt at an implementation of the inevitable stack example, corresponding to the header file, **stack.h**, containing the following interface:

```
void init();
void push(int);
int pop();
int isempty();
```

A brief explanation of the code is given below for those unfamiliar with the details of C.

The header file **stack.h**, which will be the externally visible interface of the "module" is **#include**d to allow the compiler to check that it is, in fact, compatible with the operation implementations. C comments are enclosed in the "/*" "*/" brackets.

The data structure is declared as an array **store** of 100 integer elements, together with the top of stack pointer **tos**. The type of **tos** is "pointer to **int**", as indicated by the "*" declarator. This is used to exploit the C duality between arrays and pointers, which recognizes the name of an array as a pointer to its first element, and thus permits the assignment of **store**, i.e. a pointer to **int**, to **tos**, in the initialization function **init()**.

---

1. The include mechanism is a feature of the C compiler pre-processor that causes files nominated in an expression of the form **#include** *"filename"* at the head of a source file to be merged into it before compilation. Note that this is quite different from the Ada/Modula-2 library mechanism, which merges the *compiled* components of library units.

```
#include "stack.h" /* to ensure compatibility */
int store[100] ;
int *tos ; /* stack top pointer */

void init() /* initialise stack */
        {
                tos = store;
        }

void push(int elem)
        {
                *++tos = elem;
        }

int pop()
        {
                return *tos--;
        }

int isempty() /* returns 0 if not */
        {
                return tos == store;
        }
```

Figure 6.1 C implementation of a stack.

C functions are headed by the type of the returned value, which is **void** if there is no value, followed by the name and the, possibly empty, formal parameter list; this consists of the types of the parameters, with optional names[2] (e.g. **elem** in **push()**). The body of the function then follows as a block enclosed by "{" "}", the C equivalents of **begin** and **end**.

The **push()** and **pop()** operations depend respectively on the incrementing (++) and decrementing (--) operations applied to the top of stack pointer. In each case the pointer is dereferenced by "*" to allow assignment to/from the current stack top. This occurs *after* the incrementing and *before* the decrementing, as indicated by the position of the operator relative to **tos** in each case.

The C assignment operator is "=", and the equality test "==". There is no **boolean** type in C; the result of a relational operator is 0 if false and 1 if true.

---

2. Note that this is a feature specific to the later version of the language, known as ANSI C.

6.2.3 Data encapsulation

The use of declarations to permit external references may also, less desirably, be applied to data items. A data declaration qualified by the **extern** qualifier, referencing a data item defined externally in a separate file, provides global access to the item. Thus, a file containing the declaration **extern store** would, when compiled and linked with the file (**stack.c**) containing the implementation of the stack, enable assignments to be made directly to the array within which the stack is implemented, sidestepping the operations that maintain the LIFO discipline. This would appear to be a severe blow to any possibility of creating a genuinely encapsulated data abstraction. Fortunately, however, help is at hand in the form of the **static** storage class.

static appears in two guises. The first, and perhaps more intuitive, provides the facility (mentioned in Ch. 3) of making local variables survive individual invocations of their enclosing functions. Although not irrelevant to data abstraction, as we have seen, this type of facility is not adequate to support a satisfactory realization. It is in its application to external data items that **static** achieves a considerable significance to data abstraction, because it has the effect of making such items invisible to external references – in other words it encapsulates them within their enclosing file. The data definitions shown in Figure 6.2, therefore, cannot be accessed outside their file, and thus may be manipulated only by the operations declared in the related header file. The combination of the two, therefore, provides a perfectly adequate realization of a stack data abstraction.

6.2.4 Limitations

The support for data abstraction that we have discussed here is limited by the fact that only objects, realized as individual modules, can be created. In other words, a program that required two stacks would have to include two modules along the lines shown above – the technique cannot provide abstract data types, which may be used to declare an indefinite number of stack objects.

It *is* possible in C to create a type whose instances are collections of functions, or rather function types. The means of doing this is the C *structure*, which fulfils the same role as the **record** type in Modula-2 and Ada – i.e. a composite type with heterogeneously typed "slots" or fields, known as *members* in C. For example, a structure holding fields for the data structure of a stack might be declared as:

```
struct stackst{
            int store[100];
            int *TOS;
        };
```

```
static int store[100];
static int *tos ; /* stack top pointer */

void init() /* initialise stack */
        {
                tos = store;
        }

void push(int elem)
        {
                *++tos = elem;
        }

int pop()
        {
                return *tos--;
        }

int isempty() /* returns 0 if not */
        {
                return tos == store;
        }
```

Figure 6.2 C implementation of a stack with encapsulated data.

The keyword **struct** indicates the declaration of a structure type. In this case there are two fields enclosed within the braces, and the type is given the name, or "tag", **stackst**, which can be used to declare variables in exactly the same way as **int** or **char**.

As in the case of the Pascal/Ada record, the dot notation is used to select fields from structures:

```
struct stackst st1, st2;
st1.TOS = st1.store;
```

In addition to data type fields, **structs** may also contain "function type" fields, albeit indirectly. Consistently with its comprehensive support for the use of pointers, C provides for the creation of pointers to functions. Practically, these are simply pointers to the entry points of the functions concerned. As in the case of pointers to data areas, C, despite its reputation, attempts to allow the compiler to check that what is being pointed at is, at least, of the correct type. What is the type of a function? It is the pattern of parameter types and the return type – the information provided by the prototype of the function: the interface. For example, the declaration of a pointer type to a function that takes two **char** parameters and returns an **int** value, is as follows:

```
int (*) (char, char);
```

The type can be given a name using the **typedef** facility:

```
typedef int (*PFICC) (char, char );
```

This causes **PFICC** to name a type that is a pointer to any function with two character parameters that returns an **int**. A variable of type **PFICC** can be made to point to a "real" function by an assignment to the address of such a function. In fact, in a manner analogous to arrays, function names denote pointer values, and so a function name can be assigned directly to an appropriate pointer.

This means that the **stackst** structure can be extended to include function pointer fields that define the prototypes of the operations associated with a stack, as shown below:

```
typedef void (*PFVV) (); /* returns void,
 no parameters */
typedef void (*PFVI) (int); /* returns void,
 int parameter */
typedef int (*PFIV) (); /* returns int,
 no parameters */
struct stackst{
                int store[100];
                int *TOS;
                PFVV initp;
                PFVI pushp;
                PFIV popp;
                PFIV isemptyp;
        };
```

As we can see, the structure now provides a type definition that captures the essential features of the stack. This would now permit the declaration of an indefinite number of **stackst** variables, each possessing members corresponding to the data structure and associated operations of a stack. Unfortunately, however, the C structure is inadequate to allow for a useful implementation of abstract data types, for the following reasons:

1. The apparent elegance of the idea is ruined by the need to assign actual functions corresponding to the function pointer members.
2. The functions assigned to the function pointer members in each case would have no special access to the data members. They would have to access them using the name of the variable in each case. So each structure variable would have its own unique set of functions.

3. There is no protection afforded to the fields within a structure; it would be possible therefore to manipulate the data fields without using the operational interface.

It can be seen, therefore, that the standard C structure provides an imperfect image of what an implementation of abstract data types might be. To find an adequate implementation it is necessary to turn to C++.

6.3 Data abstraction in C++

6.3.1 Structures in C++

As we have seen, the C structure goes some way towards providing the ability to define abstract data types, but is eventually inadequate. We have also seen that a quite different approach can be used to support data abstraction, in the sense of a module capable both of exporting a set of operations and of encapsulating the data structure manipulated by these operations.

In C++ the concept of the structure is extended to confront the problems noted at the end of the last section, and to provide a module construct that is actually defined in the language, rather than as a matter of conventional usage. One of the important ways in which C++ extends the C structure is in permitting the inclusion of function declarations. These are given directly as *prototypes*, indicating the return type, name and formal parameter types (optionally with parameter names), rather than as function pointer types. This provides the ability to define a self-contained operational interface, without the need for **typedefs**. The effect of this is to provide a construct for the definition of an operational interface that looks not unlike an Ada package specification or Modula-2 DEFINITION MODULE. For example, using the hallowed stack, with **int** elements (note that C++ supports both the C comment brackets "/*" "*/" and a line-terminated version introduced by "//"):

```
struct stack {
            void init(); // initialize stack
            void push(int elem);
            int pop();
            int isempty(); // returns 0 if not
};
```

There is, however, a very important difference from the equivalent Modula-2/Ada construct – a structure defines a *type*, not a program unit, the tag being recognized as a type name. So the way in which **stack** is used is, as for any other type name, to declare variables, possibly with derived types, e.g. arrays of stacks. A program using the **stack** struct might include the following:

```
struct stack s1;
struct stack svec[10];
```

declaring, respectively, a **stack** variable and an array of 10 **stacks**. Function stack members are referenced in the same way as data members using the structure member selector operator " **.** " **Push** operations on each might appear therefore as follows:

```
int ival = 1;
s1.push(ival);
svec[2].push(ival);
```

As these examples show, the operations are associated with the stack *objects* in a very direct way – they may be invoked only by selection on the object's name, rather than from a program unit to which the object is passed as a parameter. C++ structures, then, provide the basis for realizing abstract data types in a way that is very faithful to the theoretical concept, certainly in comparison with Ada private types or Modula-2 opaque types.

6.3.2 Data structure encapsulation – the class

So far our stack structure possesses an adequate operational interface, but lacks the essential data structure to maintain its internal state. Suitable data members can be added without difficulty to support an array-based implementation:

```
struct stack {
            void init(); // initialize stack
            void push(int elem);
            int pop();
            int isempty(); // returns 0 if not
            int store[100];
            int *TOS;
        };
```

However, in the previous discussion of the shortcomings of the C **struct** it was noted that all the fields are externally accessible, using the selection operator " **.** ". This attribute remains unchanged in the C++ version, and so it is impossible to protect the data members from direct modification, and thus to guarantee the maintaining of the stack semantics.

A possible answer might have been to avoid the inclusion of data members in the interface declaration – to adopt the Modula-2 solution in effect and encapsulate them in a separate construct. This was not done, however, for much the same reason that data declarations appear in the private parts of Ada package specifications – to allow the compiler to determine the memory required for each object.

Instead, and in a manner somewhat similar to Ada in this respect, C++ provides the ability to control access to individual members. As this represents a quite new characteristic Stroustrup felt it was appropriate to introduce a new construct into the language, the *class*, which possesses all the attributes of the structure, and indeed the same basic format with **struct** replaced by **class**. The first major difference that the class exhibits over the structure is its support for *access levels*.

Access levels

Every class member possesses an *access level*, which determines its accessibility. There are three access levels, but for the moment we will restrict the discussion to two: *public* and *private*; the third is relevant only to inherited classes and will be described later. In a fairly natural manner, public class members are accessible from anywhere in the program containing the class. Private members are accessible only within the scope of the class, and are thus protected from external access.

The default access level that class members possess is private; this can be overridden by the appearance of the **public:** label in the sequence of member definitions: those following **public:** then possess the public access level. Hence the need to precede the operations for **stack** by **public:** Although strictly unnecessary because of the default, it is good practice to use the **private:** label to precede and identify the private members in a class declaration. This is enforced by the convention that the public members (typically functions defining the interface) of a class appear before the private members that comprise the encapsulated data structure.

We may now convert the stack structure example into a class, so as to include an encapsulated data structure for an array-based implementation, as follows:

```
class stack {
          public:
              void init(); // initialize stack
              void push(int elem);
              int pop();
              int isempty(); // returns 0 if not
          private:
              int store[100];
              int *tos; // stack top pointer
          };
```

An important point to note is that initializations may not appear in a class declaration, thus the perhaps natural initialization of **tos** to the first element of **store** is not permitted. Initialization of class members is (very comprehensively) supported, but this is a future topic.

Operation implementation – the scope operator
The previous discussion of the shortcomings of the C structure identified two further problems, apart from its inadequate support for encapsulation. These are both concerned with the relationship of the implementations of the operations – the function bodies – to the interface declaration. How is this relationship to be specified, and how is access to the data members provided?

It is obviously necessary for the operations of an abstract data type to be able to access the encapsulated data structure – the operations of **stack**, for example, need access to both **store** and **tos**, despite their private access level, which restricts access to within the scope of the class. As this would appear to be delimited by the braces surrounding the declaration, how can access be provided?

The answer is provided by the *scope operator*, which takes the form of a double colon "**::**" When this is used to conjoin a class name with the definition of a function declared within the class, it has the effect of extending the scope of the class over the whole function definition, thus providing access from within the function to the private members of the class. (Recall the distinction between a function *declaration*, which simply provides the interface of the function – its prototype – and its *definition*, which also includes its implementation.)

We may now supply the bodies of the **stack** operations:

```
void stack::init() // initialize stack
            {
              tos = store;
            }
void stack::push(int elem)
            {
              *++tos = elem;
            }
int stack::pop()
            {
              return *tos--;
            }
int stack::isempty() // returns 0 if not
            {
              return tos == store;
            }
```

(It should be noted that, consistent with earlier illustrations, this implementation is deficient in providing no error checking, particularly in the use of a bounded array. This is for the sake of clarity, and is not intended as a style model.)

Inline member functions

It is permitted to avoid using the scope operator and to supply the *definition* of a member function within a class declaration, i.e. including the function body. This has the effect of causing the function to be *inline expanded* which means that the complete compiled code of the function is inserted into the program at the point of each call made to it, rather than using the standard call mechanism. This produces an improvement in speed efficiency, but obviously at the cost of an increased program size, and is intended to be used only with very small, and frequently called, functions. The inclusion of function definitions in a class declaration also serves to reduce its readability.

File usage

Unlike Modula-2 or Ada, C++ does not provide language support for library modules, so the compiler will not allow a program to include calls to library functions that are not actually declared in the program. A program wishing to use the **stack** class would be obliged, therefore, to include the *declaration* of **stack**. As we have seen the conventional way of doing this in the C context is to create the declaration in a separate header file. This convention is continued in C++, the header file, (i.e. with a **.h** extension, is **#include**d into the **.c** files holding the data structure and operation implementations, and the program.

6.3.3 Class management members

So far we have covered the language structures, particularly the class, that C++ provides to support abstract data types: types whose instances are data abstractions. Besides providing what is, as has been remarked, a very intuitively natural syntactic support, C++ also provides *pragmatics*, i.e. features actually concerned with the use of the language, designed to facilitate object-based programming. The visible counterparts of these features are a set of conventional operations, or *function members*, that commonly appear in C++ classes – members whose existence is largely unaffected by the specific application to which the class is devoted. These function members are referred to as *class-management* members, and an important category of these are concerned with object initialization and deletion, known respectively as *constructors* and *destructors*.

Constructors and destructors

The initialization of a data abstraction requires, to say the least, special consideration. Generally it will involve giving initial values to part or all of the underlying data structure, yet of course this will be hidden from direct assignment of values. At the same time the importance of initialization is hard to exaggerate – research has shown that a very considerable proportion of program bugs arise from the failure to initialize variables correctly, and data abstractions, in this context, are simply complex variables. It is for this reason that Modula-2 and Ada extend Pascal's notoriously inadequate facilities for initialization. Both languages complement their support for data abstraction by the provision for an "initialization section" at the end respectively of the relevant IMPLEMENTATION MODULE or package body. This is a piece of code with full access to the encapsulated data structure, which is executed at the initiation of the program, indeed actually before control is passed to the "entry point". In this way the initialization of the data structure is guaranteed before any external reference is made to it.

The initialization section idea is quite adequate for modules or packages that are implementations of individual data abstractions. It is less satisfactory where a package, for example, exports an abstract data type in the form of a private type. There may be any number of instances of such a type created during the running of the program, each of which will possess its own data structure, which will need initializing. The code of the initialization section will have completed its execution before the creation of any of these data structures, and so is effectively irrelevant.

As we have seen, Ada provides discriminants for the parameterization of abstract data types, but these are inadequate to accomplish the initialization of dynamic data structures, which require the execution of memory allocators and the assignment of pointers. The only recourse for the designer of a package implementing such a type is to include an initialization *operation* in the interface provided for the type, in the pious hope that users will remember to call it before doing anything else. There is no way that such a requirement can be enforced, and this is particularly serious where, as is often the case, the data structure involved is dynamic.[3]

C++ classes, as we have seen, define types and are therefore used to declare variables in indefinite numbers and at any point during the execution of the enclosing program. When the type is an abstract data type, so that the variables are data abstractions, the need for a powerful initialization mechanism is particularly marked, and is comprehensively satisfied by the constructor concept.

A constructor is a class member function intended to be called whenever an instance of the class is created, i.e. it is synchronized with the birth of the instance objects, rather than the initiation of the program. As might be anticipated, to avoid the problems of normal "initialization operations" constructors are called *implicitly*, i.e. automatically by the C++ system rather than explicitly by the programmer. In some circumstances, however, object initializations *simulate* explicit calls to their constructors.

---

3. Ada 95 introduces a feature for the implicit invocation of a user-written initialization of program objects.

A constructor is distinguished textually by the fact that its name is the same as the class in which it is declared; the other noteworthy feature about constructor declarations is that they do not have a returned type specification (not even **void**), as constructors may not return a value. The provision of constructors by the class designer is optional. In the absence of a constructor the system will create a "default constructor", which may or may not perform in the way that the designer wishes; an understanding of this, and other "default behaviour" is necessary on the part of the user of C++, which possesses a number of hidden pitfalls.

Complementary to constructors are destructors, which are called when an object is destroyed, typically to free up the memory occupied by the object. The destructor for a class has the name of the class prefixed by a tilde (~); like constructors, a destructor declaration does not specify a return type. Again destructors are optional, and are certainly normally restricted to a particular category of class implementations.

The sequencing of implicit calls to constructors and destructors within the execution sequence of a program depends on the way in which the objects for which they are called are created. There are three ways in which an object can come into existence during the execution of a C++ program, which result in the object possessing *static*, *automatic* or *dynamic extent*.

Static objects   In C++ global objects, i.e. those defined externally – outside any enclosing structure other than the file that contains them – possess static extent and come into existence before the commencement of the execution of **main()**, the "program root" function. If such an object is an instance of a class then a constructor, if it has one, will be called when the program begins to execute, i.e. before the execution of **main**. In effect the constructor for this kind of object is equivalent to an Ada package initialization section and, as such, is useful in providing for the initializations of libraries. A destructor will be called after the termination of **main**.

It is also possible for local variables to be declared as **static**, which, as we have seen, means that their values survive the invocation of the function to which they are local. Objects of this kind are initialized only once – on the first invocation of the function within which they are declared – the constructor for a class instance declared as **static**, therefore, is called only once.

Automatic objects   The lifetimes of automatic objects, typically denoted by variables declared within functions, are determined by the structure of the program text, which defines the variable scopes. When a function call is executed, memory for the variables local to the function is allocated within the *activation record* placed on the top of the *run-time stack*. The activation record remains at the top of the stack until execution returns from the function, at which point the stack top is collapsed and the activation record, including all the local variables, destroyed.

The interaction of constructors and destructors with this mechanism occurs invisibly as far as the programmer is concerned – a constructor is called implicitly when execution reaches the scope of the variable that denotes the object, and memory for it is allocated on the stack; the destructor is called implictly when execution leaves the scope of the variable and the memory is deallocated.

Returning to the **stack** class example, we may replace the **init()** operation by a constructor, which will avoid relying on the user of the class having to remember to call **init()** before making any use of a stack object. The revised declaration is shown below, together with the implementation of the constructor and an illustration of its use:

```
class stack {
            public:
              stack();
              void push(int elem);
              int pop();
              int isempty();
            private:
              int store[100];
              int *tos;
          };

    stack::stack() // initialize stack
          {
              tos = store;
          }
    int main()
          {
              stack s; // constructor called here
```

It should be emphasized that the allocation and deallocation of memory for automatic objects is – automatic (hence the name). There is therefore little requirement for the provision of destructors for them, *unless* their implementation involves the use of dynamic memory, which will be discussed in the next section.

Dynamic objects A characteristic of object-based systems is the dynamic management of objects, and the linking of object lifetimes to the textually defined scopes of the variables that denote them, as in the case of automatic objects, is overly constraining for some applications. A more fine-grained level of control is provided by the use of *dynamic objects*, which are created within memory allocated in the "free store" available to the program.

Heap management Every C++ program is provided with a pool of "free store", i.e. memory that does not have objects allocated in it by the compiler, often called the *heap*. Free store is used for the creation of *dynamic* objects, i.e. objects explicitly created during the running of the program and effectively unknown to the compiler. They are contrasted with automatic objects for which memory is *implicitly* allocated, on the run-time stack. Dynamic objects can be accessed only via pointers into the heap.

In C++ free store allocation is performed, rather like Ada, by the **new** operator. **new** takes a type name as its (right) operand and returns a pointer to the allocated memory if the operation is successful, or 0 otherwise. This value is assigned to an appropriately declared pointer, or used to initialize such a pointer in its declaration. For example:

```
int *ip;
ip = new int;
// or ..
int *ip = new int;
```

As noted above, objects created by **new** have dynamic extent, and will continue to exist until the memory allocated to them is returned to the free store pool by means of the **delete** operator, which takes as its operand a pointer to the object that is to be "destroyed". In fact the object is not destroyed – its memory becomes available for new allocations, which may or may not occur.

The simple allocation and deallocation of memory, however, is inadequate to support the level of object management that is required in the use of abstract data types; in particular there is the need to provide for the initialization of objects as they are created, and in a manner that can coexist with the encapsulation of their internal structure. Thus the invocation of constructors and destructors for dynamic objects is tied in with the memory allocation/deallocation operations that delimit their existence.

To illustrate this we may create a dynamic, rather than an automatic, stack object by declaring a **pointer to stack** object, which is then made to point at a stack created on the heap, as shown below. (Note that no use is made of the heap *by the constructor*, which remains the same. We will come to "internal" use of the heap by constructors shortly.)

```
int main()
    {
    int val;
    stack* ps;
    * * * // statements
    ps = new stack; // constructor called here
    // get a value for val
    while (val) {
                ps->push(val);
                // get another value for val
            }
```

(Note the expression **ps->push**, which is shorthand for **(*ps).push**, i.e. the "**->**" symbol selects the member named by its right operand from the class object *pointed to* by its left operand. Also the inclusion of the assertion "**assert (ps != 0)**" causes the program to terminate if the heap allocation fails, and **new** returns 0.) As indicated by the comment, the implicit call to **stack::stack()** is made when the memory for the stack is allocated by **new**, and is thus decoupled from the function block structure.

Once memory has been allocated on the heap it remains allocated until being specifically deallocated by **delete**, which takes as its operand a pointer to the area in question. (Note that it is possible for such a pointer to go out of scope, in which case the memory is lost to the program.) The dynamic stack created in the last example, therefore, could be destroyed by:

```
delete ps;
```

and this will implicitly call the destructor. In this case the destructor does very little because the creation of stack objects by the constructor involves no memory allocation.

Constructors with parameters

The example constructor considered so far, that for the **stack** class, is a parameterless function, and thus the nature of the stack objects created in conjunction with this function is fixed, with no possible variation. With a small amount of effort we may imagine a requirement to create stacks of different sizes, and the obvious mechanism to achieve this is to supply a parameter to the constructor that specifies the size of the array **store**. The prototype of the constructor would then become:

```
stack (int);
```

As the decisions about the size of each stack might well be taken at run-time, in response to data input to the program, it is clearly impossible to have memory for **store** allocated by the compiler. Instead, heap space must be used, with an implementation along the lines of:

```
stack::stack(int len) // len is size of stack
    {
        store = new int[len];
        assert ( store != 0 );
        tos = store;
    }
```

(Note the form of the type name for the use of **new** to allocate heap space for an array, which gives the element type followed by the size in the vector brackets "[ ]".)

As the creation of a **stack** object involves the allocation of heap memory, it is necessary for the destructor to deallocate the memory to avoid "memory leakage":

```
stack::~stack()
    {
        delete store [];
    }
```

The **delete** operator takes a pointer to the memory in question, in this case **store**, which is followed by the square bracket pair indicating that the memory is occupied by an array.

Member initialization lists   In the example constructor the initialization of the private data members **store** and **tos** is done by assignments in the body of the function. An alternative method is provided by C++, which emphasizes the special nature of initialization as a "one-off" event that may therefore be granted certain privileges.

A *member initialization list* takes the form of a list of expressions, separated by commas if there is more than one, each of which looks like a call to a function with the name of a data member. The "actual argument" supplied in parentheses is an expression, usually involving one or more of the formal parameters of the constructor, whose value is used to initialize the data member. The list is preceded by a colon and is placed between the formal parameter list and opening "{" of the constructor body. For example, if we introduce a new data member **length**, holding the size of the **store** array, its initialization can be achieved as follows:

```
stack::stack(int len):
    length(len)
        {
            store = new int[len];
            assert (store != 0);
            tos = store;
        }
```

The significant point about member initialization lists is that they can be used to initialize constant data members. The new data member **length** denotes a variable quantity as far as the program is concerned – it can be set to different values in each of the stack objects declared – but as far as each stack object is concerned it is a fixed value, and should be protected from modification. C++ provides the means to do this with the **const** qualifier. A variable declared as a constant in this way cannot be altered by assignment; however, when such a variable is a class data member its value *can* be changed, *from being undefined*, by an item in a member initialization list. So if the declaration of **length** is:

```
const int length;
```

the above code will work; this would not be the case for an assignment within the body of the function.

Passing parameters to a constructor As we have seen, constructors are called implicitly, and this raises the obvious question of how the actual parameter(s) may be passed to a constructor. The answer is by the use of a simulated explicit call to the constructor, although for an automatic object the standard way is to use a shorthand version that appends the actual parameter list to the variable name in its definition:

```
stack s(50);
```

This is actually shorthand for:

```
stack s = stack(50);
```

The shorthand form is rather less confusing, but cannot be used for a dynamic object, where the explicit form must be used:

```
stack *ps = new stack(50);
```

Default parameter values We can still retain the ability to have a default stack size by giving the parameter a default value, in the prototype of the constructor:

```
stack (int = 100);
```

It would be more normal, and better practice, to *overload* the constructor, i.e. provide one for the default case, and another with the size parameter.

Alternative constructors

It is standard practice to provide several constructors within a class declaration. All will be named with the tag name of the class, which is then said to be *overloaded*. The overloadings must have different parameter profiles to permit the compiler to distinguish between them. The class declaration might, therefore, include the following:

```
stack();
stack(int);
```

This is a typical pattern in a class declaration – a constructor that takes no parameters called the *default* constructor and one that has one or more parameters of built in types, which provides in effect a "conversion" from its parameter types to the type of the class (e.g. **int -> stack** in this case).

Default constructor The default constructor is used when no parameters are supplied in the declaration of an object, for example:

```
stack st;
stack *sp = new stack;
```

Note that an attempt to invoke the default constructor as follows:

```
stack st();
```

is in fact a declaration of a parameterless function with a result type of **stack**.

The default constructor is also necessary if it is wished to declare a vector of objects, for example:

```
stack st_vec[10]; // vector of 11 stacks
```

this is because there is no way of passing parameters to the constructor invoked by such a declaration.

It is also standard practice to provide an overloading that allows an object to be initialized to the value of another object (obviously) of the same class, for example:

```
stack st1;
stack st2 = st1;
```

this overloading is often referred to as the *copy constructor*.

The copy constructor   In the absence of a copy constructor in the class declaration, an object declaration of the form shown above (in which the new object is initialized to the value of an existing object) the initialization is performed by *default member-wise* copy, i.e. an exact copy of the data members of the existing object. An inevitable problem, which is analogous to those that arise with Modula-2 opaque types, occurs when these data members include pointers. A default member-wise copy simply copies pointer values, so that the two objects end up addressing the same area of heap memory. This is not only almost certainly what the programmer did not intend, but can cause disaster if **delete** is called in the destructor, because it will be called twice for the same area of memory – an action that should be avoided at all costs.

The copy constructor, then, should perform what is known as a *deep copy*, which reproduces the structure of the object, as contrasted with the *shallow* default copy, that just copies its pointer values. In the case of a **stack** object, for example, this will necessitate the allocation of heap space and the copying of the values held in the existing stack into the new area.

The C++ compiler recognizes a copy constructor by its prototype. This has one parameter, which is "read-only, reference to"[4] the type of the class in whose declaration it appears, i.e. for a class **x** the copy constructor will have the prototype **x(const X\&)**. A copy constructor for the **stack** class might look as follows:

---

4. C++, unlike C, allows for the use of parameters called by reference – i.e. where the actual parameter itself, rather than a copy of it, is accessible within the function – such parameters are distinguished by the "**&**" declarator. Reference parameters may be protected from modification, made read only, by the use of **const**.

```
stack::stack(const stack &ost): // create a new stack
    length(ost.length), store(new int[ost.length])
    {
        assert (store != 0);
        tos = store;
    // copy the old stack into it
        for (int *otos = ost.store;
         otos != ost.tos; )
        {
                *++tos = *++otos;
        }
    }
```

The importance of the copy constructor is not restricted to initialization in declarations. For example, when an object is passed *by value* to a parameter declared with a type that is a class with a copy constructor, the copy constructor is invoked to create the value of the formal parameter. The importance of this is perhaps not so much what happens if a copy constructor exists, but what happens if one does not exist: a default member-wise copy is generated. Where the class involved uses pointers, this will result in side effects that may not be obvious to the programmer.

Under certain circumstances the copy constructor is also invoked when an object of a class type is passed back as the returned value from a function.

It will be seen that in C++, as in Ada, the inevitable use of pointers in the implementation of abstract data types requires specific measures to deal with the indirection involved. This is true not only in the context of constructors – particularly the copy constructor, but also the overloadings of the assignment and equality test operators.

Overloading for orthogonality
So far the discussion of class management members has been restricted to constructors and destructors; although highly important, these do not exhaust the subject. Typical application independent classes include a number of members designed to make their use more "natural" in the sense of being like the built-in types such as **int, char,** etc., and also common derived types such as vectors. C++ classes resemble Ada limited private types in that they have no test for equality operations by default, and so the provision of these is a common requirement. Perhaps surprisingly they are provided with assignment by default, although the factors invalidating a default test for equality apply to assignment; this is discussed below.

The major facility of C++ in this context is *operator overloading*. We recall that to overload an operator means to provide an alternative implementation that will allow the operator to be applied to operand(s) with types different from that of the existing version(s). Overloading introduces ambiguity – the operator in question standing for several different things – that the compiler must be able to resolve by examining the type pattern of the operands. These therefore must be unique in each case.

An overloaded operator is declared as a member function with a name consisting of the operator symbol prefixed by **operator.**

The assignment operator   In the absence of an explicit overloading of the assignment "=" operator an assignment of a class object to another will be implemented as a member-wise copy. For much the same reasons that were adduced in respect of the default copy constructor this may well not be acceptable, particularly for classes whose implementation involves the use of pointers. Again, the similarity to the copy constructor extends to the mode of the parameter (the "right-hand operand"), which is read-only and called by reference, and indeed to the implementation code.

The main difference, in fact, derives from the requirement in a faithful emulation of the semantics of the assignment operator to permit the composition of the operator, i.e. to permit statements like **a = b = c**, which is interpreted as **a = (b = c)**. For this to work the assignment must return a value that can itself be assigned, i.e. rather than just overwriting the left-hand operand; this is accomplished by dereferencing the pointer to the current object, which is provided in C++ by the implicitly declared variable **this**, to obtain the returned value (note the use of a reference type). **this** is also used to test for the case in which an object is assigned to itself – a necessary check because the assignment operation initially destroys its left-hand operand; the read-only parameter mode would prevent this but a run-time error would occur. An implementation of the overloaded assignment operator for **stack** is shown below:

```
stack& stack::operator= (const stack& rst)
     {
     if (&rst == this){
         return *this;
     }
     delete store;
     store = new int[rst.length];
     tos = store;
     for (int *rtos = rst.store;
             rtos != rst.tos; ){
             *++tos = *++rtos;
     }
     return *this;
     }
```

The equality test operator   Unlike Ada and Modula-2 equivalents, the test for equality operator "==" is overloaded by default only for the built-in types; an attempt to use the operator to test for the equality of two stacks, say, in the absence of a user-defined overloading, will be treated as an error. This is a reasonable approach, as the reasons that invalidate the use of the member-wise copy in many cases, notably where class implementations involve pointers, would apply also to the naïve use of the test for equality. Intuitively, in the case of **stack** objects, for example, equality means possessing identical element values at each level in the structures. This is a property that could not be determined by a straightforward comparison of the data members. An implementation of the test for equality is shown below.

```
int stack::operator== (const stack &rst)
            {
            int *lsp = store;
            int *rsp = rst.store;
            while (((lsp != tos) && (rsp != rst.tos))
                    && (*lsp++ == *rsp++))
            return (( lsp == tos ) &&
              ( rsp == rst.tos));
            }
```

6.3.4 Singleton classes

C++ classes define types, which may generally be used in the declaration of an indefinite number of variables during program execution. In certain rather rare circumstances it may be necessary to restrict the number of instantiations of a class to one, i.e. to define a data abstraction, rather than an abstract data type. A payroll program, for example, would require only one payroll object. Such a class, known as a *singleton* class, can be declared by using the **static** storage class specifier for one or more of the data members of the class. Such data members may be manipulated only by function members with **static** in their prototypes. A class defined in this way may not have constructors or a destructor.

6.3.5 Friends

In certain circumstances it is useful to be able to pierce the encapsulation of an abstract data type in a controlled way, to allow access to the hidden data structure. In C++ this is provided for by the existence of *friends*, which may be either functions or classes, and which are permitted direct access to the non-public members of the class that declares them as friends. The declaration of a friend consists of the word **friend** followed by the function prototype or class name.

A common use of a friend is to make available an overloading of the stream output operator "<<" for a user-defined type (i.e. a class). The operator, rather confusingly known as the "insertion" operator, because it inserts a printable representation of its right-hand operand into the "output stream object", such as cout, specified as its left operand. In C++ the statement part of the "hello world" program is:

```
cout << "hello world \n";
```

There are a number of standard overloadings of "<<" to allow the output of ints, chars, character strings, etc., but, of course, the stream library designer could not be expected to cater for any possible user-defined class. The overloading of "<<" is slightly special in comparison with other standard overloadings, because it is stylistically awkward to supply it as a member function. This arises from the format of calls to class member functions, which always have the name of the instance of the class on the left-hand side – the "implied parameter" – of the call. So if "<<" is defined as a function member for a stack class, say, then a call to it would look like: stack1.<<(cout); which fails to match the standard format. To maintain orthogonality, we need to overload "<<" by a function outside the class declaration.

If we consider supplying an overloading of "<<" for stack we can imagine that the operator will produce an ordered list of the elements contained in the stack, perhaps in a vertical column. A practical insertion operator, then, will need to access the encapsulated data members of the stack, and this is done by the inclusion in the class declaration of:

```
friend ostream& operator<< (ostream&, const stack&);
```

Friend declarations may appear anywhere in a class declaration; conventionally they appear immediately after the " { " so that their existence is obvious to the reader.

The definition of the function might be as follows:

```
ostream& operator << (ostream& os, const stack& s)
            {
            int* tp = s.tos;
            while (tp != s.store) {
              os << *tp-- << endl;
            }
            return os;
            }
```

The function is completely outside the scope of the stack class, but is able to access the hidden instance variables tos and store by virtue of its status as a friend. Once defined as shown, it may be used in the same way as for the standard overloadings:

```
stack s;
/*
  input some values
*/
cout << " stack contents are " << endl
     << s << endl;
```

The use of friends is dangerous, in that it compromises the encapsulation of the befriended class; a change to the internal structure of such a class may well make the friend(s) invalid. The class designer does, however, at least have control over which friends are permitted access.

6.4 Summary

C++ provides very comprehensive facilities in support of data abstraction, particularly the class construct, which provides for the implementation of abstract data types in a way that is close to the theoretical concept, and which permits them to be used with the same kind of freedom as provided for built-in types. The constructor/destructor mechanism is a very powerful facility for the initialization and tidying up of the kind of complex, dynamic data structures on which significant abstract data types are frequently based. Although C++ goes a considerable way in "civilizing" C, the language contains a number of pitfalls for the unwary, particularly in the shape of "default" behaviour.

6.5 Further reading

C++ is reasonably well served by text books. S. Lippman, *A C++ primer*, 2nd edn. (Reading, Mass.: Addison-Wesley, 1993), can be recommended, as can the B. Stroustrup & M. Ellis (no relation), *Annotated C++ reference manual* (Reading, Mass.: Addison-Wesley, 1990).

PART II

Data abstraction in design and specification

CHAPTER 7

Information hiding – a case study

7.1 Introduction

In this chapter we consider a very well known case study of the application of data abstraction to program design. The case study is taken from one of the most significant papers to have been written on the subject of data abstraction – significant enough to have introduced a related term into the language of computing, and indeed to have formed the basis of a new design methodology. The paper in question is by David Parnas and is entitled, with a rare clarity, "On the criteria to be used in decomposing systems into modules". As the reader will see, the title at least would appear to indicate some relevance to the subject matter of this book.

Parnas' paper was published in 1972 in the *Communications of the Association for Computing Machinery*. It is therefore not a new paper, although a surprising number of popularizers of program design methodologies seem oblivious to its existence. The material in this chapter is heavily borrowed from the paper and the author would like to acknowledge both it and Parnas' general contribution to modular program design concepts.

7.2 The problem

The case study is based on the problem of the generation of a KWIC (which stands for Key Word In Context) index. A KWIC index is formed from a list of phrases, normally titles of books or papers as might be found in a library catalogue. Each title contains a number of significant or *key* words that give a strong pointer to the contents of the book or paper. The title of Parnas' own paper contains the obvious key words *criteria, decomposing* and *modules* with others such as *the* that are obviously not key words. The KWIC index consists of a list of all the key words in all the titles, sorted in alphabetical order and shown (emphasized in some way) within the titles from which they are extracted – hence "in context". Every title will therefore appear the number of times in the index that it possesses key words.

Clearly, words like "module" can hardly be expected to be unique in an index concerned with computing topics, and the question arises as to how repeated key words are to be ordered. The answer is that in such cases the *remainder* of the titles in question, viewed as a sequence of key words, are compared alphabetically comparison. So, if an index contains the titles:

On the criteria to be used in decomposing systems into modules and
A metric for determining the coupling between modules

the ordering of the appearances of "modules" is determined by forming the "circular shifts" of the titles concerned, so that the key word appears in the first position in the line:

modules On the criteria to be used in decomposing systems into and
modules A metric for determining the coupling between

and then by determining the lexical, or alphabetic, ordering of the shifted titles, considering the key words only. In this case the first will appear before the second because its remainder *criteria* . . . is alphabetically prior to *metric* . . . .

The complete, if somewhat short, index generated from the two titles would be, therefore:

A metric for determining the **coupling** *between modules*
On the **criteria** *to be used in decomposing systems into modules*
On the criteria to be used in **decomposing** *systems into modules*
A **metric** *for determining the coupling between modules*
On the criteria to be used in decomposing systems into **modules**
A metric for determining the coupling between **modules**

It will be seen that the problem is unlikely to require anything like a large program. It is not completely trivial, however, and is significant enough to illustrate some important principles.

7.3 The algorithm

Parnas suggests a straightforward solution to the problem with the following algorithm:

1. Input the titles.
2. Form the circular shifts for all the titles (so that every title has a set of circular shifts containing one for each key word in the initial position).
3. Sort the circular shifts alphabetically.
4. Create the index by outputting, for each circular shift in the sorted order, the title from which the circular shift was generated, with the word in the initial position of the circular shift emphasized.

7.4 Design – the conventional approach

In considering the design of the program to generate the KWIC index Parnas first adopts what he characterizes as the obvious or conventional design approach. This approach might well be derived from a data flow diagram of the realization of the algorithm, showing the data flows between the *processes*, which correspond reasonably enough with the stages of the algorithm and are therefore *input, circular shift, sort* and *output*. A typical such data flow diagram is shown in Figure 7.1.

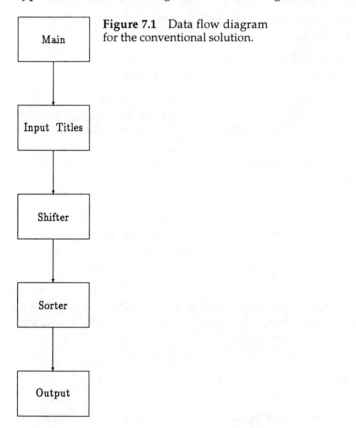

Figure 7.1 Data flow diagram for the conventional solution.

The next obvious conventional step is to modularize the design into a partitioning suggested by the data flow diagram, i.e. with a module corresponding to each process, together with a "main" module that controls the sequence in which the "process" modules execute. Each of the process modules is called, in turn, by the main module to perform its single, discrete function, and might be thought of as a very powerful program statement or command. This approach to modular design, which emphasizes the *imperative* aspect of modules, is known as *procedural abstraction*, because it allows for the creation of procedures, or commands, that are abstracted away from the machine-orientated level of the ordinary program statements. The sequence of process modules effectively forms a program, comprising a "pipeline" that accomplishes the transformation from the input list of titles to the output index.

The "structure chart" representation of the design is given in Figure 7.2 showing the simple modular structure and straightforward execution sequence, i.e. without loops. (The reader may recall that modules derived in this way possess "procedural" strength according to the classification described in Ch. 2.) It might be noted that Parnas' view of what was "conventional" in 1972 would be unlikely to cause many surprises to one of the practitioners of the many currently well marketed methodologies based on data flow diagrams and structure charts.

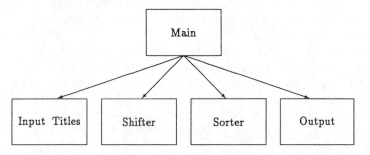

Figure 7.2   Structure chart for the conventional solution.

The next step, and the first interesting one in the context both of Parnas' paper and this book, is to evaluate the suggested design from the point of view of the criteria that have been discussed in earlier chapters.

7.5 Analysis of the conventional design

It takes relatively little analysis to discover that the proposed design is a very poor one from the point of view of module coupling. If we consider the interface between the **input** and **circular_shifter** modules we see that it must consist of a data structure, containing the entire set of titles from which the index is to be generated, populated by the input process. The nature of the input module is defined by the structure diagram as the first of a sequence of functions, which is never invoked again. This implies that the input set of titles must be handed over "all of a piece" via what must inevitably be a wide and complex interface.

The nature of this interface may be parameterized, i.e. the call by the main module to **input** may return the data structure or, more likely, a pointer to the data structure, which may then be passed to **circular_**

shifter on its invocation. But this is a perfect example of a parameterized interface being almost indistinguishable from a global data area because the data structure involved is so large. Additionally, the data structure must provide for a nested structure of titles and words within titles and then characters within words – perhaps a list of lists of lists, or a "ragged-edged" two-dimensional array. Whatever data structure is chosen it will be complex and, importantly, place a heavy commitment to it on both the communicating modules. (It is assumed that **main** performs no processing of the data structure but simply transmits it between **input** and **circular_shifter** and so would be relatively uncommitted.)

We can see then that the proposed design exhibits a high level of coupling between the first two modules in the sequence, with the characteristic problems of modifications to one having profound effects on the other. If we imagine an initial implementation based on an array structure a subsequent change to a list-based approach would necessitate a complete rewrite of both modules.

When we turn to the next interface, between **circular_shifter** and **sorter**, we see that the situation is even worse than is the case for the first. Again a large data structure must be handed over. Not only is its size a multiple of the first, because of the generation of several circular shifts for each title, but, more crucially, another level of nesting and thus complexity must be provided to represent the relationship between titles and their circular shifts.

Again, the level of coupling is very high, and it is clear that the whole "pipeline" is inextricably committed to a large and complex interface, that will allow any modifications in an earlier module to "ripple through" the remainder. From the point of view of achieving the benefits of modularity the design can hardly be said to be modular at all.

7.6 Improving the design by narrowing interfaces

The above analysis may well have struck some resonances in the reader's mind. The essential cause of the shortcomings of the "conventional" design is the necessity for each module to hand over, in a single action, the large data structure that the next module is to work on. On seeing the phrase *data structure*, the related concept of the data abstraction should be asserting itself in a positively Pavlovian way. Clearly a possible approach to improving the design might lie in the encapsulation of the data structures so that their implementation details are hidden, and thus cannot form part of an interface commitment. If we consider the nature of a collection of titles as a rather complicated multi-level list, with character strings at the bottom level (to hold the words), and recall the character string data abstraction introduced in Chapter 3, we may see how to elaborate the latter so as to provide the semantics of the former.

7.6.1 A titles data abstraction

What then are the requirements a data abstraction for a collection of titles must satisfy? We can see its essential nature is that of a "data repository" that simply allows the titles to be inserted into it and extracted from it, but over an interface requiring no commitment to its internal structure. Like its counterpart in the character string data abstraction this interface is basically one character wide, but with an additional complexity necessitated by the nested structure of the titles.

As is often the case, a good starting point for its design is to imagine a piece of (pseudo) code that actually uses the data abstraction, say as part of the **input** process. The code has just read a title and is about to transfer a character from it into the titles data abstraction. Normally, in a manner that should be familiar from the discussion of *iterators* in Chapter 3, the transfer will be accomplished by a **SET_NEXT_CHARACTER_TO** operation, but of course the transfer must reflect the structuring of the input into words and titles, and so it is necessary to provide operations corresponding to *start a new word* and *start a new title*.

The code to read the set of titles and to insert it into the data abstraction might therefore appear as shown in Figure 7.3 using an Ada-like pseudo-code and assuming that the data abstraction is implemented as a package called **TITLES**. The corresponding constructor operations of the **TITLES** package specification would be declared as follows:

```
package TITLES is
--
        procedure START_NEW_TITLE;
        procedure START_NEW_WORD;
        procedure SET_NEXT_CHARACTER_TO(CHAR : character);
--
```

```
TITLES.START_NEW_TITLE;
while some_input_characters_left
loop
        read (next_character); -- from input stream
        if end_of_word
        then
                if end_of_title
                then TITLES.START_NEW_TITLE;
                end if;
                TITLES.START_NEW_WORD;
        else TITLES.SET_NEXT_CHARACTER_TO(next_character);
        end if;
end loop;
```

Figure 7.3   Inserting into the **TITLES** data abstraction.

(This example shows the Ada versions of the **while** and **if** statements. The former follows the Pascal model quite closely, apart from the use of the **loop .. end loop** brackets instead of a compound statement. The latter again uses a self-bracketing terminator, **end if**, in a way that is quite consistent in the language.)

The complementary set of observer operations must provide for the extraction of the complete collection of titles from the data abstraction. Clearly an iterator is required, but again we must take account of the three-level structure and provide observer operations that allow for the detection of the end of words and the end of titles. The following Ada declarations provide a possible realization:

```
function SOME_TITLES_LEFT return boolean;
-- returns TRUE until all titles read
--
function SOME_WORDS_LEFT return boolean;
-- returns TRUE until the current title is exhausted
--
function SOME_CHARACTERS_LEFT return boolean;
-- returns TRUE until the current word is exhausted
--
function NEXT_CHARACTER return character;
```

A piece of code to extract all the titles from the abstraction might then look something like the following:

```
-- set up data areas, counts etc.
while TITLES.SOME_TITLES_LEFT
loop
        while TITLES.SOME_WORDS_LEFT
        loop
                while TITLES.SOME_CHARACTERS_LEFT
                loop
                        NEXT_CHAR := TITLES.NEXT_CHARACTER;
                        -- transfer NEXT_CHAR to local area
                end loop;
                -- initialize next word
        end loop;
        -- initialize next title
end loop;
-- all titles extracted
```

At the risk of labouring what should be a fairly obvious point, by the introduction of the **TITLES** data abstraction we have narrowed the interface, over which the entire set of titles may be transmitted, to the width of one character. In the context of the design for the KWIC index program this

```
package TITLES is
--
-- constructor operations
--
     procedure START_NEW_TITLE;
     --
     procedure START_NEW_WORD;
     --
     procedure SET_NEXT_CHARACTER_TO(CHAR : character);
--
-- iterator
--
     function SOME_TITLES_LEFT return boolean;
     -- returns TRUE until all titles read
     --
     function SOME_WORDS_LEFT return boolean;
     -- returns TRUE until the current title is exhausted
     --
     function SOME_CHARACTERS_LEFT return boolean;
     -- returns TRUE until the current word is exhausted
     --
     function NEXT_CHARACTER return character;
     --
  end titles;
```

Figure 7.4   Ada realization of a titles data abstraction.

interface may be established between the **input** and **circular_shifter** modules so as to reduce their coupling and interface commitment drastically. It can be seen that the operations provided by the **TITLES** package/data abstraction require no commitment to the underlying implementation – either an array or list-based data structure could be used, and indeed changed one to another without affecting the external operations and, thus, the implementations of the two "process" modules.

The complete package specification corresponding to the **titles** data abstraction is shown in Figure 7.4.

Before considering the other interfaces we will examine Parnas' own abstraction, which differs somewhat from the above.

7.7 Parnas' solution

Parnas suggests the addition of a data abstraction (although he does not use the term), which he calls **LINE_STORAGE**. Its role in the design is essentially the same as the **TITLES** package but it provides an index-based interface rather than one based on an iterator.

The constructors of the interface are an **INITIALIZE** operation and an operation, called **PUT_CHARACTER_FROM**. In addition to the value of the character to be inserted, the latter takes parameters giving the number of the line (i.e. title) in which the character occurs, the number of the word within the line within which the character occurs and then the number of the character within the word. There are thus four parameters, one character and three *natural*, i.e. positive integers or zero. The interface provided by **PUT_CHARACTER_FROM** is thus slightly more complex than that of the corresponding operation in the **TITLES** package, but it still represents a very low interface commitment – integers and ASCII characters are unlikely to be affected by implementation changes.

The observer operations for **LINE_STORAGE** consist of a main index-based function that performs the mirror image of the **PUT_CHARACTER_FROM** operation, i.e. it returns the value of the character at a specified line, word and character number. Additionally, because of course the writer of a routine using the data abstraction does not know how many titles there are, how many words there are in each title or how many characters in each word, natural valued observers are provided to allow these to be extracted. An Ada realization of the interface to **LINE_STORAGE** is shown in Figure 7.5. The way in which the operations exported by this package may be usedto extract the complete set of lines is shown in Figure 7.6. (Figure 7.6 shows the Ada version of the **for** statement, in which the body of the loop, enclosed by the **loop .. end loop** brackets, is executed once for every value that the control variable takes. The control variable follows the word **for** and takes, successively, each value in the range specified after **in**.)

The reader may recall that in the discussion of the string data abstraction in Chapter 3, the use of the indexed style of interface was criticized on the grounds that it was an "over specification" of what is conventionally thought to be appropriate to a character string. That is to say, it provided a functionality, particularly in supporting random access to any character

```
package LINE_STORAGE is
    procedure INITIALISE;
    procedure PUT_CHARACTER_FROM(LINE_NO,WORD_NO,CHARACTER_NO:
                                            natural;
                        CHAR : character);
    function NO_OF_LINES return natural;
    function NO_OF_WORDS_IN (LINE_NO : natural) return natural;
    function NO_OF_CHARACTERS_IN(LINE_NO,WORD_NO : natural)
                                        return natural;
    function GET_CHARACTER_FOR(LINE_NO,WORD_NO,CHARACTER_NO:
                        natural) return  character;
end LINE_STORAGE;
```

Figure 7.5   An Ada realization of the **LINE_STORAGE** module interface.

```
LINE_NO := 1;
for LINE_NO in 1 .. LINE_STORAGE.NO_OF_LINES
loop
        for WORD_NO in 1 ..
            LINE_STORAGE.NO_OF_WORDS_IN(LINE_NO)
        loop
                for CHARACTER_NO in 1 ..
                LINE_STORAGE.NO_OF_CHARACTERS_IN(LINE_NO,WORD_NO)
                loop
                        NEXT_CHAR := LINE_STORAGE.GET_CHARACTER_FOR
                                        (LINE_NO,WORD_NO,
                                        CHARACTER_NO);
                        -- transfer NEXT_CHAR to local area
                end loop;
        end loop;

end loop;
```

Figure 7.6 Code to extract the titles from LINE_STORAGE.

position within the string, over and above what might be required for any application involving character strings. By contrast, the iterator style of interface appeared to match more naturally the semantics of character strings.

As we have seen, Parnas' approach to the KWIC index program, at least as far as the LINE_STORAGE data abstraction is concerned, is very definitely based on the indexed style, and the obvious question arises as to why he chose this type of interface. The first version that we have discussed is based on the use of an iterator, and we have seen how the entire collection of titles may be extracted via this interface. Is there any deficiency in the use of the iterator style that dictates the use of the indexed approach? In order to discuss this question in more detail we need to look at the remaining inter-modular interfaces.

7.8 The circular shifter interface

The essential functionality that the circular_shifter must support is to enable the sorter to extract the collection of circular shifts generated from the titles. We have seen how the addition of a data abstraction, along the lines of either TITLES or LINE_STORAGE, can narrow the interface between input and circular_shifter to an acceptable level. We should also note specifically that the nature of this interface has changed from the original version in that it involves a (large) number of calls to the operations of the data abstraction. We have abandoned the "single-shot" approach.

115

Should the interface between `circular_shifter` and `sorter` be similarly provided with a separate data abstraction, to perform a corresponding service? A moment's thought shows this is unnecessary, because we can modify the interface of `circular_shifter` itself to provide the low coupling that we are trying to achieve. The interface is closely modeled on that of the `TITLES` or `LINE_STORAGE` data abstraction but replaces `title` by `circular_shift`. An Ada realization of this interface, utilizing the Parnas indexed style, is shown in Figure 7.7.

```
package CIRCULAR_SHIFTER is
    procedure INITIALISE;
    function NO_OF_SHIFTS return natural;
    function NO_OF_WORDS_IN (SHIFT_NO : natural) return natural;
    function NO_OF_CHARACTERS_IN(SHIFT_NO,WORD_NO : natural)
                                            return natural;
    function GET_CHARACTER_FOR(SHIFT_NO,WORD_NO,CHARACTER_NO:
                            natural) return  character;
end CIRCULAR_SHIFTER;
```

Figure 7.7   An Ada realization of the `circular_shifter` interface.

The main difference, apart from the substitution of **SHIFT** for **LINE**, is the lack of an input or **PUT** operation. This is replaced by the internal operations of the `circular_shifter`, comprising calls to **LINE_STORAGE** in the manner shown previously in Figure 7.6.

An immediate design decision concerns the necessity for `circular_shifter` to contain its own data structure within which the shifts are stored as they are generated, presumably in response to the **INITIALIZE** operation. This seems a natural approach, but a viable alternative is for the module to generate the shifts "on the fly" – that is, as the **sorter** repeatedly calls **GET_CHARACTER_FOR** in order to construct the collection of shifts prior to sorting them, the code of `circular_shifter` extracts the titles from **LINE_STORAGE** as they become needed. The difference between the two implementations is a trade-off between memory occupancy and code complexity, but the important point is, that either can be used without any need for alterations in any other modules. This is the direct consequence of the decoupling effect of the narrow interface supported by the data abstraction.

7.9 The sorter interface

It is when we come to the interface between **sorter** and **output** that the choice of design style, namely iterator *versus* indexed, adopted for the interface to **TITLES**/**LINE_STORAGE** necessitates significant differences in implementation. The basic functionality of **sorter** must enable **output** to extract the collection of circular shifts, sorted in alphabetic order *together* with sufficient information to allow, for each shift, the reconstruction of the title from which it was generated. If the indexed style of interface design has been adopted for **TITLES/LINE_STORAGE** then the **sorter** interface can be simplified to one providing an iterator for the extraction of pairs of natural numbers. The number pairs are supplied in an order determined by the alphabetic sort. One number gives the line number of the title from which the "next" shift was derived, the other gives the position of the key word that is to be emphasized in the output (this is the same as the number of key words that the shift was rotated).

An appropriate package specification is shown below.

```
package Sorter is
    --

        procedure INITIALIZE;
          -- must be called before NEXT_SHIFT
          --
        procedure NEXT_SHIFT
          (LINE_NO,KEY_WORD_NO : out natural);
    --
    end Sorter;
```

It is at this point that the apparent over-specification of the indexed style of the interface to **LINE_STORAGE** can be seen to be justified, because its random access capability allows **output** to extract lines in any sequence as dictated by **sorter**. **output** may therefore look like the following:

```
SORTER.NEXT_SHIFT(LINE_NO,KEY_WORD_NO);
word_count := LINE_STORAGE.NO_OF_WORDS_IN(LINE_NO);
for word_no in 1 .. word_count
loop
        emphasized := word_no = KEY_WORD_NO;
        for CHARACTER_NO in 1 ..
            LINE_STORAGE.NO_OF_CHARACTERS_IN(LINE_NO,WORD_NO)
        loop
                    NEXT_CHAR :=
                    LINE_STORAGE.GET_CHARACTER_FOR
                        (LINE_NO,WORD_NO,
                        CHARACTER_NO);
                    -- transfer NEXT_CHAR to output area
                    -- if emphasized is true then emphasize
                    -- the word
        end loop;
    end loop;
```

Once again it may be noted that, as compared with the first version of the design, the interface presented by the **sorter** to **output**, consisting of pairs of natural integers, requires a very low level of commitment. The sorting algorithm and, importantly, the data structure on which it is carried out, are completely hidden. This is made possible both because of the encapsulation of **LINE_STORAGE**'s data structure, and also because of the relationship between the **LINE_STORAGE** and the other modules, which involves many invocations throughout the various phases of the processing, rather than the single delivery of the complete set of titles. The modular structure no longer reflects closely the processing sequence of the program but is more determined by the significant data structures – procedural abstraction has given way to data abstraction.

7.9.1 An iterator-based interface

The question now arises as to whether or not the iterator style as exhibited by the specification of the **TITLES** package in Figure 7.4 is in fact capable of supplying a functionality adequate to support the requirements of **output**. The answer is that it is, but at the cost of a considerably more complex implementation of **output**, which is obliged to provide a reverse circular shift in order to recreate each title. This recreation is necessary because the iterator-based **TITLES** package is incapable of providing a random access to individual titles and so cannot be used by **output** to obtain the reordered sequence. Instead, the titles must be provided, each in the form of one of its circular shifts, in the correct sequence by the **sorter**. The interface of the iterator-based version of the **sorter**, shown in Figure 7.8, thus closely resembles that of the **circular_shifter** with an additional

```
Package sorter is
          function SOME_SHIFTS_LEFT return boolean;
          function SOME_WORDS_LEFT return boolean;
          -- returns TRUE until the current shift is exhausted
          -- at which point the following operation:-
          function KEY_WORD_POSITION return natural;
          -- returns the position of the first word in the shift
          -- in the original line
          --
          function SOME_CHARACTERS_LEFT return boolean;
          -- returns TRUE until the current word is exhausted
          --
          function NEXT_CHARACTER return character;
          --
end sorter;
```

Figure 7.8 Interface of an iterator-based **sorter** module.

operation that returns, for each shift, the ordinal number of the key word in the original title (that is, the number of key words that the shift must be reversed in order to recreate the title). The additional operation is a function that may be called after the characters for the shift in question have been extracted. The word to be emphasized in the output is identified by the fact that it is the first in the shift, of course. When the two variations in interface style are compared it is fairly clear that what has been defined as Parnas' indexed style provides for a simpler **sorter** interface and **output** functionality. Indeed, in the iterator-based version it might with some justification be suggested that the **output** module should be supplemented by a "reverse shifter" module to balance out the functionality.

7.9.2 A hybrid interface

Whilst accepting that the random access to lines supported by the indexed interface produces a better design we might still query the need for random access to words and characters. This is clearly not necessary, as the words, and the characters that form them, are always extracted in their order as input. We might finally, therefore, adopt a hybrid version for the

```
package TITLE_STORAGE is
    procedure INITIALISE;
    --
    --    constructor operations
    --
        procedure START_NEW_LINE;
        procedure START_NEW_WORD;
        procedure SET_NEXT_CHARACTER_TO(CHAR : character);
    --
    --    observers
    --
        function NO_OF_LINES return natural;
        procedure SET_CURRENT_LINE_TO(LINE_NO : natural);
        --
        function SOME_WORDS_LEFT return boolean;
        -- returns TRUE until the current title is exhausted
        --
        function SOME_CHARACTERS_LEFT return boolean;
        -- returns TRUE until the current word is exhausted
        --
        function NEXT_CHARACTER return character;
        --
end TITLE_STORAGE;
```

Figure 7.9   A hybrid interface to **TITLES/LINE_STORAGE**.

119

TITLES/LINE_STORAGE data abstraction that provides indexing for lines, but an iterator for words and characters – a compromise that seems to pitch the level of functionality appropriately over the whole interface. This hybrid interface is shown in Figure 7.9, realized as the specification of a package called, appropriately, TITLE_STORAGE. The iterator operates on the "current line", which is established by the SET_CURRENT_LINE operation.

7.10 The circular shifter revisited

The designer of a data abstraction must ensure that its interface is sufficient to enable users fully to exploit its functionality. The reader may have wondered about the interface of the circular_shifter module – is it adequate for the sorter to carry out its task? In particular, how can the sorter identify the source line from which each circular shift is generated?

The answer is that this is possible only if the sorter makes some specific assumptions about the way the circular_shifter works: in particular, that the circular_shifter generates all the circular shifts from one line in an unbroken sequence, and the shifts for line k are all generated after those for line j, if $k > j$ in the line number sequence generated by LINE_STORAGE. The sorter can determine how many shifts there are for each line by invoking the NO_OF_WORDS_IN function from the LINE_STORAGE package and so, by monitoring the count of shifts as they are extracted, associate the set of shifts generated from each line with its number. However, this technique is based on some assumptions that although quite reasonable are assumptions nevertheless, and place a commitment to a particular implementation on the two modules involved. The coupling between the two is thus undesirably high and could cause problems in the event of a change to the implementation of the circular_shifter. Once again we see that interface design requires considerable thought if inadvertent commitments are not to be placed on the related implementations.

The answer to this problem is to provide an operation, exported by the circular_shifter, that returns the line number corresponding to the circular shift whose number is supplied as its argument. The sorter is then not obliged to make any assumptions about the order in which the circular shifts are generated, with a corresponding reduction in the coupling of the modules involved.

7.11 Information hiding

In view of the quite dramatic improvement in the design of the KWIC index program obtainable by the use of a relatively straightforward data abstraction, Parnas suggests that the technique might usefully form the basis of a design methodology. Essentially, the approach is to identify the large-scale decisions, particularly those concerned with data structures, that must be made in the design of a program and to *hide*, or encapsulate them, using the kind of module structure discussed in previous chapters. This approach, which Parnas (perhaps not originally) called *information hiding*, in effect transforms program construction into the identification and assembly of sets of data abstractions – known also as *object-based* programming. In comparison with the conventional functional decomposition approach, information hiding emphasizes the importance, to its modular design, of the data structures of a program rather than of the sequence of actions undertaken when the program is executed. As the case study shows, procedural abstraction tends to lead to wide and complex interfaces, because it ignores the nature of the data that is manipulated by each action in the sequence, with the inevitable implications for implementation and maintenance.

By contrast, information hiding deems the interfaces to program modules that implement data abstractions to be of primary concern in the design. Programs resulting from such a process will exhibit the benefits that modular design can achieve, providing the necessary attention is paid to interface design that has been illustrated in the case study.

7.12 Summary

In this chapter we have considered a design case study illustrating the potential the data abstraction possesses for providing the basis of good modular design. The necessity for care in the design of data abstraction interfaces has been discussed, particularly in the context of the design approach termed information hiding.

In the next chapter this question of design methodologies is developed considerably to provide a discussion of *object-oriented design*, on which Parnas' information hiding may be seen as a major influence.

7.13 Further reading

There is little to add to the acknowledgement in the text: D. L. Parnas, "On the criteria to be used in decomposing systems into modules" *Communications of the ACM* **15**, 1,053–8, 1972.

CHAPTER 8

Object-oriented design

In the preceding chapters we have looked at the problems arising in the construction of large software systems and, it is hoped, the reader will have been convinced both of the desirability of the modular approach and of the utility of the data abstraction in providing the basic architectural unit for this approach. So far, however, the subject has been treated in an analytical way: we have established some criteria that enable us to evaluate the quality of a modular design and have investigated, in some depth, a programming language paradigm that, if used correctly, can ensure that good modular design is achieved.

The significant phrase here of course is "if used correctly" – perhaps "imaginatively" would capture the intended meaning better – because the software design process involves more than the analysis of designs: it must also depend on a synthetic, or creative, component that generates the design, which may then be analysed and found to meet the criteria or not. Again, and perhaps obviously, it is not particularly satisfactory to have these criteria and the knowledge of the data abstraction, if they are isolated from the creative component of design. This is perhaps the main criticism of Parnas' attempt to derive a design methodology from the idea of information hiding: to put it crudely, we have got too far down the design track by the time we know what information we want to hide – in other words, information hiding is essentially a desirable quality that a design may exhibit rather than a technique that may be followed from the start.

What is additionally required is a way of guiding the design process, a methodology to use the somewhat pompous terminology, so that it will result in a design that meets the criteria for good modularization. As an initial step it seems reasonable to examine the well established conventional design methodologies in the light of this requirement. Before looking at such a methodology it will be as well to remind ourselves of the context and nature of software system design.

8.1 Conventional methodologies

Until recently most established design methodologies were based on an analysis of the data flows in the application, leading to the production of a hierarchy of *data flow diagrams*. A data flow diagram, or DFD, is a directed graph in which the nodes represent *processes* that effect *transformations* on the data, linked by arcs that show the data flows between the transformations.

The hierarchy of DFDs is generally created in a top-down fashion. At the highest level the *context* DFD shows the data flows between the system and its environment. Each transformation at the context level is then elaborated, by decomposing it into sub-transformations and internal data flows, into a DFD at the next lower level. This process is continued until the transformations are sufficiently limited in their extent as to be realizable as modules.

As this description suggests, methodologies based on data flow analysis tend to identify modules with data transformations, and it is worthwhile investigating this approach from the point of view of the quality of the modularization to which it is likely to lead. A data transformation produces one or more output data flows from one or more input data flows. A characteristic transformation is a sort as, for example, in the initial modularization in Parnas' KWIC index case study. Modules derived in this way are essentially procedural abstractions – they are very large-scale "program statements" that carry out the transformations necessary to generate the output data flows from the inputs. As we have seen, such modules tend to exhibit procedural strength. Importantly, in the context of this discussion, any information hiding exhibited by such a modularization will be either fortuitous, or imposed *after* the modular structure has been defined. Nothing in the technique of data flow analysis assists in the identification of the significant data structures on which the design will depend; such considerations are essentially secondary. The technique cannot, therefore, be expected to arrive at a modularization in which the idea of encapsulating the data structures is a primary concern. Clearly, then, conventional DFD-based methodologies are unlikely to satisfy the quest for a technique leading to good modular design.

It is also the case that conventional methodologies possess shortcomings other than those relevant to modular design. The nature of these derives from the longevity of the methodologies (DFD techniques were established well before the end of the 1960s) and the character of the software design process. By a remarkable coincidence, as we shall see, the approach to avoiding these shortcomings will provide the basis for the kind of methodology for which we are searching. The first thing to do, then, is to step back from detailed consideration of particular design techniques and to undertake a brief philosophical enquiry into the nature of the software design process.

8.2 Software design

The characteristic problem of software design centres on the discontinuity, or dissimilarity, between two worlds, or *"domains"* as they have become known. The term domain has become rather overworked of late. It has a very precise meaning in an area of mathematics called, appropriately enough, *domain theory*, which is certainly relevant to computing but is beyond the scope of this book. In the more informal usage of the term that we are concerned with the essential concept is that a domain is a self-contained fragment of the world, or universe if you take a more cosmic view of things. The idea is used quite often in non-technical contexts. We are all used to reading phrases like "the world of . . ." where the ". . ." may be anything from "small-bore rifle shooting" to "Viennese opera". The implication underlying the use of such a phrase is a well understood set of rules, conventions, terminology, and so on. The term "domain" is roughly equivalent to "world" as used in "the world of . . .".

8.2.1 Domain mismatch

The production of software systems inevitably involves two domains: the *problem domain* and the *implementation domain*. The problem domain is populated by the "real-world" objects that are significant to the application in question – people, aircraft, inventory items, whatever. The implementation domain is populated by the objects that can be manipulated by the computer on which the system is to run, or, more precisely, by the objects that are available to the designers and programmers of the system. This distinction is made because it is now (fortunately) rare to find systems written in assembler, and so normally the objects of the implementation domain are the more abstract, less machine-oriented, constructs that can be manipulated by the programming language being used to write the system. Software design is essentially concerned with modeling the objects of the application domain using the objects of the implementation domain: its characteristic difficulty arises from the dissimilarity – or *mismatch* – between the two domains noted above.

The reader may ask, why is this mismatch between the two domains important? The answer is that because the objects of the two domains are often so dissimilar it is almost impossible to recognize features in the implementation that correspond with those of the problem domain. This gives rise to a number of characteristic difficulties. It is the common complaint, for example, of customers of software systems that "it works all right but it doesn't do what we wanted". The reason for this is that, in the process of translating the objects of the problem domain into the quite different implementation domain, the details of the former became obscured. The designers, who are experts in computing, not the application, naturally tend to concentrate on the implementation details – the wood that obscures the problem domain trees. When the mismatch between the two domains is great, the analysts – who are supposed to act as the custodians of the functionality of the system on behalf of the customer – often cannot understand the implementation in sufficient detail and so it takes on a life of its own, related to but often quite distinct from the intentions of the original requirements specification. For the same reason maintenance programmers, who were rarely involved in the original design process, have considerable difficulty in correcting bugs or implementing enhancements that are identified or specified in terms of the application.

The principle to be drawn from this is that considerable benefits are to be obtained from the use of program constructs that, as far as possible, reflect or resemble the "real-world" objects of the problem domain.

The relevance of this discussion to considerations of design methodology is that the conventional methodologies approach the problem of the discontinuity between the problem and application domains by emphasizing one – the implementation domain – in order to enable the modeling. One way of characterizing DFD-based methodologies is that they require the designer to describe the problem domain in terms of the implementation domain (entities, data flows and transformations) that are easily translated into the entities of a typical first-generation language. This was, of course, quite natural when such languages were all that was available. There have, however, been developments in programming language design in the intervening years, as described in earlier chapters, that make possible an alternative to this dominance of the implementation domain, with its typical shortcomings arising from the decomposition, and obscuring, of the objects of the problem domain.

8.3 Real-world objects

In order to present an alternative approach to design, one that does support the retention of the problem domain objects in the implementation, it will be useful to consider in more detail the characteristics of what have been up to now referred to merely as "real-world objects". Obviously the nature of these objects is, in their full reality, infinitely varied. The list of computer applications is lengthening daily. As each new application area is addressed, a new domain of objects, with their associated concepts, attributes, and network of relationships, must be accommodated by the software. Now it is very clear that the objects of an application domain are represented only by *models* within the relevant application software. Programs cannot *really* contain cars, ships, people, molecules, and so on. Rather, a collection of information sufficient to represent the objects *for the purposes of the application* is required – a model, in other words.

So, the model of an employee adequate for the purposes of a payroll program contains such information as name, rate-of-pay, tax-code, pay-to-date etc. Characteristics of the real human being such as colour of hair, musical ability, political opinions, etc., are irrelevant and are therefore excluded from this particular model. On the other hand, a model of the same person maintained by a police security system might well include these details.

The question then arises as to whether the models of real-world objects have a sufficient similarity in order for generalizations to be made about them; in other words, is there a modeling technique that is generally applicable to many different problem domains?

8.3.1 Behaviour

It is clear that these models must be capable of maintaining the association within their respective collections of data over periods of time. It is also clear that a simple passive collection of data is not a very satisfactory general representation of a real-world object.

Consider a program that contains a model of an electrical circuit containing a number of components exhibiting variously resistance, capacitance and inductance. These attributes of the circuit components can certainly be represented by values held in a straightforward array data structure, but the modeling of the response of the circuit to an input waveform requires *computation* – the active evaluation of a set of program statements that must exist in addition to the data structure and access it. Thus an adequate model of the circuit must consist of both passive data and active statements, and these two are logically interdependent in the sense that neither is meaningful without the other.

This requirement for the association of computation with the data values defining the characteristics of an object arises from the fact that in nearly every significant case the objects modeled within an application system exhibit *behaviour*, the representation of which is essential if the software models are to be adequate for the purpose. Typical examples of behaviour exhibited by objects are:

- the accumulation week by week of pay-to-date by an employee;
- the change in position of an aircraft as it continues in level flight or undertakes a manoeuvre;
- The change in value of a stock bond as the result of market movements.

When we discuss the behaviour of objects it is very natural to do so in terms of *stimulus* and *response* – how does the object *react* to an externally applied input? This approach is so general as to underlie much of our thought and language about the real (external) world: the need for an active or computational component in adequate models of real-world objects, as discussed above, clearly reflects it. It seems very appropriate, therefore, that the program structures used to model real-world objects should do so in a way that allows them to exhibit behaviour in this kind of stimulus–response way.

In conventional programming languages the closest representation of the stimulus–response pattern is provided by the subprogram call, with its corresponding return, the procedural abstraction of the subprogram encapsulating the computation underlying the response. The basis of object behaviour modeling, therefore, is the provision of subprograms that will provide appropriate responses, in the form of returned data values, to stimuli in the form of calls, possibly with input data values. The nature of the responses of a particular object will be determined by the data associated with it, which generally will be modified as the result of the calls stimuli made to the object, and from which the returned data will be derived.

By this time the reader is almost certainly prepared for what is about to come, bearing in mind the content of earlier chapters: *the program objects that can most appropriately model real-world objects are data abstractions*, because they provide the unified association of the subprograms, which provide behaviour modeling, with the underlying data that determines the individual nature of the object.

Having accepted the viability of this approach from the perspective of the requirements of faithful modeling, we are also guaranteed, because of the properties of the data abstraction, a sound basis for good modular design – two birds with one stone in fact. This duality of beneficial roles for the data abstraction on the one hand provides the architectural unit for good modular design, on the other, a flexible and powerful program object that can model a huge variety of real-world objects. This is one of those inspiring discoveries that comes somewhat rarely in any branch of applied science, and perhaps particularly in software engineering.

8.4 Object-oriented design

The foregoing discussion has led to the notion of a design methodology based on the use of the data abstraction to model the real-world objects of the problem domain, an approach that has become known by the term *object-oriented design*. Object-oriented design presents two beneficial aspects corresponding to the analytic/synthetic split referred to at the beginning of this chapter.

- *Analytic* – the end product of the technique is the specification of a collection of data abstractions defined *by their external interfaces*. As we have seen in previous chapters, this is a prescription for good modular design *provided that the data abstractions are appropriately chosen*.

This last proviso may strike the reader as the inevitable let-out clause, but of course it is possible to arrive at a collection of data abstractions including members that are too large – whose internal complexity causes design problems within the modular structure. The complementary problem – data abstractions that are too trivial – at the level of a straightforward program variable say, is unlikely to be serious in itself but indicative of an unbalanced design that includes over-complex members as well. Clearly the role of an object-oriented design methodology is to arrive at a well balanced, compatible set of data abstractions.

- *Synthetic* – the combination of data and operations that the data abstraction supports provides a far more natural modeling unit than the more traditional methodologies, which fail to support the association between computation and data that is characteristic of faithful models of real-world objects, and thus fail to allow the carrying through of the objects of the problem domain into the implementation domain.

There appear to be clear advantages, therefore, both to the design process and to the resulting program structure, in using object-oriented design – a design methodology based on the data abstraction as its main architectural building block.

8.5 The methodology

In arriving at this conclusion we have hinted fairly strongly at the starting point and the destination of the object-oriented methodology. We start with the problem domain and finally arrive at the specifications of a number of data abstractions and abstract data types; the former corresponding to single, unique objects, the latter to replicated objects, in the problem domain. If we are using a language such as C++ or Ada the end-product of the design process will be a set of class declarations or package specifications, in the latter case some of which will declare private or limited private types, implementing abstract data types. There are a number of stages in this process:

- identify the objects of the problem domain;
- define the behaviour of the objects in terms of operations associated with them;
- establish the dependency relationships between these objects;
- design the interfaces that the objects present;
- design the implementations that support these interfaces.

The first question that needs to be answered is: how are the objects of the problem domain to be identified so that they may be satisfactorily modeled by an interdependent collection of data abstractions? When the methodology was first introduced this question exercised the object-oriented community to a level that might be described as obsessive. Before we go on to discuss it in detail the point might be made that the proponents of more conventional design methodologies, typically based on the use of data flow diagrams, never in the experience of the author explain from where the "processes" and "data-flows" are derived. They are presumably so obvious as to require no extraction from the requirements specification, but spring fully defined from the brow of the designer. This thought might be kept in mind in the following discussion.

8.5.1 Booch/Abbott

The term "object-oriented design" was originally applied to a methodology devised and popularized by Grady Booch, with at least an initial input from Russell Abbott. Booch's methodology was originally presented in the context of the Ada language, although there is no reason why it cannot be applied, with suitable and fairly minor modifications, to other language contexts, certainly including C++.

At its introduction, Booch's approach provided a novel contrast with the diagram-based methodologies. The novelty, relating specifically to the identification of the objects and the elaboration of their behaviour, was revealed by the title of an article written by Abbott in which it was first discussed: "Program Design by Informal English Descriptions", (Abbott 1983). Abbott's article describes a technique whereby the objects of the problem domain, their behaviour and thus the operations associated with them can, it is suggested, be derived from a grammatical analysis of a statement of the *informal strategy* devised to provide the solution of the problem.

The essential nature of the grammatical analysis rests on the idea that *nouns* – "naming words" – can be used to identify objects. More specifically, common nouns identify abstract data types. Proper nouns identify single, individual objects, or data abstractions. Verbs and adverbial expressions identify operations.

A more detailed exposition of the methodology is as follows:
- Develop an informal strategy for a solution of the problem. This, according to Abbott, should be "at the same conceptual level as the problem itself" – in other words it should not attempt to describe an implementation of a program solution, but should be written, in English, using the terms of the problem domain.
- Formalize the strategy by:
  - identifying the data types – by finding the common nouns in the informal strategy.
  - identifying the objects – by finding the proper nouns and direct references.

- identifying the operations to be associated with the objects (Booch uses the phrase "suffered by the objects", which may strike the reader as a more illuminating terminology) – by finding the verbs, adverbs and descriptive expressions.

The descriptions of this analysis included in both Abbott's article and the first edition of Booch's book *Software engineering with Ada* include examples of its application to several "informal strategies" that show the nouns and verbs etc., actually underlined in the text. The phrase "underlining the nouns" seems to have become indissolubly associated with the technique, usually mentioned in a rather disparaging way by its detractors.

Booch developed the technique both in the second edition of his first book, and also in the more recent *Software components with Ada* and *Object-oriented design with applications*. In these later versions of the methodology, the emphasis placed on the importance of grammatical analysis has been reduced in favour of a straightforward "examination of the problem domain", with whatever assistance might come to hand, including the identification of nouns and verbs in the specification, but also conventional aids such as flowcharts and data flow diagrams.

8.5.2 An example – counting leaves

Booch gives as an example the problem of counting the leaves of a binary tree. The informal strategy is given as follows:

> Keep a pile of the parts of the tree that have not yet been counted. Initially, get a tree and put it on the empty pile; the count of the leaves is initially set to zero. As long as the pile is not empty, repeatedly take a tree off the pile and examine it. If the tree consists of a single leaf, then increment the leaf counter and throw away that tree. If the tree is not a single leaf but instead consists of two subtrees, split the tree into its left and right subtrees and put them back on the pile. Once the pile is empty, display the count of the leaves.

The basic form of the algorithm suggested by this description is a simple loop. The number of iterations of the loop is determined by the (initially unknown) number of subtrees, and so a condition-controlled, rather than a count-controlled, loop is appropriate. The "program" may be sketched in Ada as follows:

```
add_to_pile(get_tree_from_somewhere);
leaf_counter := 0;
while not_empty(pile)
loop
    current_tree := next_tree_from_pile;
    if is_a_leaf(current_tree)
```

```
        then leaf_counter := leaf_counter + 1;
        else
            add_to_pile(left_subtree_of(current_tree));
            add_to_pile(right_subtree_of(current_tree));
        end if;
    end loop;
    display(leaf_counter);
```

The reader may well object that this is hardly distinguishable from the initial stage of a process of design by functional decomposition, simply rendering into pseudo-code a straightforward algorithm. In fact this is the case – the difference being at the next stage. In functional decomposition the next stage would be to take the various "high-level" operations such as **add_to_pile** and decompose them into more implementation-oriented lower-level operations. In object-oriented design, the objects/data abstractions are defined by examining the required operations. If we list the operations:

- **get_tree_from_environment** – the informal description is very vague on this point – we simply assume a function that returns a tree (object), as a rather specialized *initialize* operation;
- **add_to_pile** – inserts a tree object into the pile;
- **next_tree_from_pile** – returns a tree. The implication is that the read-out must be destructive – not simply a copy, so that once removed a tree cannot be re-read. It is the equivalent of a stack "pop" operation but provided for the pile. Note that the requirement to "throw away" trees is satisfied by this property of a **pile** operation, rather than an operation suffered by **tree**;
- **is_empty_pile** – a Boolean operation on the pile;
- **is_leaf** – a Boolean operation on a tree;
- **left_subtree, right_subtree** – operations respectively returning the left and right subtree of a tree argument;
- **display** – an operation exported by the user interface object. As the values to be displayed will be positive integers there is little further analysis required.

It takes very little analysis to identify two major objects: **pile** and **tree**. The two are entirely distinct. **pile** is a single, unique object that is essentially a "store and yield" object, with its only slightly unusual feature being the "destructive" nature of the "yield" or "pop" operation.

On the other hand **tree** is indefinitely replicated. Also, the fact that the operations on each tree are subject to a condition test by the main program means that a tree object must exist in the main program, as the value of a declared variable – so that it can be tested and, if it is not a leaf, split. These requirements dictate that **tree** must be an abstract data type, i.e. a limited private type in the Ada context, a conventional (non-singleton) class in C++.

Staying with Ada, we can now define, or formalize, to use Booch's terminology, the interfaces of these objects. First it is necessary to determine the dependency relationship between them, in other words to decide on the visibility of one from the other. This is an issue that can become tricky – to the level of pathologically circular dependencies. However, in this case it is fairly clear that the **pile** object must be dependent on the **tree** abstract data type: the operations associated with the **pile**, such as **add_to_pile**, have parameters that must be of type **tree**, which is obviously exported from a package "**with**ed" by the package realizing the **pile** data abstraction. The package specifications are shown in Figure 8.1.

```
package trees is
----
-- A package exporting an abstract data type that provides the
-- semantics of the binary tree for objects of the type.
--
        type TREE is limited private;
        function GET_TREE_FROM_ENVIRONMENT return TREE;
        --
        procedure ADD_ITEM_TO(T : in out TREE; E: ELEMENT);
        --
        function IS_LEAF(T : TREE) return BOOLEAN;
        --
        function LEFT_SUBTREE_OF(T: TREE) return TREE;
        function RIGHT_SUBTREE_OF(T : TREE) return TREE;
private
        type TREE_STRUCTURE;
        type TREE is access TREE_STRUCTURE;
end trees;

package pile is
--
        procedure INITIALISE_PILE;
        --
        procedure ADD_TREE_TO PILE(T : TREE);
        function NEXT_TREE_FROM_PILE return TREE;
        function PILE_IS_EMPTY return BOOLEAN;
end pile;
```

Figure 8.1 Package specifications defining objects for the leaf-counting problem.

8.6 Developments of the methodology

The original version of object-oriented design, as illustrated by this example, seems limited to "problems" whose solutions are individual algorithms. The examples given by Booch: the determination of the number of days between two given dates, even the KWIC index problem, are typically single algorithm problems. The technique has been criticized therefore, for example in Nielson & Shumate (1987), as being unsuitable for the design of large systems in which there are many algorithms and where the technique would simply be too time-consuming and unwieldy if applied to the complete "informal strategy", or design specification, of the system. Again, although the original technique's output, as a set of abstract data type definitions, is certainly quite consistent with the view of design recommended in Chapter 1, which emphasizes the importance of the "mortar" before the "bricks", it is hardly adequate in providing for the specification of the behaviour that the abstract data types are to capture. They are left as static, syntactic definitions of sets of operations, with little guidance to the implementor how the corresponding objects behave *dynamically* as they interact in the executing system. These limitations have led to the enrichment of the methodology with a number of techniques intended to support the modeling of the dynamic behaviour of the system.

8.6.1 Scenarios and use cases

Although slightly discredited in its original form, the use of English prose is still important in the initial stages, in the form of *scenarios*. A scenario is a description, normally written in English, of the steps that the system takes to perform one of its functions. An example is the following (rather imaginative) example, from Chonoles and Gilliam, of the steps taken by a cash dispenser system when presented with a stolen credit card:

> Customer inserts card into reader
> Card reader reads magnetic strip
> Account number sent to account server
> Stolen card message returned by account server
> Police summoned
> Card coated with instantaneous acting sleeping drug
> Card returned to user

In a large system there may well be many such scenarios. A subset is known as *use cases*. These are scenarios involving *actors*, which are entities outside the system that interact with it. Actors may be human, as in the cases of the stolen card user above, or objects within another system. Use cases enable the characterization of the external behaviour of a system, in terms of the stimuli it recognizes and the responses it makes as a result.

Scenarios are not primarily written to facilitate the identification of the objects of the system (although they may be suggestive in this area), but rather to provide the "raw material" from which the interactive behaviour of the objects may be derived. Each scenario defines a sequence of events undergone by the objects involved in it – a sequence of stimuli from object to object. Such sequences can be captured in a revealingly systematic way by an *event trace diagram*.

8.6.2 Event trace diagrams

These diagrams consist of a number of vertical lines, one for each of the objects in the associated scenario, between which horizontal arrows are drawn. An arrow from one vertical to another represents an interaction, in the form of a stimulus or message, from the source object to the receiver object as indicated by the direction of the arrow, which is labelled with an abbreviated English version of the message involved. Time flows down the diagram – arrows representing later events appear below those representing earlier events. The event trace diagram for the stolen card scenario is shown in Figure 8.2.

8.6.3 State transition diagrams

As the complete set of scenarios, and their associated event trace diagrams, for a system is built up, the behaviour of individual objects, or

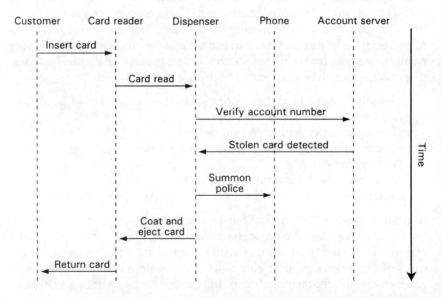

Figure 8.2 Event trace diagram for stolen card.

abstract data types, can be extracted. This is done by concatenating related verticals for the particular object/type, from all the event traces, their attached events, and source/destination object/types where the object/type appears.

With a remarkable degree of consistency, in virtually all the contemporary successors of Booch's original methodology, the means used to model this object or type behaviour is the *state transition diagram*. A state transition diagram is a directed graph in which each node represents a state of the entity it represents, and interconnections between the nodes represent possible transitions between states. The transitions are generally labelled with the stimulus causing the transition from the source state to the destination state.

A partial state transition diagram for the cash dispenser system showing that part of its behaviour including the stolen card scenario is given in Figure 8.3. This example shows an extension to the basic state diagram in the form of dashed arrows showing the transmission of events to related objects, represented as rectangles.

As implied above, Booch's monopoly over object-oriented design has been eroded, and there are a number of well established competitors. Probably the most significant is OMT (Object Modeling Technique) devised by

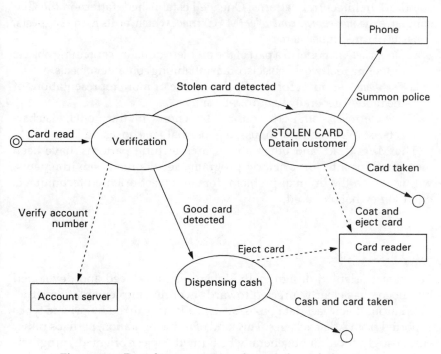

Figure 8.3 Partial state transition diagram for cash dispenser.

Rumbaugh *et al*. The reader is recommended to consult the further reading at the end of the chapter for a number of references to OMT and others.

8.6.4 Standard object patterns

As we have seen, the typical problem domain is populated by real-world objects. When we come to design a specific computer application designed to provide a solution to some aspect of the problem domain, it is necessary to take into account that the application will contain more than simply a model of (part of) the problem domain. It will contain objects whose existence derives from the fact that it is a *computer* application, and have no counterparts as problem domain objects. Examples of these are objects concerned with the support of the user interface, which may be numerous, and subject to complex interrelationships where this is a GUI. Again, it is very common to find the requirement for "containers" for problem domain objects; Parnas' line storage data abstraction is one such object; the hallowed stack is another.

Obviously an analysis of the problem domain is of little help in identifying these application domain objects – precisely because they have no counterparts in the problem domain. Instead, the designer must rely on experience and a degree of intuition, often assisted by the existence of standard architectural patterns. One well established pattern in the GUI context is the *model view controller* (MVC) *triad*, which, as its name suggests, consists of three subsystems:

1. *The model* – a model of a part of the problem domain, containing objects modeling real-world objects, often inhabiting container objects.
2. *The view* – support for the display of one or more representations of the model, generally windows-based.
3. *The controller* – support for user interaction with the model, via characteristic GUI entities: mouse, menus, dialogue boxes, etc.

The MVC triad, and other similar architectural patterns, have been incorporated into proprietary program development environments, within which the original problem domain object-oriented technique is often somewhat obscured.

8.7 Inheritance

The object-oriented design methodology, as introduced and developed by Booch, was clearly directed towards eventual implementation structured around abstract data types, specifically as realized by private types exported from Ada packages. This kind of implementation, perhaps rather surprisingly, would not generally be termed "object-oriented" programming; instead the term "object-based" is conventionally used. The distinction between object-based and object-oriented *programming* is the utilization of *inheritance* by the latter.

In the object-oriented methodology, the primary focus is on the identification of the objects of the problem domain. Many domains contain very large numbers of objects, and if it were necessary to treat them as unique individuals the object-oriented technique would be impractical, because of the need to create correspondingly large numbers of uniquely defined data abstractions. We are nearly always able to reduce this multiplicity drastically by recognizing similarities between objects, so that they can be treated as instances of sets of characteristics, or abstract data types to use the standard terminology. Thus the initial focus on the identification of objects is succeeded by the attempt to discover similarities between them, so that abstract data types, or *classes* as they are sometimes termed, can be derived.

All the instances of an abstract data type possess the same structure, and the same *potential* behaviour, although this will typically vary from individual to individual because it is dependent on the life history of the instance concerned. Thus, the "similarity" that objects must exhibit in order to be represented as instances of a class must be quite strict – their characteristics must be identical in so far as they are modeled by the class.

It is clear that in many application domains the objects may fail to exhibit this level of strict similarity, but still possess what can be recognized as similarity, at the level, say, of "family resemblances". The valves controlling the flow of chemicals in a plant, for example, may well have a common set of operations including **open, close, report_position**, etc. Some will possess more specialized characteristics, such as **set_to_ default, set_percent_open**, etc., and the question naturally arises as to whether there are advantages to be gained by recognizing these family resemblances, in a manner analogous to those obtained by the use of classes.

In fact this is clearly the case. To continue the example – in many scenarios the differences between valve variants will be irrelevant, and so a simplification of the problem domain, a *raising of the level of abstraction*, can be achieved by ignoring these differences. So compelling is the naturalness of this approach, many exponents of object-oriented design regard the recognition of this kind of relationship between objects, or rather between the classes of which they are instances, called *inheritance*, as fundamental to the whole object-oriented philosophy. The sequence of analysis of the problem domain is extended therefore, to include an attempt to discover similarities between the classes identified previously.

The proponents of inheritance point to the ubiquitous nature of *classification* in human thought, citing, for example, the taxonomies of botany and zoology as the basis of the power of the technique.

When inheritance is included in the object-oriented design picture, the process of identifying objects and their characteristics becomes subtly changed. The process becomes not so much one of *identification* but of *recognition* – to find characteristics that are largely exhibited by an existing object, and then to define the specialization necessary to characterize the object in question.

For example, let us consider a system concerned with cars: perhaps a car-hire management system. The "family resemblance" of cars – their common attributes and operations – include items such as maker's name, engine size, accumulated mileage, and so on. If we assume that an abstract data type exporting this set of operations is already in existence, then the creation of more specialized cars – limousines, estate cars, sports cars – can be seen as a matter of adding alternative sets of additional characteristics to the general, parent car type. A tree-structure of relationships growing from a general root to specialized leaves can easily be envisaged.

8.7.1 Class hierarchies

Inheritance introduces a new dimension into the abstract data type theme that has permeated this book up to this point. By allowing the recognition of a weaker form of resemblance than strict identity, inheritance provides a new abstraction technique permitting differences between similar objects to be ignored, where these are irrelevant. The inheritance relationship allows for the construction of a new kind of structure – the *class hierarchy* – in which a class at one level is a specialization, i.e. possesses a superset of the characteristics, of one or more in the level above, and a generalization, i.e. possesses a subset of the characteristics, of one or more in the level below. The scope of the associated abstraction extends over the whole of such a hierarchy, in that an instance of any class in the hierarchy can be treated as an instance of a class at its top level.

Although obviously a powerful abstraction mechanism, inheritance would remain only an interesting intellectual exercise if it could not be carried through into the implementation phase, and this is clearly dependent on significant features of the programming language used. Specifically, the language must allow for class hierarchies to be defined. In the descriptions of the support for data abstraction by a number of languages so far, abstract data types have been characterized by their splendid isolation, and it is not immediately obvious how hierarchies can be constructed while still retaining the beneficial qualities of data abstraction. We shall return to inheritance, and its support by a number of languages, including C++ and Ada, in the last part of this book.

8.8 Summary

In this chapter we have discovered the relevance of data abstraction to the synthetic component of software design, and discussed the methodology that recognizes this relevance – object-oriented design. A particular approach to this methodology, associated with Abbott and Booch, has been investigated, together with an indication of more recent developments that have been introduced to increase the representational power of the methodology, particularly in its modeling of dynamic behaviour. Finally, we have introduced the concept of inheritance – a very significant abstraction tool, which, with the associated concept of class hierarchies, will be central to much of the material of the last part of this book.

8.9 Further reading

R. J. Abbott "Program design by informal English descriptions", *Communications of the ACM* **26**, 882–94, 1983, was closely related to G. Booch's book referred to above (in its first edition). It is certainly worth reading, if only to gain an appreciation of the complexities to which such an apparently simple approach can lead.

K. W. Neilson & K. Shumate, "Designing large real-time systems with Ada," *Communications of the ACM* **30**, 695–715, 1987, includes a consideration of the Booch methodology in the real-time context, and finds it wanting. Their own methodology might be regarded as a modified version of object-oriented design, tailored specifically to real-time systems. R. J. A. Buhr, *System design with Ada* (Englewood Cliffs, New Jersey: Prentice-Hall, 1984), also adopts what might be termed a modified object-oriented approach.

A description of the technique of discovering objects by identifying agents of behaviour is given in E. Gibson, "Objects born and bred", *Byte Magazine* (October 1990), 245–54.

The standard work on the most significant "post-Booch" methodology is J. Rumbaugh, M. Blaha, W. Premerlani, F. Eddy, W. Lorenson, *Object-oriented modeling and design* (Englewood Cliffs, New Jersey: Prentice-Hall, 1991). Also see D. Embley, B. Kurtz, S. Woodfield, *Object-oriented systems analysis* (Englewood Cliffs, New Jersey: Yourdon Press, 1992); R. Wirfs-Brock, B. Wilkerson, L. Wiener, *Designing object-oriented software* (Englewood Cliffs, New Jersey: Prentice-Hall, 1993); M. Priestley, *Practical object-oriented design* (Maidenhead, Berks: McGraw-Hill, 1996) and, of course, G. Booch, *Object-oriented design with applications* (Menlo Park, California: Benjamin/Cummings 1991).

See also: M. Chonoles & C. Gilliam, "Real-time object-oriented system design using the object modeling technique (OMT)", *Journal of Object-Oriented Programming* **8**(3), 16–24, 1995.

CHAPTER 9

Software reusability

9.1 Introduction

At a conference on software engineering some years ago, one of the wittier participants delivered himself of the following: "In software engineering we should stand on the shoulders of those who have gone before us. In fact we stand on their feet." This sums up rather well the very general and regrettable tendency for the wheel to be reinvented constantly in software engineering. Rare indeed is the software product that is not written "from the ground up", with virtually every module actually designed and written by the project team, from the high, application-specific level to the low, general routine level, which contains much that is common to many applications. Normally, little attempt is made to exploit existing software "off the shelf".

This is perhaps a slightly black picture. Every user of a high-level language unavoidably reuses software in the form of input/output facilities, which may be built into the language or provided as separate, standard libraries as in C++ or Ada. On a more significant level from considerations of functionality, a few areas have developed a strong dependence on reusable software. The notable example of this is in computer graphics, where libraries such as GINO-F and the various language "bindings" of the Graphical Kernel System (GKS) have achieved wide penetration – within a relatively small volume of actual use, however. Even here though, the reused software is normally essentially peripheral in nature, excluded from the central core of the application, and this seems typical of reuse in general.

9.1.1 Component software

In the context of this kind of discussion software engineering is often compared unfavourably with electronic systems engineering. The electronic system designer charged with the design of, say, a radar transmitter does not either begin or end the process by designing the resistors or even transistors that form the "atomic" components of the design. Instead, the design is expressed in terms of components that are "one level down" in complexity from the transmitter itself: amplifiers, modulators and so on. Typically these components are not only not designed by our designer but they are, in many cases, not produced by the manufacturer for which he or she works. These components are supplied with well defined interfaces and functionality, catalogued in sufficient completeness to allow their incorporation in a design still at the "paper" stage.

Design, in this environment, is therefore largely a matter of devising the best collection of components, from those available, to satisfy constraints such as price and performance. As such, in being concentrated at one level of abstraction, it is intrinsically simpler than the "deep structure" characteristic of software products, with a correspondingly higher chance of being successfully carried out.

This is, of course, a picture seen through the rose-tinted spectacles of the software engineer. In practice electronic components frequently react in unpredictable and awkward ways when connected into assemblies, and much of the time of the designer is occupied in solving the resulting problems. The picture does contain a good deal of truth, however, certainly sufficient to provide a model or ideal towards which software engineering might well aspire. The question then arises as to whether software can be "componentized" so as to achieve, or at least approach, this ideal. Clearly there are some stringent criteria involved, and it is to the consideration of these that we now turn.

9.2 Criteria for reusability

The component software idea is obviously dependent on a basic level of compatibility. The traditional absence of reuse in software engineering stemmed not from any absence of motivation, but from an absence of the minimal technological support required. The multiplicity of machine architectures, operating systems, language dialects, character codes and so on, made the transfer of any significant piece of software between different platforms, to use the current jargon, a difficult business. This picture has changed radically as a result of the ever-widening use of portable operating systems, of which Unix provides the most important example, based on a 32-bit architecture. The introduction of languages with very strongly enforced standardization, such as Ada, has also tended to enable the transferability of software.

Given that the minimal technological support for component software is now widely available, what characteristics should software items possess to make them likely candidates for reuse?

9.2.1 Negative criteria

The first criteria that must be met are negative in the sense that the absence of the qualities to which they relate guarantees *non* reusability. These are *correctness* and *efficiency*. Clearly no item of software will be even considered as a candidate for reuse if it is full of bugs, or if it is too large, or too slow.

Mention of correctness immediately raises the question of specification, for the assertion of the correctness of a software item is meaningless in the absence of its specification. This is an area of considerable importance in the context of reusable software, to which we shall return shortly.

9.2.2 Functionality

Turning to criteria related to qualities that positively support reuse, the most obviously important concerns functionality. A software item is more likely to be reused the more it exhibits a functionality applicable in many contexts, performing some useful and significant task common to many applications.

There are the makings of a contradiction here: *useful* and *significant* are highly subjective terms, but it is clear that in each application they will be relative *to the purposes of the specific application.* This would seem to conflict with the next criterion.

9.2.3 Independence

A software item will be reusable only if it is sufficiently free of any bias towards a particular application. "Sufficiently" in this context is relatively easy to define: the reuse of a software item should not require the distortion of its new environment to simulate the characteristics of the environment in which the item was first developed.

Reusable items are therefore required to be significant contributors to every application within which they are employed, while remaining independent of each of them – a difficult balancing feat.

9.2.4 Robustness

A further important requirement is that the item should be *robust*, i.e. it should be capable of being transplanted to many different environments without compromise to its correct and efficient operation. The designer of such an item must be able to control completely the way in which external units interact with it. Robustness is the syntactic complement to the semantic criterion of independence and must be present to underpin the latter.

9.2.5 Fail safety

The "contract model" is often invoked in the context of reusable software. The idea is of a (normally unwritten) contract between the users of a software item and its implementor, with the implication that both parties incur responsibility for its successful use. (Use here means incorporation into a system.) The users agree to abide by the requirements of the public interface, in return for which the implementor guarantees the correct operation of the software.

This agreeable analogy is rarely extended to the inclusion of penalty clauses: what can the user expect if the requirements of the interface are not complied with? The usual answer is probably chaos, but this is hardly satisfactory. The user of a reusable item should be protected from the results of his or her folly as far as possible, with a policy of damage limitation constantly observed by the designer.

A *fail safe* design in software terms means something rather different from that employed in other areas of technology. The major requirement is that the user must never be left in ignorance of the fact that something has gone wrong. A "helpful" software component that tries to compensate for its misuse is highly dangerous: if misuse does occur then the (mis)user must be informed, preferably in a way that cannot be ignored.

9.2.6 Data abstraction: the basis for reusability

The list of criteria given above points inexorably towards a particular kind of software construct as being the most suitable vehicle for reuse. The requirement for significant functionality suggests that subprograms are unlikely to be adequate in the general case, because of their inability, in most languages, to maintain an internal state over several invocations. Robustness can be guaranteed only by encapsulation – which can be provided only by subprograms or (it can finally be revealed) the data abstraction. The separation of interface from implementation detail, and the hiding of the latter, makes the data abstraction the natural form for reusable software components. This is not to say, of course, that all the criteria mentioned will be satisfied by adopting this approach – the conflict between application-specific significance and independence mentioned above is still a major problem, for example.

9.3 Genericity

A major contribution towards the solution of this problem arises from the possibility of *parameterizing* some of the types involved in the interface of a software component. This possibility comes about where the characteristics of the types concerned are either irrelevant, or need be recognized to only a very limited extent. An example of the first kind is provided by container structures such as our old friend the stack. The type of the items pushed into a stack is quite irrelevant to the operations of the stack, which require only the ability to assign the items to and from the internal data structure. The items are treated as black boxes, with no operational interface whatsoever.

An example of the second possibility is provided by a sort routine. Again the items to be sorted are treated as black boxes with no discernible features, other than sufficient individuality to permit an *ordering relation* to be determined between them. In other words, the possibility of sorting is dependent on the possibility of deciding that one item is, in some sense, less than another. Apart from this, no sorting algorithm requires any further access to the internal details of the items to be sorted. It should also be noted that the items must be held within a structure that allows the ordering relation to be represented – a container, again.

The natural implication is that it should be possible to take advantage of the irrelevance of the types of the items involved in these two examples by constructing, for example, a *generic* stack abstract data type capable of accepting any item type. (The term generic means "applicable to a whole class or group".) This possibility would have obvious benefits for reusability in freeing a component from inessential detail deriving from a specific application, and can be recognized as another way of raising the level of abstraction.

9.3.1 Problems of strong typing

In a strongly-typed language like Pascal, however, this kind of "type blindness" cannot be permitted – every subprogram parameter must possess a type, and the types of the parameters of a subprogram are part of its declaration: change a parameter type and a different subprogram is defined.

This has the unfortunate result that routines must be replicated if they are to accommodate different types, even if these are completely irrelevant to the operations involved. It also prejudices the reusability of the software components concerned because of the complete lack of flexibility involved. An application that required the use of a stack holding, say, pointers, would not be able to use a stack declared for unsigned integer items, despite the probable similarity of the sets of values involved.

It would appear then that what is required is the ability to declare parameters as having no type at all, or "don't care". This approach can be adopted by a user of Modula-2, which provides a type WORD that, when used to declare a formal parameter, allows substitution for it by an actual parameter with any type that occupies one word of memory. The specific size of a word is not defined in the language but is dependent on the implementation. Typically, a word will be of 16-bit or 32-bit extent and capable of holding INTEGERs, CARDINALs and, again depending on the implementation, BOOLEANs.

The applicability of this feature is greatly extended by using type WORD in conjunction with the Modula-2 *open array* type constructor, which permits the declaration of one-dimensional array formal parameters with unspecified index ranges – itself a form of genericity.

Such a parameter may be declared, for example, as being of type ARRAY OF INTEGER. This means that any one-dimensional array with INTEGER components may be substituted for it. The procedure to which the formal parameter belongs is able to determine the last, or highest, index value by the inquiry routine HIGH; the lowest index value of an open array is always 0.

An open array with components of WORD is obviously more nonspecific still, and this generality is increased by the fact that a parameter declared to be ARRAY OF WORD is not even constrained to be substituted by an array, and so actual parameters of any type may be used. ARRAY OF WORD, therefore, fits more or less exactly the idea of a "don't care" type.

It must be pointed out, however, that this feature of Modula-2 is *not* provided to allow the recognition of the irrelevance of the types of some of the parameters to certain software components. It is provided to allow the language to be used as a systems programming language, for example in writing operating systems, where the constraints of strong typing are sometimes inconvenient. The feature is specifically included to provide a well defined breach in the iron-clad defences of strong typing, to be used only in the direst circumstances and with the responsibility for any ensuing disaster placed firmly on the head of the foolhardy programmer concerned. As can be seen, this is certainly not an appropriate basis for constructing highly reliable software components whose use in any hands can be safely guaranteed. The sort of abuse that might be perpetrated can be illustrated as follows, given a definition module for a queue:

```
DEFINITION MODULE QUEUE;
    TYPE Queue;
    PROCEDURE Initialize (VAR Q : Queue);
    PROCEDURE EnQueue (Q : Queue; Item : ARRAY OF WORD);
    PROCEDURE DeQueue
      (Q : Queue; VAR Item : ARRAY OF WORD);
    PROCEDURE IsEmpty (Q : Queue) : BOOLEAN;
END QUEUE.
```

Then the following program fragment would incur no protest from the compiler:

```
VAR     Rec : RECORD
                IntVal : INTEGER;
                FloVal : REAL
            END;
        INTVAL : INTEGER;
        RecsQ : Queue;
BEGIN
        Rec.IntVal := 10;
        Rec.FloVal := 1.0;
        Initialize(RecsQ);
        EnQueue(RecsQ,Rec);


            *     *     *


        DeQueue(RecsQ,INTVAL);
```

with probable catastrophic results at run time caused by the overwriting of the memory area following that allocated to **INTVAL** by the additional extent of **Rec**.

Clearly, then, simply permitting "don't care" types is not adequate – the compiler needs to "care" enough to prevent the kind of situation sketched above. The minimal requirement would seem the ability to check that *the same* type is involved in logically related cases such as **EnQueue** and **DeQueue**, even though other characteristics may be ignored. Such an ability is provided by the Ada *generic* facility and, more recently, the equivalent C++ *template* facility.

9.3.2 Generics in Ada

As part of its design aim to support component software, Ada provides the means for writing certain program units, specifically subprograms and packages, as *templates* with parameters that are normally types. These templates may not be compiled into executable code but must be *instantiated*, with actual parameters "plugged into" them in order to produce normal program units. To give a (the!) simple example, a generic routine to swap over its two parameters is shown in Figure 9.1. The body of the generic procedure is preceded by the reserved word **generic**, the generic formal parameter type **ANY_TYPE** and its *specification*, which has the same form as in a package specification and consists of its name and parameter list, terminated by a semi-colon. There is no need for the body to follow immediately after the *generic specification*: it may appear anywhere in a declarative region within the scope of the specification and indeed in some circumstances it is necessary for the two to be separated; hence the need for the apparent duplication.

```
generic
type ANY_TYPE is private;
procedure GEN_SWAP ( LEFT,RIGHT : in out ANY_TYPE );
procedure GEN_SWAP ( LEFT,RIGHT : in out ANY_TYPE ) is
TEMP : ANY_TYPE;
begin
        TEMP := LEFT;
        LEFT := RIGHT;
        RIGHT:= TEMP;
end GEN_SWAP;
```

Figure 9.1   A generic swap procedure.

This generic template could then be instantiated with, say, **integer** and **character**, to produce procedures for swapping parameters of the nominated type; indeed, it could be instantiated with *generic actual* parameters of *any* type: this is the implication of the *generic formal* declaration **private**. Note the plurality of the word "procedures" in the last sentence – one ordinary unit is produced for every instantiation of a generic; it is *not* like the Modula-2 pattern where one unit can handle any kind of parameter type.

Although any type may be substituted for **ANY_TYPE**, the fact that it defines the type of both the parameters of the procedure, and the type of the local variable **temp**, means that the compiler can check that *the same* "any type" is used in each particular case. The use of generics involves no breach in strong typing, therefore, and so the facility can be used to provide software components with all the protection that strong typing affords.

The swap generic might be instantiated as follows:

```
procedure INT_SWAP is new GEN_SWAP(integer);
procedure CHAR_SWAP is new GEN_SWAP(character);
```

with the generic actual parameter in parentheses after the name of the generic. The instantiations appear in a declarative region and have the same significance as an ordinary procedure specification and can be used to swap, respectively, integer and character variables.

The generic facility is essentially a *compile-time* mechanism – generic program units must be instantiated with the actual parameters required before they can be compiled into run-time units. There are thus, typically, two sets of parameters associated with a generic unit such as **GEN_SWAP**:

1. *the generic parameters* that are substituted at compile time to produce a normal unit;
2. *the run-time parameters* that are substituted when the instantiated unit is invoked at run-time, in exactly the same way as for an ordinary unit.

The instantiations of a generic unit are indistinguishable from an ordinary unit as far as the final stage of compilation is concerned. The generic

```
generic
      type Item is private;
package Queues is
--
      type Queue is limited private;
--
      procedure initialise(Q : in out queue);
      procedure enqueue(I : Item; Q : queue);
      procedure dequeue(I : out Item; Q : queue);
      function is_empty(Q : queue) return boolean;
--
      QUEUE_UNDERFLOW : exception;
private
      type queue_struct;
      type queue is access queue_struct;
end Queues;
```

Figure 9.2   A generic queues package specification.

facility is, therefore, essentially a text substitution mechanism confined completely to the source program.

The generic mechanism can be used to define a template for a package also; the Ada equivalent of the **Queues** module is shown in Figure 9.2. The corresponding package body is written in the same way as for a normal, non-generic package, using the generic formal parameter where appropriate.

Exceptions

The declaration of **QUEUE_UNDERFLOW** as apparently a variable of type **exception** is, in fact, an illustration of Ada's *exception mechanism*, which provides for the kind of fail-safety mentioned earlier. The exception mechanism is not restricted to generic program units, but a brief description seems appropriate at this point.

An exception is associated with an error condition that is detected either by the run-time system, such as overflow or exhaustion of memory, or by tests written into the program. When such an error condition occurs an exception is *raised*, automatically in the case of a system-detected condition, or explicitly by a **raise** statement in the case of a program-detected condition. Once an exception is raised the normal execution of the program is disrupted – thus providing the means whereby the user of a component is "not left in ignorance" that an error has occurred.

The exception mechanism provides a means whereby an exception may be trapped, or *handled*, allowing the execution of the program to continue, presumably after some corrective action has been taken. But the writer of a component can ensure that this error handling must be provided by the external user simply by failing to incorporate it within the component. Exceptions declared in the specification of a package, like QUEUE_ OVERFLOW, which is raised on an attempt to dequeue an item from an empty queue, will invariably be intended for this purpose. Such an exception is intended to be exported to external units and is not, therefore, handled internally.

Constrained genericity

In the queues example there is no problem in allowing for any type of parameter to be substituted. In some contexts, though, such freedom could lead to incompatibilities that the compiler could not accept. A good example is a generic formal parameter that is to be the index type of an array. Ada permits only discrete types to be used for indexing arrays, in common with all structured languages. It would not, therefore, be appropriate for the declaration for such a generic formal parameter to specify private, meaning "any type". Instead Ada provides the means for constraining generic parameters so that the range of possible actual parameters falls within a particular class. The declaration of a generic formal parameter that may be substituted only by a discrete type takes the form of the following example:

```
INDEX_TYPE is (<>);
```

Such a parameter could then be used as part of the declaration of an array formal generic parameter, as follows:

```
INDEX_TYPE is (<>);
type ELEMENT is private;
type GEN_VECTOR is array(INDEX_TYPE) of ELEMENT;
```

GEN_VECTOR is thereby declared as a generic formal that may be substituted by any one-dimensional array type with any component type and indexed by any discrete type – the most abstract form of such an array.

Operation parameters

In the previous discussion that led up to the idea of genericity the example of a sort routine was mentioned. It was suggested that a sort needs rather more than the ability to distinguish the identity of different objects – in particular it needs to be able to *order* objects of the type that it manipulates: to determine for each pair of objects in the set submitted to it which is the larger, in some sense. In the case of a generic sort procedure there is an obvious problem – if the objects that it is to sort are of a parameterized type that has the formal declaration private, meaning "any type", how can it determine an ordering over them, in ignorance of the type used as the actual parameter in each instantiation? It is not even possible to determine whether such an ordering is defined.

149

In order to overcome this problem Ada allows for the specification of generic parameters that are *operations* – subprograms, in Ada terminology – to permit such attributes as an ordering relationship to be parameterized. In other words, a generic parameter may be supplied with its own version of the "<" operator: defined with itself as the operand type. Ada allows an operator such as "<" to be *overloaded*, that is given an additional meaning in terms of its operand types. Ada, like C++, allows *user-defined* overloadings of the arithmetic and logical operators. Such an overloading is achieved by specifying a function with a name of the form "<", which is then used in its conventional infix form, i.e. placed between its operands, rather than in the prefix form conventional for functions. The complete generic specification for a sort routine, capable of being instantiated to sort any one-dimensional array with elements of any type, might look as shown in Figure 9.3 therefore.

```
generic
    type ELEMENT is private;
    type INDEX is (<>);
    type GEN_VECTOR is array(INDEX) of ELEMENT;
    with function "<" (LEFT,RIGHT : ELEMENT) return boolean;
procedure GEN_SORT(VECTOR : in out GEN_VECTOR);
```

Figure 9.3 Generic specification for a sort routine.

An operation parameter is given as a subprogram specification preceded by the reserved word **with**, so that the compiler does not assume that it is the start of the generic unit.

Someone wishing to use **GEN_SORT** would have to provide an appropriate overloading of "<" for the particular actual parameter type corresponding to **ELEMENT**. For example, assuming that a user wishes to sort an array of records, with the following type:

```
type CAR is record
            FLEET_NUMBER : positive;
            MANUFACTURER : string(1..20);
            MODEL : string(1..10);
            REGISTRATION : string(1..7);
            ENGINE_SIZE : positive;
            PURCHASE_YEAR: YEAR_RANGE:
            MILES_TO_DATE: positive;
        end record;
```

a particular application might require a listing of cars in order of their recorded mileage, and so an appropriate overloading would be:

```
function "<" ( L,R : CAR) return boolean is
begin
        return L.MILES_TO_DATE < R.MILES_TO_DATE;
end "<";
```

defining "<" for type CAR in terms of the corresponding operation for positive, which is defined as a standard operation.

9.3.3 Templates in C++

The incorporation of a generic facility into C++ occurred some time after the initial versions of the language. Stroustrup was characteristically keen to avoid inefficiency in its provision, and for this reason it is a noticeably more "lightweight" facility than the Ada equivalent. Both classes and functions may be specified as templates with type parameters. In this brief description we will restrict consideration to template classes, as being more relevant to the themes of this book.

The declaration of a template class is distinguished by being introduced by the reserved word template followed by a formal parameter list enclosed in angle brackets. Type formal parameters are preceded by the word class. A template for a stack class with the type of the items parameterized is shown below:

```
template <class itemType>
class stack {
            public:
                stack();
                void push(itemType elem);
                itemType pop();
                int isempty(); // returns 0 if not
            private:
                itemType store[100];
                itemType *tos; // stack top pointer
            };
```

The template can then be used to instantiate classes for, say, int and char stacks, used to declare variables in the same way as non-template classes, as follows:

```
stack<int> istk;
stack<char> chstk;
```

the actual type parameters being supplied in angle brackets, mirroring the definition.

The use of the compound name, such as stack<int>, as a class name is a deliberate design decision, providing in effect a "generic name". This

151

contrasts with the Ada instantiation mechanism, which imposes no requirement on the form of the name of an instantiation. In C++, however, **typedef** can be used to avoid the compound.

Non-type parameters may also be declared, typically to provide size information for the instantiations:

```
template <class itemType, int siz>
class stack {
        public:
            stack(): store(new itemType[siz])
                                {tos = store;}
            void push(itemType elem);
            itemType pop();
            int isempty(); // returns 0 if not
        private:
            itemType *store;
            itemType *tos; // stack top pointer
        };
```

Constraints and operations

In keeping with the general "lightweight" philosophy, the C++ template facility does not directly provide for the specification either of constraints over the kinds of type that may be supplied as actual parameters, or for operations such as overloadings of "<". The C++ inheritance facility, to be described in Chapter 12, can be used together with templates to achieve the same effects; this is an area where the language is still evolving.

9.3.4 Genericity – summary

Genericity as supported by Ada and C++ provides a powerful means of escaping from the "not specific enough to be useful – too specific to be widely reused" dilemma that was discussed earlier. The generic facility supports the ability to produce templates with a level of abstraction appropriate for reused components – application-specific features can be abstracted away, leaving essential functionality that can be tailored to many different application contexts by a suitable choice of generic parameters. Probably the most significant classes of reusable components are "container classes" – abstract data types such as lists, stacks, queues, vectors, trees, etc., which are employed in virtually every significant application and are very suitable for implementation as generic templates. In this context a significant recent development has been the development of a *standard template library* for C++ by Stepanov & Lee (1995), whose description of the benefits of genericity can hardly be bettered:

If software components are tabulated as a three-dimensional array, where one dimension represents different data types (e.g. `int`, `double`), the second dimension represents different containers (e.g. vector, linked list, file), and the third dimension represents different algorithms on the containers (e.g. searching, sorting, rotation), if i, j and k are the size of the dimensions, then $i*j*k$ different versions of code have to be designed. By using template functions that are parameterized by a data type, we need only $j*k$ versions. Further, by making our algorithms work on different containers we need merely $j+k$ versions.

Polymorphism

Both genericity and overloading are examples of a more general concept: that of *polymorphism*. As classical scholars will immediately recognize, the term means "possessing many forms". In the context of computer programming it has come to mean strictly "capable of possessing more than one type", although it is generally applied to operations – routines or subprograms – in relation to which it means "able to be applied to parameters of different types". Parametric polymorphism, of which the Ada and C++ generic template mechanism is an example, requires the specification by means of type parameters of each of the types that a polymorphic unit is to deal with, as its name suggests. Parametric polymorphism is particularly relevant to reuse; another kind of polymorphism, of which overloading is a rather restricted example, is a powerful aid to abstraction. This subject will be examined in more detail in a later chapter.

9.4 Design and reuse

Booch (1986) has suggested a basic portfolio of reusable components, which includes the standard data structures such as linked lists, stacks, queues, trees and directed graphs, all defined as abstract data types with generic parameters defining the elements/nodes of the structures. More recently, as we have seen, a standard template library for C++ has been published. It is worthwhile considering briefly the effect on the software design process that the general adoption of these portfolios might have.

The discussion of object-oriented design in Chapter 7 characterized the output from the design process as a set of abstract data type interface specifications – package specifications, in the Ada context. It seems obvious that this picture requires some modification, or at least clarification, when the existence of reusable software is taken into account. The existence of the possibility of software reuse would appear to necessitate the recognition of two reasonably distinct design activities:
- the design of reusable components;
- design for the reuse of components.

153

The first of these has been discussed briefly in the earlier sections. Suffice it to add that the requirements for quality assurance of reusable components must be stringent enough to give prospective reusers the necessary confidence in their integrity.

The second activity reflects a shift in the way in which design is carried out towards the idealized view of electronic systems design mentioned earlier. The objective of the design process becomes the generation not of a collection of module specifications but a "pick-list" of reusable components forming the basis of the design, possibly with some "glue" in the form of a few specially-written modules to make the whole thing work. To a certain extent this process must involve the imposition of the structures exhibited by the available reusable components onto the structure of the problem domain, or at least the *recognition* of these structures in the problem domain. For this to be done without undue distortion of a specific application obviously places considerable demands on the generality of the reusable components, as we have seen.

As important is the requirement for a change in the attitudes and methods of the software designer, who must perhaps lose some of the attributes of the "master architect", carrying through the design from its broad outlines to the mass of implementation detail, becoming instead more like a medical practitioner: recognizing a set of symptoms and applying the appropriate "cure" in the form of a reusable component. The idea of "egoless" programming is not a new one, nor was it deployed in the context of software component reuse, but it does convey the idea of the need to take some of the individuality, and perhaps creativity, out of software design that reuse implies.

9.5 Extensibility

As we have seen, the possibility of reusing software components is greatly enhanced by the ability to tailor them to the specific requirements of a new application context. The generic facility provides considerable support for this idea, but the range of possibilities of tailoring a particular component to different contexts is circumscribed by the limits of the abstraction concerned; they will all have the "family likeness", which is, of course, implied by the word "generic".

A more developed version of this idea is generally referred to as *extensibility*, implying not just the kind of syntactic tailoring that genericity of the Ada model provides, but adding functionality to what exists already – actually modifying the semantics of the abstraction. There is a considerable grey area between the two: the functionality of an Ada generic unit can be modified very considerably by the choice of an operation parameter, after all, but extensibility carries the suggestion of a change to the intrinsic functionality.

Once again we risk being impaled on the horns of a dilemma: the kind of modification that will qualify as being characteristic of extensibility seems incompatible with the strict encapsulation that has been identified as a hallmark of data abstraction. There are cases where this penetration of encapsulation is not required – where the functionality of one abstraction can be constructed on top of the external interface of a lower level one, with no need for any additional access to the data structure. As an example, the **Queues** package might well be built on top of a linked list package, with the specification shown in Figure 9.4.

The package provides operations for an abstract data type that is an abstraction of the conventional linked list – a linear structure of cells or nodes related by their positions in the sequence, i.e. by the "next" relationship. The interface is based on the idea of an imaginary pointer that identifies the "current" element for purposes of insertion into the next place, deletion or read access. The current element pointer may be moved up and down the list by the "navigation" operations, with the complementary predicates (Boolean functions) allowing for the detection of the current element being the first or last in the list.

The functionality of the **gen_lists** package is rather sparse – too sparse for a "real" component: it lacks any support for indexing, for example. It does provide sufficient to support the **Queues** package, however, as we shall demonstrate. The first question concerns the underlying data structure of a queue. Obviously this must be derived in some way from the **List** type exported by **Gen_lists**, which must therefore be instantiated in the body of **Queues**. The generic formal parameter of **Queues** is used as the actual for **Gen_lists**:

```
with Gen_lists;
package body Queues is
--
-- instantiate Gen_lists to provide queue data structure
--
    package Q_list is new Gen_lists(item);
```

The **list** type exported by the instantiation **Q_list** may now be used to create a data structure for a queue, supplying the implementation for the incomplete declaration **queue_struct**. In addition to incorporating a list it includes a **natural** variable to maintain a count of the number of elements. A record structure is therefore appropriate.

```
type Queue_struct is record
                       items : Q_list.list;
                       count : natural;
                     end record;
```

```
generic
     type element is private;
package gen_lists is
--
     type list is limited private;
     procedure initialize(L : in out list);
--
-- navigation operations for 'current element'
--
     procedure set_current_first(L : list);
     procedure set_current_last(L : list);
     procedure set_current_right(L : list);
     procedure set_current_left(L : list);
     function current_is_first(L: list) return boolean;
     function current_is_last(L: list) return boolean;
     --
-- insert/delete operations
     --
     procedure insert_right_of_current(E : element;
                              L : list);
     -- leaves current element as newly inserted one
     -- 'current' is imaginary in the empty list
     --
     procedure delete_current(L : list);
     -- leaves current element as one to left, unless the
     -- first one is deleted, when it's the one to the right
     --
-- access operation : read out the current element
     --
     function the_current_from(L : list) return element;
     --
     LIST_EXHAUSTED : exception; -- fallen off either end
     --
private
     type list_structure;
     type list is access list_structure;
end gen_lists;
```

Figure 9.4 A generic linked-list package.

The **Initialize** operation may now be implemented, using the corresponding **gen_lists** operation:

```
procedure initialize(Q :in out Queue) is
begin
        Q := new Queue_struct; -- Q points to the new
                                -- queue_struct object
        Q_list.initialize(Q.items);-- gen_lists operation
        Q.count := 0; -- no items in a new queue
end initialize;
```

The remainder of the operations may now be constructed straightforwardly using the operations exported by **Gen_lists** as shown in Figure 9.5.

It must be admitted that this is a somewhat special case, and that functionality cannot often be extended in this, encapsulation respecting, way. Since the original launch of Ada, in its 1983 version, there has been an increasing tendency to regard the encapsulated component model, enshrined in the language, as being too rigid, particularly in the very limited scope that it provides for code reuse by incrementation, or "programming by difference".

```
procedure enqueue(I: item; Q : queue) is
begin
        Q_list.set_current_last(Q.items);
        Q_list.insert_right_of_current(I,Q.items);
        Q.count := Q.count + 1;
end enqueue;

procedure dequeue(I : out item; Q : queue) is
begin
        if Q.count = 0 -- empty queue?
        then raise QUEUE_UNDERFLOW;
        end if;
        Q_list.set_current_first(Q.items);
        I := Q_list.the_current_from(Q.items);
        Q_list.delete_current(Q.items);
        Q.count := Q.count - 1;
end dequeue;

function is_empty(Q : queue) return boolean is
begin
        return Q.count = 0;
end is_empty;
end gen_queues;
```

Figure 9.5 Queue operations implemented using list operations.

9.5.1 Inheritance – programming by difference

The idea of programming by difference is based on the conviction that the *re*users of a software component are generally different from its users, and should accordingly be granted certain privileges: specifically in being provided a limited access to its implementation details. This access is not sufficient to allow destructive changes to be made to the original, but does allow the addition of further implementation detail, which may reference the original.

The mechanism supporting this kind of extensibility is that of the class inheritance hierarchy, which made a brief appearance in the last chapter. It is indicative of the extent that these ideas have become accepted that the 1995 revision of Ada has incorporated the mechanism into the language.

9.6 Summary

In this chapter we have discussed some of the concepts of software component reuse, and noted the significant place amongst these occupied by data abstraction. The fundamental problem of significance versus application independence has been described together with an exploration of genericity, as exemplified by the facilities provided by both Ada and C++. The developing awareness of the limitations of the encapsulated component model, and its correlative – programming by difference using the inheritance mechanism – have been introduced. The discussion of extensibility, and the introduction of the concept of polymorphism, are precursors of a more extended discussion of related matters in a later chapter.

9.7 Further reading

Software reuse has yet to become a popular topic outside the realm of research papers. The outstanding example is G. Booch, *Software components in Ada* (Menlo Park, California: Benjamin/Cummings, 1986), which is a worthy, although perhaps not totally compelling, attempt at a logically-derived taxonomy of reusable Ada components. The C++ standard template library is described in a report by A. Stepanov & M. Lee, *The Standard Template Library* (Palo Alto, California: Hewlett Packard Laboratories, 1995).

A polemical celebration of the potential of reusable software is given B. J. Cox in "There is a silver bullet" *Byte Magazine* (October 1990), 209–18, and the ubiquitous D. L. Parnas has contributed to "Enhancing reusability with information hiding" in *Software reusability: concepts and models*, T. J. Biggerstaff & A. J. Perlis (eds), 141–57 (Reading, Mass: Addison-Wesley 1989).

CHAPTER 10

Formal specification of ADTs

10.1 Introduction

One of the significant phases in the object-oriented design technique is *formalize the interfaces of the objects*. In practice this means defining the operations that are available for manipulating the data abstractions, or abstract data types (ADTs), within a syntactical structure such as a class declaration in C++ or an Ada package specification. Importantly, the "formalization" involved is purely a syntactical one: each operation is defined by its name and parameters, with their types and modes, but there is no corresponding formalization for the definition of the *semantics* of the operations – what they actually "mean", or "do".

In many cases there is a well understood conventional semantics – the stack and the queue, for example, have functionalities that are generally known and require little interpretation. But when less well known (and hackneyed) examples are considered the definition of their semantics cannot be left to the intuition of potential users. In the case study contained in Chapter 5, the `Pile` data abstraction exported the operation `next_tree_from_pile`, which was distinguished from a conventional read operation by the fact that it was "destructive": more like a "pop" operation. Nothing in the syntactic definition of the operation suggests this, and so the additional semantic information must be conveyed separately. One possibility would be simply to allow the user to inspect the code that implements the data abstraction. But this would run strongly counter to the whole idea of data abstraction and is not an acceptable technique. The most common approach is to supply the additional information in the form of comments within the interface specification, aided by the use of suggestive operation names.

10.1.1 The need for formal specification

In comparison with the syntactic specification of abstract data types, the semantic specification by the use of comments is, often highly, informal. As such, it frequently demonstrates all too clearly the propensity of natural language to encourage vagueness or ambiguity or both. This is not a trivial matter because, as has been remarked a number of times, the important feature of an abstract data type, from the point of view of those who are to use it, is its external interface. So the nature of this interface, in the sense of "what it does", must be clearly understood by its users, otherwise the whole exercise of designing the abstract data type, implementing it and making it available for use, is futile.

There is, therefore, a correspondingly strong motivation to ensure that the semantic specifications of abstract data types are clear and unambiguous. In this field, as in others, the surest way of achieving this objective is by the use of mathematical techniques, because of the intrinsic economy and precision of mathematical notation. It turns out that, in addition to their desirable properties in relation to program architecture and the design process, there is a close relationship between abstract data types and a particular kind of mathematical structure – *algebras* – which facilitates their treatment as mathematical entities. This chapter presents an introduction to the particular mathematical or *formal* specification technique that depends on this relationship, which is commonly known as *algebraic* specification.

10.2 A familiar example

Initially, we will approach this formal technique in a somewhat informal way, showing the construction of an algebraic specification of our old friend the stack.

The first part of such a specification consists of an abstract version of the kind of structure with which we have become reasonably familiar – the interface definition of an abstract data type, as realized by a definition module or package specification. Consider first an appropriate Ada package specification as shown in Figure 10.1. The only unusual feature of this specification lies in the exclusive use of functions to provide the operations associated with the abstract data type. The reasons for this will be explored later. For the moment the main points to notice are that the functional style requires a slight change to the "normal" stack interface, in that the **pop** operation does not remove the top element from the stack *and* return the value of the top element: it simply returns the truncated stack. The additional **top** operation is required to provide the value of the top element. It should be noted that this is not the only way in which the operations can be defined – this way is shown because it is the closest to the "normal" version.

Before considering the mathematical equivalent of this specification it will be useful to remind ourselves of the nature of the information that it conveys. The first point to make is that this information is really very

```
generic
     type element is private;
package stacks is

     type stack is private;

     function initialise return stack;

     function push (S : stack; E : element) return stack;

     function pop (S : stack) return stack;

     function top (S : stack) return element;

     function is_empty (S : stack) return boolean;

private

     type stack_struct;

     type stack is access stack_struct;

end stacks;
```

Figure 10.1   Ada generic specification for a stack ADT.

limited, as can perhaps be more easily seen if the conventional operation names are replaced by ones that are less suggestive of the stack (see Fig. 10.2).

It seems clear that a program fragment such as:

```
if not splurge(stk1)
          then e2 := tosh(stk1)
```

is considerably less meaningful than:

```
if not is_empty(stk1)
          then e2 := top(stk1)
```

but the relative clarity of the latter derives completely from the familiarity of the operation names – nothing is added to or taken from the intrinsic meaning of the specification, which is restricted to defining the names of the operations and the types of their arguments and results, by a systematic renaming of the kind shown in Figure 10.2. The implication of this is that the identifiers appearing in such a specification, both operation and type names, have a completely *symbolic* significance – they are "placeholders" showing only where the various types associated with the operations are the same or not. For example, the **slush** (**push**) and **slop** (**pop**)

```
generic
    type element is private;
package splodges is

    type splodge is private;

    function splodgise return splodge;

    function slush (S : splodge; E : element) return splodge;

    function slop (S : splodge) return splodge;

    function tosh (S : splodge) return element;

    function splurge (S : splodge) return boolean;

private

    type splodge_struct;

    type splodge is access splodge_struct;

end splodges;
```

Figure 10.2   The stack specification with systematic renaming.

operations both return values of the same type. (The one exception to the purely symbolic names in the specification is **boolean**, which has a well defined meaning deriving from outside this specification.)

The arrangement of the "place-holders" defines a pattern that many implementations might be devised to fit. For example, the operation named **top** or **tosh** in some versions might always return the value of type **element** that was the second argument of the first invocation of the **push** or **slush** operation. This would not be consistent with the behaviour of a stack, but an implementation that does provide a conventional stack behaviour is only one of many possibilities – further emphasizing the need for semantic, or behavioural, specification.

10.2.1 An algebraic specification of the stack

The corresponding algebraic structure possesses a similarly symbolic relationship with a number of possible mathematical "implementations", or *interpretations*, as they are more properly known. Unlike the Ada specification the operation names denote, or are "place-holders" for, actual mathematical functions, rather than subprograms that are in some sense "functional". The features of an algebraic specification that correspond to the symbolic types of an Ada specification are symbols for the sets of values from which the arguments and results of the functions are drawn. These symbolic set names are known as *Sorts*, and it is conventional to list the sorts involved in an algebraic specification at its head.

The sorts involved in the algebraic version of the stack obviously include *stack* and *element*, but also required is a mathematical model for **boolean**, as there is no equivalent of "pre-defined types" in an algebraic specification. For the purposes of the algebraic specification of a stack abstract data type this model requires nothing more than a set containing two distinguished values that can be thought of as representing *true* and *false*, and named as such. This set is denoted by the sort *bool*. The sorts of the specification, which are conventionally preceded by the heading *SORTS*, would appear as follows:

SORTS   *element stack bool*

The remaining differences between a package specification and the corresponding section of an algebraic specification are simple matters of notation. If we look at the package specification we can see that the essential information is the set of operation names and the types of the parameters of the functions, and their result types. Parameter names, although useful for documentary purposes, are not really required for the *specification* of the stack, and the reserved words **function** and **result** are just "syntactic sugar" that can be dispensed with, provided the operations are restricted to functions. All that is required is some kind of punctuation allowing for the distinguishing of operation names, argument sorts and result sort. A common convention separates the operation name from the argument sorts by a colon, and the argument sorts from the result sort by an arrow. The specification of the *push* operation, adopting this format, would look as follows:

push : *stack element* $\rightarrow$ *stack*

The collection of operation specifications are headed by *OPERATIONS*. The algebraic equivalent of the stack package specification is shown in Figure 10.3.

This kind of structure is called a *signature* and it might be thought of as a language-independent, "pared down" version of an interface definition, and we must always bear in mind its symbolic nature as defining a pattern with many possible interpretations. The signature shown in Figure 10.3, which involves several sorts, is classified as *many sorted*.

10.2.2 Semantic specification

So far the algebraic specification technique has provided nothing more than an economical notation for conveying the same kind of information –

$$SORTS \quad element \ stack \ bool$$

$$OPERATIONS$$

$$
\begin{aligned}
initialise \ &: \ \rightarrow stack \\
push \ &: \ stack \ element \rightarrow stack \\
pop \ &: \ stack \rightarrow stack \\
top \ &: \ stack \rightarrow element \\
is\_empty \ &: \ stack \rightarrow bool
\end{aligned}
$$

Figure 10.3 Algebraic signature for a stack ADT.

syntactical information – as a definition module or a package specification. As we have seen, this information is inadequate to distinguish between the many different interpretations that can match a particular signature, most of which do not provide the desired semantics. The next step, which reveals the power of algebraic specification in comparison with its programming language equivalents, is to extend the technique so as to be able to specify the semantics of abstract data types in a formal way. The additional features that the algebraic technique requires to support semantic specification are perhaps surprisingly simple, they are:

- functional composition;
- equations.

Functional composition

We have seen previously that the use of algebraic specification requires the operations associated with an abstract data type to be defined as functions. A function is a mathematical object that resembles quite closely its namesake in programming languages. A function defines a mapping from a number of argument values ("input values") to a single ("output") value, with the constraint that each unique combination of argument values maps to only one result. The set(s) of values from which the argument(s) of a function are drawn are known as the *domain* set(s) of the function; the set of values from which its result is drawn is known as its *range* set.

The *application* of a function is the operation of mapping its argument value(s) to a result. The conventional notation for function application shows the argument value(s) in parentheses prefixed by the name of the function, the whole expression denoting the result value. So if we have a function *square* that maps integer values to their squares, the function application of *square* to the integer value 4 is written as *square*(4), an expression that denotes the value 16. Instead of using an integer value we may use a variable, say *i*, and show an application as *square*(*i*). To take this process a step further, the value to which a function may be applied may itself be obtained as the result of another function application, provided it is the correct type of value. For example: *square*(*square*(4)) denotes the application of *square* to 4, producing the result 16, and then the application of *square* to 16, producing the final result 256. There is, of course, no restriction on the nature of functions combined in this way, other than that noted above requiring the range set of the preceding application to be the same as (or a subset of) the domain of the successor. Nor is there any restriction on the number of functions involved.

This technique is called *functional composition* and it is utilized in algebraic specifications in expressing *axioms*. It is this usage of functional composition that necessitates the restriction of the operations included in an algebraic specification to functions. Procedures, the other kind of operation often used in implementations of abstract data types, do not possess a close mathematical analogue, unlike functions.

10.2.3 Axioms

The idea of an axiom is that, within obvious requirements of internal consistency, it is an unquestionable and unprovable assertion that is simply accepted. The axioms of an algebraic specification provide the means of specifying the meanings, or semantics, of the abstract data type it defines. They may be seen as constraints on the operations defined syntactically by the signature. If we consider the stack example, there are several characteristics that are inseparable from the idea of *stackness*, as follows:

- If a top operation immediately follows a push operation, then the value returned by the top operation is the value of the element pushed onto the stack.
- If a pop operation immediately follows a push operation, then the stack returned by the pop operation is identical to the stack that was an argument to the push operation.

These characteristics cannot be *proved* to be uniquely associated with stacks: they simply *are* part of what the word means.

If we utilize some variables, s and e, to stand respectively for "any stack" and "any element", we can express the first of these characteristics as follows:

$top(push(s, e)) = e$

Functional composition is used to express mathematically the idea contained in the phrase "immediately follows", and the equality relation, symbolized by "=", is used to express the equivalence of the left- and right-hand sides. The equation captures formally the idea contained in an informal statement like: "The top value obtained from a stack formed by pushing an arbitrary element e onto an arbitrary stack s is e."

Similarly:

$pop(push\ (s, e)) = s$

"The value of the stack returned by a pop operation on a stack formed by pushing an arbitrary element *e* onto an arbitrary stack *s* is *s*."

In each case the form of the expression that defines the stack characteristic is an *equation*: it consists of a *left-hand side*, a *right-hand side* and an equals sign separating the two. The expressions are known accordingly as *equational axioms* in the context of algebraic specifications.

The relationships between the other operations provided by the stack may also be expressed equationally: the *is_empty* operation will obviously return the value *true* immediately after the *initialize* operation, which returns an empty stack; it will return *false* immediately after any *push* operation. These two characteristics can be expressed as follows:

   is_empty(initialize) = true
   is_empty(push (s, e)) = false

Errors
The mention of the possibility of an empty stack brings with it the corresponding possibility of applying various operations to an empty stack. Clearly there is no problem with *push*. *Pop* is more problematic – what is the effect of popping an empty stack? The usual answer is to return an empty stack, although this sounds rather like damage limitation: leaving the rather uneasy thought that it *shouldn't* have happened. But there can be no doubt that the *top* operation on an empty stack is an error – there is simply no top value to return. The immediately obvious "solution" to this problem is to invent a special value, called *error*, that is returned by the *pop* operation on an empty stack. This will necessitate a change to the range set of the *top* operation, which must be constructed from *element* and the value *error* using set union: *element* ∪ {*error*}. We can then add an axiom to this effect:

   top(initialize) = error

and it is certainly the case that a number of writers on algebraic specification, Guttag (1977) for instance, have been quite happy with this. But, as pointed out by Goguen (1978) and others, this appears to lead to some fairly uncomfortable results. For example, what are we to make of the following:

   push(s, (top(initialize)))

The value denoted by the overall expression is from sort *stack* – the result sort of the *push* operation – but the top value of the stack presumably has the value *error*, because this is the value returned by the *top* operation forming the second operand, of sort *element* ∪ {*error*}. We may imagine further *push* operations being carried out on the stack, with non-erroneous arguments, and then we would be left with a stack with a hidden *error* somewhere in its depths – obviously not an acceptable arrangement.

A more natural approach would be to regard any stack with *error* pushed into it as totally erroneous, perhaps as signified by a special error value of sort stack. In turn, we must then consider what the effect of *is_empty* on an *error_stack* would be – obviously neither true nor false is appropriate and so an additional error value must be included in *bool*, and so on. The result is a considerable proliferation both of error values, whose symbolic status is rather unclear, and of error axioms. The appealing elegance of the algebraic technique is rapidly obscured.

A number of techniques have been suggested to confront the problem of error handling in algebraic specifications. A common approach is to permit the specification of some of the operations as denoting *partial* functions – that is, functions defined over only a subset of their domain values. In the context of the stack this would allow the *top* and *pop* operations to be defined only for stacks that are not empty, the corresponding undefinedness of these operations on empty stacks implicitly defining erroneous applications.

Goguen introduces the idea of *subsorts* to support this approach, being symbolic subset names. In the case of the stack a subsort *ne_stack* might be declared to symbolize the subset of *stacks* whose members are non-empty, permitting the appropriate specification of the *top* and *pop* operations, as shown in the complete specification in Figure 10.4. As can be seen, the subsort is declared under a separate heading and is shown in relation to its "super-sort": in this case *stack*. This approach has the advantage of avoiding the somewhat dubious association of error values with sorts, which are purely symbolic entities after all.

10.3 An alternative semantics

We can illustrate the power of the use of equational axioms to specify semantics by providing an alternative set for the same signature that was used in the *stack* specification, so as to define a first in first out list, or queue, rather than a last in first out list, or stack.

Informally, the axioms that capture the essential qualities of the queue are as follows:

- The insertion, or pushing, of an element into a queue affects the front, or top, of the queue only if it was empty to start with.
- The composition of a queue following a push and a pop operation is unaffected by the order in which the operations are applied, except when the queue is initially empty.

Clearly, this affects both the queue equivalents of the **pop** and **top** operations, perhaps more conventionally called **De_queue** and **Front**. In both cases, the expression of an equivalence requires the evaluation of a condition – specifically that the queue in question is empty, and in order to

$$STACK$$

$$SORTS$$

element stack bool

$$SUBSORTS$$

ne_stack < stack

$$OPERATIONS$$

initialize	:	→ stack
push	:	stack element → ne_stack
pop	:	ne_stack → stack
top	:	ne_stack → element
is_empty	:	stack → bool

$$VARIABLES$$

s : stack e : element

$$EQUATIONS$$

top(push(s, e))	=	e
pop(push(s, e))	=	s
is_empty(initialize)	=	true
is_empty(push(s, e))	=	false

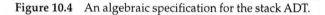

Figure 10.4 An algebraic specification for the stack ADT.

capture this in a notationally convenient manner the language of algebraic specifications is conventionally extended to include *conditional expressions*, usually adopting the *if .. then .. else* format.

Within the context of algebraic specifications, the *if .. then .. else* construct defines a family of functions with three arguments, the sort of the first of which is *bool*, that of the second and third determined by the application. The semantics of the construct can be concisely expressed using equations:

if true then a else b = a
if false then a else b = b

Armed with this additional expressivity we may now define the characteristic semantics of the queue:

top(push(e, q)) = if is_empty(q)
            then e
            else top(q)

and:

168

$$QUEUE$$
$$SORTS \qquad element\ queue\ bool$$
$$SUBSORTS \qquad ne\_queue < queue$$
$$OPERATIONS$$

$$
\begin{aligned}
initialize \quad &: \quad \rightarrow queue \\
push \quad &: \quad queue\ element \rightarrow ne\_queue \\
pop \quad &: \quad ne\_queue \rightarrow queue \\
top \quad &: \quad ne\_queue \rightarrow element \\
is\_empty \quad &: \quad queue \rightarrow bool
\end{aligned}
$$

$$VARIABLES \qquad s : queue\ e : element$$
$$EQUATIONS$$

$$
\begin{aligned}
is\_empty(push(e, s)) \ &= \ false \\
is\_empty(initialize) \ &= \ true \\
top(push(e, q)) \ &= \ if\ is\_empty(q) \\
&\qquad then\ e \\
&\qquad else\ top(q) \\
pop(push(e, q)) \ &= \ if\ is\_empty(q) \\
&\qquad then\ initialize \\
&\qquad else\ push(e, pop(q))
\end{aligned}
$$

Figure 10.5 Algebraic specification of a queue ADT.

$$
\begin{aligned}
pop(push(e, q)) = \ &if\ is\_empty(q) \\
&then\ initialize \\
&else\ push(e, pop(q))
\end{aligned}
$$

These may be incorporated into the complete specification with, as promised, the same signature as the specification for *stack*, but with the sort changed to *queue* for the sake of avoiding confusion, as shown in Figure 10.5.

The reader may be experiencing some feelings of doubt at this point – these equations seem somewhat slight to express everything that is characteristic of queues. What about, for example, the requirement that, given a queue containing two elements, the one that was inserted first should be revealed first by the **top** operation? This does not seem immediately obvious from the equations we have defined and obviously, if the specification does not support this interpretation, it will call into question the usefulness of the technique. The question arises as to whether it is possible to "test" a specification to see whether appropriate implications can be drawn from it. In this case we wish to assure ourselves that, given two element values, distinguished say as *e1* and *e2*, then the sequence of operations represented by:

   top(push(e2, push(e1, initialize)))

whereby *e1* is pushed into the queue before *e2*, will produce the result *e1*.

10.3.1 Term rewriting

Fortunately such a technique does exist, in the form of *term rewriting*. Each equation is interpreted as a *rewrite rule*, which specifies how its left-hand side may be rewritten as its right-hand side. If we examine the expression above we see that it has the form of the following axiom:

   top(push(e, q)) = if is_empty(q)
        then e
        else top(q)

with *q* replaced by *push(e1, initialize)*. The appropriate axiom tells us that

   is_empty(push(e1, initialize)) = false

and so the expression may be replaced by, or rewritten as, the *else* alternative value:

   top(push(e1, initialize))

This reduced expression also has the form of the same axiom, but now the queue to which the *push* is applied *is* empty and so the *then* alternative is used, giving the expression *e1*, and so the "correctness" of the specification is confirmed.

A more complex test is shown below, involving a *pop* operation in addition to the two *push*es. In each stage of the proof the sub-expression that is to be rewritten is shown underlined. The identification of the appropriate axiom, or rewrite rule, is left as an exercise for the reader.

To show that:

   top(pop(push(e2, push(e1, initialize)))) = e2

   top(pop(push(e2, push(e1, initialize))))
 = *top(push(e2, pop(push(e1, initialize))))*
 = *top(push(e2, initialize))*
 = *e2*

10.4 Implementation bias

The significant point about this type of specification is that the semantics of the operations are always shown by the interaction of two or more of them: they are never defined in isolation. Moreover, the semantics are defined without the use of any other set of entities, but purely in terms of the set of operations associated with the abstract data type. In this the algebraic specification technique differs from the two other well established techniques: *operational semantics* and *denotational semantics*. In operational semantics the meanings of operations are defined in terms of their effect on an idealized machine. In denotational semantics, they are defined in terms of their effects on mathematical entities such as sets, which are considered to be the denotations of program data structures.

In both cases, operations are defined in terms of "something else" – something intrinsically better defined and understood than any particular program structure, which thereby obtains "well definedness" by association with this underlying reality.

In the context of abstract data types there is an obvious parallel between the underlying data structure that provides the basis of the "real", or implementation, view, and the underlying machine or mathematical structure that provides the "real" semantics of the applicable operations. But, of course, the encapsulation characteristic of the abstract data type is intended to *hide* the "reality" of the implementation, and there is therefore something unsatisfactory about formally specifying an abstract data type by defining its semantics in terms of some underlying implementation, no matter how abstract.

By contrast, algebraic specifications do not define semantics by recourse to some better defined, different domain, but each is defined in terms *of itself* – a feature that often tends to inspire vague feelings of disquiet in newcomers to the technique, but which provides precisely that analogy with information hiding that the other two techniques mentioned cannot provide.

In fact there *is* an underlying object associated with an algebraic specification, which is the *initial algebra* of the specification. A brief introduction to the concept of initial algebras is given below, but we may summarize their significance by noting that such an algebra contains nothing more than what the corresponding specification requires. There is no sense in which it might be thought to be better-defined or "more real" than the associated specification – it is simply different in a way analogous to the way that, say, an implementation module is different from its associated definition module. The initial algebra for a specification might be thought of, therefore, as capturing its essence in a way that, to employ a well known slogan, introduces "no junk and no confusion".

In this algebraic specification contrasts with denotational and operational semantics, both of which provide a general set of operations: the "instructions" of the ideal machine on the one hand, the standard set-theoretic operations on the other. There is therefore the risk, in using either of these techniques, of incorporating influences deriving from operations that are not intimately concerned with the specification in question – a tendency known as *implementation bias*. Implementation bias may be thought of as the analogue of an imperfectly encapsulated abstract data type, in which the nature of the underlying data structure is allowed to determine its use in addition to the defined operational interface.

10.5 Algebras and specifications

The non-mathematical reader, and indeed the mathematical reader with a conventional mathematical background, may find the plural "algebras" in the introduction to this chapter, and the last sub-heading puzzling. Surely there is just *algebra*, a branch of mathematics in which letters are used to stand for quantities? This is certainly the view of algebra imparted by school mathematics courses, but the term has a more specialized meaning in the context of a comparatively recently developed branch of mathematics, derived from set theory.

As might be anticipated from this derivation, the central concept involved in algebras is that of the *set* – the essentially simple idea of a collection of unique individuals with some kind of common characteristic, which may be simply membership of the same set. The set is a peculiarly appropriate mathematical object for modeling the world, viewed as being inhabited, in the widest possible sense, by many unique individual objects, even if this uniqueness is a matter only of position in space and time.

As a result of the simplicity of the concept, there are an infinite number of sets that can be defined. A few crop up very frequently, however, particularly in the context of formal specification, including the set of all integer (whole) numbers, often called I or Z, the set containing all the positive integers and 0, called N or *Nat*, and the set containing the two truth values *true* and *false*, called *Bool*.

An important result that follows from the common characteristics of all the members of a particular set is the fact that *operations*, in the form of functions, may be defined that can act on any, or all of them. (The mathematical phrase is that such operations are defined *over* the set in question.)

With the rather small number of concepts that we have introduced so far, we have enough to define what an algebra is – it is a mathematical structure that allows one or more sets, known as the *carrier*, to be associated with a collection of operations defined over them, together with a number of members of the set(s) called *distinguished values*. An example of an algebra comprises:

- N the set of natural numbers (the positive integers plus 0);
- the successor operation, which maps every natural number to its successor in the ordered sequence;
- the value 0.

The algebra might be represented as a list:

$< N, +1, 0 >$

An algebraic specification is a symbolic structure containing symbols representing the salient features of a family of algebras – symbols for sets and operations, and for terms constructed from the operation symbols. Distinguished values, or constants, are represented by symbolic operations with zero arity (i.e. no argument types). The symbolic sets of a specification, known as sorts, are employed in the signature part of the specification, to characterize the domains and ranges of the symbolic operations. The signature defines a pattern that must be respected by any algebra that *satisfies* or *is a model of* the specification; such an algebra must possess a set for each sort of the signature, an operation for each operation symbol, with domain and range sets matching the pattern defined by the signature. The algebra described above is clearly a model for the following signature:

SORTS Nat_0
 OPS
 $succ$: $Nat_0 \rightarrow Nat_0$
 $zero$: $\rightarrow Nat_0$

with an *interpretation* that assigns denotations to each of the symbols, as follows:

$Nat_0 \rightarrow N$, *the set of positive integers* + 0
$succ \rightarrow$ *the successor function for integers* "+1"
$zero \rightarrow$ *integer zero*

Clearly, the constraints imposed by this signature are very general, and many alternative models may be found for it.

The members of the carrier, with the exception of 0, may be denoted by terms consisting of compositions of the $succ$ function applied to $zero$. For example, under the above interpretation the integer value 3 is denoted by $succ(succ(succ(zero)))$. Although not a practical notation it can be seen that every member of N can be denoted in this way, and that every member is denoted by a unique term. This latter property is lost if we introduce another operation like *plus*, a binary addition function. The signature might then become:

SORTS Nat_0
 OPS
 $succ$: $Nat_0 \rightarrow Nat_0$
 $plus$: $Nat_0\, Nat_0 \rightarrow Nat_0$
 $zero$: $\rightarrow Nat_0$

The algebra extended by this additional operation permits the terms 0 and $plus(0, 0)$, amongst others, to denote the same member of the carrier. To give a slightly more significant example, using m and n to stand for arbitrary values of the carrier, the following terms:

$plus(m, succ(n))$
$succ(plus(n, m))$

also denote the same member of the carrier. These equivalences define the behaviour, or semantics, of these operations and may be incorporated as *equations* into the specification to provide constraints on any (other) algebras that satisfy it. The addition of the equations section extends the format of the specification to its characteristic two-component structure as shown below:

$$
\begin{aligned}
SORTS \quad & Nat_0 \\
OPS \quad & \\
succ : \quad & Nat_0 \rightarrow Nat_0 \\
zero : \quad & \rightarrow Nat_0 \\
plus : \quad & Nat_0\, Nat_0 \rightarrow Nat_0 \\
VARIABLES \quad & m, n : Nat_0 \\
EQUATIONS \quad & \\
plus(n, 0) = \; & n \\
plus(n, succ(m)) = \; & succ(plus(n, m))
\end{aligned}
$$

Models

Algebraic specifications like the ones shown above might be thought of as *schemas*, or templates, for families of algebras, each member of the family satisfying the specification. This idea is sometimes a little hard to grasp because the characteristic examples used to motivate the concepts, such as the Nat_0 examples above, are so obviously identified with the conventional system of natural number arithmetic – in other words, the *interpretation* defined above, with *plus* modeled by the ordinary integer addition operator conventionally written as "+". This is so natural as to be hardly worth writing down, but the important point is that it *is* only one interpretation and that there are others that are equally valid, although less natural. One valid alternative model is one in which *succ* is +2 in conventional notation, and the sort Nat_0 denotes the set of all positive *even* integers.

Initiality

The fact that an algebraic specification may be modeled by a whole family of algebras gives rise to a number of questions: what is the resemblance between the members of such a family; is there one member that in some way captures the essential qualities of the whole family?

Structural similarity between algebras exists when a so-called *structure-preserving* mapping can be shown to exist between them. Such a mapping is defined as follows. Given two algebras that model a specification, a mapping between them, from the *source* to the *target*, is actually a collection of functions from the source carrier to the target carrier that contains what might be termed a *conversion function* for each sort in the specification. This function converts the set denoted by the sort in the source algebra to the corresponding set denoted by the sort in the target algebra.

The idea implied by the phrase "structure-preserving" is that each pair of source/target functions denoted by an operation of the specification can be made interchangeable by the application of the appropriate conversions. In other words, the members of the carrier sets of the target algebra can be generated either by converting the result values of the source algebra functions, or by applying the target algebra functions to converted values from the source carrier. Such a structure-preserving mapping is called a *homomorphism*.

The formal expression of this idea is rather complicated in its full generality, but the principle can be illustrated reasonably straightforwardly with reference to a single-sorted specification, where only one conversion, or mapping, function is involved. Given two algebras S and T (source and target) that are models for such a specification, with carriers S_c and T_c, a homomorphism from S to T will comprise a function, say f, with domain S_c and range T_c such that, for each operation σ of the specification, with arguments $a_1 .. a_n$:

$$f(\sigma_s(a_1 .. a_n)) = \sigma_t(f(a_1), .., f(a_n))$$

where σ_s and σ_t are the denotations of σ in respectively S and T.

Homomorphisms come in various classifications that determine a measure of the similarity between the algebras in question. The highest degree of similarity that may be determined is where an *isomorphism* exists, which means that every value in the target carrier is mapped to, and that there is a one-to-one relationship between the members of the two carriers. This means the relationship is a symmetrical one, i.e. inverted functions will map the two carriers the other way. Isomorphism may be seen as defining equivalence to a level that "fails" only in being unable to discriminate between algebras with sets that differ only in their names.

The family resemblance between the algebras that model a particular specification involves a number of special members of the family, known as the *initial algebras* for the specification. The special feature of an initial algebra is that a *unique homomorphism* exists between it and *each* member of the family. It is also the case that all the initial algebras for a specification are isomorphic to each other, and so are "identical" within the slightly blurred perspective mentioned above. This means that "the" initial algebra provides the answer to the first of the questions posed above, in that the notion of family resemblance can be defined in terms of derivability, by a family of mappings, from "the" initial algebra.

Initiality, then, is a property of models, not specifications, and specifically of the "best" models for a particular specification, in the sense of capturing its essential qualities: providing the answer to the second question. This quality may be illustrated by considering again the specification:

$$
\begin{aligned}
SORTS \quad & Nat_0 \\
OPS \quad & \\
succ : \quad & Nat_0 \rightarrow Nat_0 \\
zero : \quad & \rightarrow Nat_0 \\
plus : \quad & Nat_0 \, Nat_0 \rightarrow Nat_0 \\
VARIABLES \quad & m, n : Nat_0 \\
EQUATIONS \quad & \\
plus(n, 0) = \quad & n \\
plus(n, succ(m)) = \quad & succ(plus(n, m))
\end{aligned}
$$

Consider an interpretation of the signature of this specification that assigns the set of integers Z to Nat_0, whilst retaining all the other "standard" assignments. This model would certainly satisfy the equations of the specification, but it suffers from the fact that one half of the members of the carrier, the values from -1 to minus infinity, cannot be denoted by terms that can be constructed from the operations: the anchoring of the specification to "zero", and the additive nature of the operations of the model make this so. The term "junk" has been adopted to refer to undenotable members of carriers, and obviously a model containing junk can hardly be said to be capturing the essence of the specification of which it is an interpretation.

Another possible deficiency of models is *confusion*. If we take the standard interpretation of the specification above and change the assignment of the *succ* operation to "+0" the resulting model satisfies the equations quite satisfactorily. But it also has the unfortunate property of making the denotations of quite dissimilar terms such as $succ(succ(succ(0)))$ and 0 indistinguishable, even though there is nothing in the specification to suggest they are equal. Like junk, the presence of confusion in a model disqualifies it from being considered a faithful interpretation of its associated specification.

It is the fact that initial models contain, in Burstall's phrase, "no junk and no confusion" and thus capture the essential qualities of their specifications, that makes *initiality*, or the properties of initial algebras, so significant to algebraic specification.

It should also be noted that an alternative approach to algebraic specification exists, notably as popularized by Guttag, which deals with the so-called *final* or *loose* semantics, defined by considering the whole class or family of algebras defined by a specification. This is not the place to discuss the pros and cons of these two approaches.

Canonical term algebras

While the foregoing discussion may have exposed the particular, and relevant, properties of initial algebras, the question as to how a useful initial algebra for a particular specification is derived has not been explored. A basis for this derivation is the *word algebra* of the specification. The word algebra is an algebra in which the operations denote character string generating functions – "production rules". For example the *succ* operation is interpreted as a function that takes a character string argument and returns a longer character string obtained by prefixing the argument with "*succ(*" and suffixing it with "*)*". The argument must, of course, be "of the right type", which means that it must be a character string generated by a function denoted by an operation with the correct range sort, i.e. *succ, plus* or, ultimately, *zero*. As usual, it is more correct to talk of the word algebras of a specification, because systematic changes may be introduced – changing case for example – which produce different but isomorphically equivalent algebras.

The terms of a word algebra will frequently be equivalent to other terms, where "equivalent to" is defined by the equations of the algebraic specification. For example, given a typical specification for *stack*, the denotation of the term:

$pop(push(e1, pop(push(e2, initialize))))$

is equivalent to that of *initialize*. The set of all terms equivalent to the term *initialize*, for example, forms an *equivalence class*. If we imagine an algebra formed from the word algebra by factoring out all the equivalent terms, then this algebra is initial. That is, an algebra of equivalence classes of the word algebra – known as *quotient algebra*.

The process of generating all the terms of the word algebra and then factoring out all its equivalence classes, whilst being conceptually comprehensible, does not appear to provide a practical method. For this we must turn to the idea of *canonical terms*, each of which is a member of a different equivalence class. It is not difficult to see that an algebra of canonical terms will be isomorphic to the quotient algebra and is therefore initial. The importance of canonical terms lies in the fact that their canonical property can often be shown, straightforwardly, to derive from their systematic generation using a subset of the operations. For example, each canonical term of the Nat_0 specification has the form:

$succ^n(zero)$

where

$$succ^1(zero) \quad = \quad succ(zero)$$
$$succ^2(zero) \quad = \quad succ(succ(zero))$$
$$\text{etc.}$$

An algebra of terms generated in this way is an initial model for the specification.

10.6 Algebraic specification and implementation

Algebraic specification, with its high level of abstraction, appears to possess clear advantages for the specification of abstract data types. The question is frequently raised as to whether the technique is *too* abstract, particularly when used in conjunction with a conventional imperative language for the corresponding implementation. An obvious problem is the restriction of the operations of the abstract data type to functions.

There are a number of responses to this type of criticism. The first concerns the nature of specification. It is important to bear in mind the objective underlying the use of semi-formal and formal specification techniques: this is to clarify its syntax and semantics to both the implementor and the user of an abstract data type, with the main requirement being firmly concerned with the semantics. As we have seen, the alternative is to use informal techniques, normally involving a natural language, with the consequent risk of imprecision this invariably brings.

Because a formal language in some ways resembles a programming language, a specification written in a formal language is often mistakenly a basis for, or high-level version of, the implementation. Algebraic specification, with its avoidance of implementation bias, is particularly uncommitted in this respect, and the lack of resemblance of specifications written using this style to implementations written in, say, C or FORTRAN, is neither surprising nor undesirable. The immediate purpose of producing such a specification is to communicate concepts to its human readers.

It is also the case, however, that some imperative languages, including the two that have received considerable exposure in this text, may be used to write program units bearing a considerable resemblance to algebraic specifications, particularly if a "functional style" is adhered to. Earlier in this chapter we moved from an Ada package specification to a related algebraic specification. The reverse process, a much more significant one in practical terms, is also possible (Priestley 1989).

Specifications are also fundamentally important to the process of proving the correctness of an implementation – for, of course, a correct implementation is one that meets, or *satisfies*, the specification from which it was derived. The precision of algebraic specifications, and their exclusive concentration on the externally visible behaviour of the abstract data types to which they relate, provide strong support for informal and semi-formal verification of correctness of implementation – either by testing or by appeal to the details of the implementation code. Naturally, this support is reinforced by the use of a language, such as Ada or Modula-2, that permits the writing of implementations that are closely related to algebraic specifications, at least in respect of their signatures.

A problem *does* arise, however, when the correctness of an implementation is to be demonstrated completely formally. As described in the last section, such a demonstration must prove that the implementation is an initial model for the specification and, as such, must depend on the characterization of the implementation as an algebra.

The problem, referred to above, is concerned with the availabilities of these *implementation algebras*, to use Goguen's term. In general, algebraic specifications of standard programming languages or machine architectures are not available "off the shelf", and their production would be a large scale undertaking, far overshadowing the effort involved in the specification and implementation of even a complex abstract data type.

These last remarks perhaps present on overly pessimistic view, based on what is really a rather extreme view of formal correctness proof. It is certainly the case that other approaches rarely, if ever, attempt to carry their proofs right down to the level of the hardware or, indeed, rely on a *detailed* formal specification of the implementation language. It is the case, however, that formal specifications of some languages, notably including Modula-2, are in existence, although, regrettably from the point of view of this discussion, not in the algebraic form. This is an area that is providing a fruitful field of research, in which many eminent workers are currently to be found.

10.7 Summary

In this chapter we have discussed the importance of formal specification in the context of data abstraction and explored in some detail one particular approach: algebraic specification. The algebraic specifications of abstract data types appearing in earlier chapters have been presented.

Algebraic specifications have been shown to provide a peculiarly appropriate technique for the specification of abstract data types, particularly in view of their ability to reflect the separation of specification from implementation detail that is characteristic of data abstraction. The theoretical basis for proving the correctness of implementations has been briefly introduced, together with an indication of the difficulties that may arise when a completely formal approach is attempted.

10.8 Further reading

The great popularizer of algebraic specification is J. V. Guttag, in numerous papers, for example "Abstract data types and the development of data structures", *Communications of the ACM* **20**(6), 396–404, 1977. A more rigorous, and perhaps better written, collection of papers is provided by J. A. Goguen, of which the seminal J. A. Goguen, J. W. Thatcher, E. G. Wagner, "An initial algebra approach to the specification, correctness and implementation of abstract data types", *Current trends in programming methodology*, R. T. Yeh (ed.), 80–149 (Englewood Cliffs, New Jersey: Prentice-Hall, 1978), is well worth reading.

A number of later publications provide more accessible treatments of the subject, for example I. van Horebeek & J. Lewi, *Algebraic specifications in software engineering* (Berlin, Heidelburg: Springer-Verlag, 1989).

A paper describing the generation of Ada packages from algebraic specifications is given in M. Priestley, "Structured specifications with annotated packages", *Ada User* **10**(supplement), 64–9, 1989.

PART III

Object-oriented programming

CHAPTER 11

The object-oriented paradigm

11.1 Introduction

In previous chapters we have examined the contribution that data abstraction may make to the general area of good modular design and its logical extension – reusable software. We have also seen that the support of data abstraction is a feature of a number of programming languages, with the notable examples of Ada and C++ having been particularly emphasized in this discussion.

The term "object-based" has come into currency to denote languages that provide this kind of comprehensive support for data abstraction. In this and the next three chapters we will discuss a family of languages that not only support data abstraction, but also a number of more-or-less closely related features, which together have become known as the *object-oriented paradigm* – the languages that support (some or all of) these features being called object-oriented programming languages (OOPls).

The features, in addition to support for data abstraction, that comprise the paradigm are conventionally identified as the following:

- object classes;
- the message-passing metaphor;
- inheritance;
- polymorphism;
- late binding.

However, a number of languages exist that are accepted as object-oriented yet omit support for at least one of the above. The remainder of this chapter is devoted to a discussion of these features of the paradigm, largely in a non-language-specific way.

11.2 Objects and classes

The deployment of the concepts of data abstraction and abstract data types in most OOPls involves a terminology based on "object" and "class". The

182

entities that are processed or manipulated by a program written in an object-oriented language are invariably referred to as *objects*. Perhaps surprisingly, there is little unanimity on an exact definition of the term *object*, although "behaviour-exhibiting entity with internal state" might perhaps gain reluctant acquiescence from a significant proportion of the object-oriented community. The idea of behaviour, as a pattern of stimulus (from the environment to the object) and response (from the object to the environment), together with that of behaviour modification as the result of history, recorded by some form of internal state, has been explored in Chapter 8. In that discussion it was concluded that the data abstraction provides a very powerful and generally-applicable program entity for modeling real-world, or application, objects. It is perhaps not surprising, therefore, to find, in the terminology that has been adopted in this book, that objects are data abstractions: they are encapsulated data structures whose interaction with the external world is entirely restricted to operations.

The underlying motivation informing this exclusive dependence on objects as the artefacts manipulated by OOPls appears to have been derived largely from a recognition of the naturalness of object-oriented design, and particularly from the benefits of structuring an application program in terms of the objects of the application problem domain – a topic also discussed in Chapter 8.

In most applications there is a requirement for the replication of objects – multiple cars, employees, aircraft seats, etc. Each of these provides the same kind of behaviour, realized as a set of operations, that its replicas provide, but with different responses to external stimuli resulting from its individual history. In the terminology of earlier chapters, this requirement is achieved, in each case, by the use of an abstract data type – a type whose instances are data abstractions, each exhibiting behaviour as a set of operations defined by the type.

Programs written in object-oriented languages are generally concerned with implementing abstract data types – the only reason for the writing of "code" in one of these languages is as part of the implementation of an abstract data type. The conventional terminology used in the context of the object-oriented paradigm uses *class* to mean an implementation of an abstract data type.

11.2.1 Instantiation

The relationship between objects and classes is generally expressed in terms of *instantiation* – an object is an *instance* of a class and thus its attributes and operations, often called *methods* in the OOPl context, are determined by its class. The conceptual difference between classes and objects is basically a very clear one: a class is an essentially *static* entity, a textual structure that may be thought of as a body of code that provides the implementation underlying the behaviour of its instances. An object is a *dynamic* entity created at run-time that can interact with other objects, in ways determined by its class. (There is a suggestive analogy with the distinction between "program" and "process", to which we shall return.)

As we shall see in the next chapter, the clarity of this distinction becomes slightly obscured in some specific examples of OOPls, although its essential validity remains unchanged.

11.2.2 Classes and types

The distinction between objects and classes is superficially similar to the distinction between variables and types in a conventional language. The similarity is described as "superficial" because there is a subtle, but significant, distinction between classes and types.

The flavour of this distinction can be gained from the fact that it is possible for two objects that are instances of different classes to be of the same type. This is because "type", in the sense of abstract data type, denotes behaviour, defined over an operational interface. As we have seen in the last chapter, the semantics of such a type may be defined independently of the underlying implementation, which is conceptually one of many possible models of the semantic specification. Thus, it would be quite possible to provide two distinct classes, each supporting an interface with the semantics of the stack, to give an original example, using different implementations. Instances of these classes would possess identical behaviour and so their types would be the same.

In practice, the relationship between class and type is generally one-to-one. The distinction between the two concepts is a significant one, however, particularly in the context of inheritance, which will be discussed shortly.

11.3 The message-passing metaphor

The underlying computational model of the object-oriented paradigm is that of a collection of independent objects, interacting in a well defined, and "arms-length" kind of way. The so-called *message-passing computational metaphor*, is a logical corollary of this model, viewing all computation, at a certain level of abstraction, as consisting solely of the passing of messages between objects. Any interaction of two objects, according to the metaphor, conforms to the pattern: the *sender* object sends a message to the *receiver* object, which returns a *response* to the sender.

As its name indicates, this model of computation is metaphorical – objects in object-oriented environments are not generally the kind of entities that are capable of "sending messages", a terminology normally implying some form of distributed processing involving communication channels. Typically, the objects of a program are implemented as structures residing within a common memory, while message-passing is realized as procedure calls. These implementation details are obscured, however, in those languages that support it, by the message-passing metaphor, which is intended to emphasize the independence of:

- *objects* – as separate exhibitors of behaviour, responding to stimuli from other, similarly independent objects;
- *messages* – as possessing an existence separate from the objects to which they are sent, and thus providing the basis for *inclusion polymorphism*, a topic that will shortly be explored.

The immediately discernible effect of the metaphor is a notational one. The typical format of the messages comprising the "statements" of a program that conforms to the metaphor is:

```
receiver selector argument(s)
```

The semantics of this format are that *receiver* is the name of the object to which the message is sent. *Selector* defines the kind of message, i.e. it specifies the service the sender wishes the receiver to perform, while the arguments, if present, may be regarded as the input data for the operation concerned. The values of arguments may, of course, be objects.

The flavour of the use of this format can be brought out by considering a reasonably close Ada equivalent. In Ada terms an object is a variable of a private type. If we imagine an Ada package as follows:

```
Package A_Class is
--
        type Object is private;
--
        procedure reset(obj : in out object;
         size : integer);
        -- reset object parameter with specified size
--
--      rest of package
--
```

Then the following fragment might be found in another unit:

```
this_Obj : A_Class.Object:
begin
        A_Class.reset(this_Obj, 100);
--
```

By contrast, a typical "message-passing" equivalent would be:

```
this_obj.reset(100)
```

The supporters of OOPls claim, with some justification, that this is a more natural representation; it is, of course, the format of a corresponding C++ statement.

11.3.1 The implied parameter – `self`

In the Ada example above the object, `this_obj`, that is to be "operated on" by `reset` is a conventional formal parameter, which can appear therefore in the code of the `reset` "method". When the message-passing format is used, the name of the "receiver object" is unknown within the method; it is an *implied parameter* to the operation, so how is it possible to refer to it there? The answer is that languages supporting the message-passing format provide a means, usually in the form of a standard variable, denoting the receiver, or "current" object. Examples of these are `self` in Smalltalk, `Current` in Eiffel and `this`, (actually a pointer to the current object) in C++.

The significant difference is the primacy of the receiver object in the message-passing format – it has a distinguished place at the start of the message rather than being just another parameter, as in the Ada version. Furthermore the class of which the receiver is an instantiation does not feature in the message, emphasizing the position of the object as the dynamic agent of computation, rather than the static code underlying its behaviour.

As we shall see in the next chapters, the message-passing metaphor is supported with various degrees of fidelity by specific examples of OOPls. Probably the most complete and consistent realization is to be found in Smalltalk, where even the summing operation represented by the arithmetic expression 3 + 1 is interpreted as a message sent to the object "3", with the method selector "+" and argument "1", producing the response "4". (As Meyer (1988) has observed, this interpretation does not seem to possess any great advantage over the conventional arithmetic one.)

An interesting possibility is the transformation of the message-passing model from a metaphor into actuality in parallel processing environment. In such a realization, the operations of every object would comprise an independent process, which is executed in parallel with the processes of all other objects in the system. At this level of realization, objects are independently active and the execution of a service by an object on behalf of a client is not like a procedure call, where a single thread of control passes from the sender, through the code associated with the receiver, to return back to the sender, but the result of a message passed between two independent processes. Message-passing provides a very natural basis for programming parallel, multi-processor systems and, importantly, their simulation on single-processor systems, *without the need to change the code at the language level*. It was for this reason that message-passing was adopted as the mechanism for inter-task (i.e. inter-process) synchronization in Ada.

11.3.2 Dynamic binding of names to objects

The execution of a typical OOPl-written program is a very dynamic affair with objects being created (and destroyed) in a way that is generally unpredictable at the time that the corresponding code is actually written. But yet the program code must be written in terms of the manipulation of objects, using names to refer to them in a manner not unlike variable identifiers in a conventional programming language. This is not a new problem – C++, Modula-2 and Ada all provide for the programming of dynamic structures, and similarly use a static collection of names to provide references to such structures, using the device of *indirection*, or the use of pointers, to handle their dynamic nature. This approach is also widely employed in OOPls, where the binding of names to objects commonly involves *reference* or pointer values: each such name denotes a location that may contain a pointer to an object. The use of this technique carries two important implications:

- Because the binding of names to objects is done at run-time, a name may reference many different objects during program execution. Indeed, this is necessary so that the dynamically-changing population of objects may be referenced by a static collection of names. This opens up the question of the types of the objects referenced by a name – can type checking be imposed in such a dynamic environment?
- The use of indirection necessitates care in both assignment and testing for equality, for essentially the same reasons that led to the incorporation of limited private types in Ada, or the significance of the copy constructor in C++; the assignment or equality testing of the pointer values is generally not the required operation.

The issue, particularly, of the typing of OOPls is an important one to which we shall return in the next chapter.

Garbage collection

As a result of this dynamic creation of objects it is generally impossible to determine the memory occupancy that will be required during the running of an OOPl program simply by inspecting the "code". For this reason memory management – the allocation of memory to objects as they are created – is an important issue in the use of OOPls. There are generally two approaches to memory management, corresponding to "pure" and "hybrid" languages.

Pure object-oriented language systems, such as the Smalltalk environment, perform memory management automatically, including the *deallocation* of memory – to make available for use again the memory occupied by objects that are no longer required. This feature is known as *garbage collection*. C++ and Ada, which are hybrid languages, as we have seen, provide for dynamic memory allocation and deallocation, but under the specific control of the programmer; they do not support garbage collection.

187

Curiously, garbage collection is a feature of one of the oldest programming languages in existence, LISP, and it is perhaps partially for this reason that there are a number of LISP-based OOPls.

11.3.3 Class definitions

As is implied by the nature of the message-passing metaphor, the internal structure of an object, defined by its class, must enable it to respond to messages sent to it. The nature of this structure will come as no surprise after the lengthy discussions of encapsulating constructs in earlier chapters: a class possesses an *interface*, in which the *attributes* and *services* it offers to the external world are defined, and an *implementation* part that encapsulates the code, or *protocol*, that supports this external interface. A variety of terminology is employed over the range of OOPls currently available to describe this structure. Classes define *methods*, *routines*, *features* or indeed *procedures* and *functions*, in order to respond to messages from their *clients*. Additionally, completing the structure of the abstract data type that each class defines, a class will typically include an encapsulated data structure consisting of items variously called *instance variables*, *attributes* or *components*. These items are often instances of other classes – objects in other words. The set of objects that are instances of the same type all have the same set of instance variables. The values of the instance variables distinguish individual objects.

It is clear that the general structure of the class will closely resemble the corresponding structures – Packages – in Ada, when these are used for implementing abstract data types, and indeed classes in C++ – particularly in their support for the separation of interface from implementation. As we shall see in the comparison of a number of OOPls in the next three chapters, this basic concept appears in a variety of guises. The major variations lie in the area of encapsulation, while the essential attribute of data abstraction, the restriction of the manipulation of data items to operations only, is preserved generally.

Classes and messages
The dichotomy between classes and objects gives rise to a conceptual problem when the creation of objects is considered. If, as has been maintained, every computation in an OOPl system is identified with message passing between objects, to what object is a message sent to cause the creation of a new object? Obviously the class of which the object is an instance must be involved, but how can a message be sent to a class – a static behavioural description? In less specialized terms, how can a static entity like a class take part in the run-time creation of dynamic entities like objects? The answer to this question is provided in different ways by the various OOPls that will be considered in the next chapter.

11.4 Inheritance

The picture outlined so far lacks a highly important, some would say the most important, feature. This is the structure of relationships that exists between the classes in an object-oriented environment, providing the basis for class hierarchies, which were introduced briefly in Chapter 8.

The basis of inheritance is the set inclusion relation, or, less formally, classification according to the "*is a*" relationship. In turn, this is the basis of the classical taxonomies of biology and zoology, in which individuals are placed within a hierarchy. For example, a kestrel is a hawk, which is a bird of prey, which is a bird, which in turn is a vertebrate, and so on. The purpose of such classifications is to impose an order on reality, so as to permit knowledge to be accumulated and related not just to individuals, but to higher level, abstract entities – such as "birds". At the same time it permits distinctions to be made between closely related, but different, entities.

Traversal over such a hierarchy in either of the possible directions, i.e. towards the "root", or highest level, or away from it, produces a change in generalization. Traversal towards the root increases generalization, or abstraction, traversal away from the root reduces generalization, or increases its complement: specialization. Specialization involves the addition of attributes to the definition of an entity at one level in a classification hierarchy, so as to produce the definition of an entity "at the next level down". This process produces a chain of relationships. For example, a shape bounded by non-intersecting straight lines is a polygon; a polygon with four sides is a quadrilateral; a quadrilateral with two parallel sides is a trapezium; a trapezium with two pairs of parallel sides is a parallelogram; a parallelogram with all internal angles right angles is a rectangle, and so on. Each of these specializations, introduced by "with" in each case, might be thought of as a test that determines whether an entity may be classified one increment deeper in the classification hierarchy (e.g. from quadrilateral to trapezium). Each level accumulates all the increments above it, or, in other words, each level possesses the attributes of all the levels above it, and so any level is defined completely by the specialization that differentiates it from the level immediately above. Consequently, because any level has the attributes of all levels above it, it "is a(n)" entity on any one of these levels, in the sense of possessing all the attributes sufficient to define one of these higher level entities – a rectangle "is a" polygon, or a shape, etc.

In the area of software design, particularly in object-oriented design (OOD), this type of classification is applied, for much the same sort of reason. As we saw in Chapter 8, the major initial phase in OOD is the identification of the objects of the application domain. Subsequently, these separate, individual objects are analyzed to determine whether any "family resemblances" exist between them, i.e. whether relationships can be identified. The purpose of this analysis is, again, to impose order and create abstractions, so that a subsequent system design can deal with coherent groups of objects, rather than scattered individuals.

Recall that two kinds of relationship are being sought:

1. strict similarity, in the sense of possessing identical sets of attributes, although with different values for them in individual cases, such as the similarity between the employees of a company;
2. a less strict "family resemblance", which can be defined as set-inclusion relation between sets of attributes, such as that between the managers of the company and ordinary employees. The managers are employees, and thus possess the "employee set", but they also possess additional attributes – in total a superset of the employee set. This is, of course, the "is a" relationship – a manager "is a(n)" employee.

The similarity relation allows the creation of classes in the object-oriented sense – a general definition applying to a collection of objects. The "is a" relation allows the identification of relationships *between classes*, i.e. the categorization of one class in terms of another, as a specialization or generalization.

Inheritance, a fundamental feature of the object-oriented paradigm, is a mechanism allowing classes to be created, related to each other by the "is a" relationship. An *inheritance hierarchy* is a tree structure, resembling a classification hierarchy, in which an entity at one level is a specialization of an entity at the next higher level. Each class in such a hierarchy (apart from that at the root) is declared in terms of a superclass, or parent, and the effect of the inheritance mechanism is to make available the characteristics of the superclass to the child, or subclass.

There are two applications of this kind of inheritance hierarchy:

1. the derivation of a new entity, by specializing an existing level.
2. the identification of a generalization, or abstraction, of an entity at a particular level by one above it.

The first of these is the basis for so-called "programming-by-difference", which we met in Chapter 9 – a form of software reuse, in which an existing class is specialized by the addition of some protocol, perhaps additional methods and/or instance variables. By the nature of inheritance, only these additional items need be specified to define the new class, provided it "claims its inheritance" from the existing class. Clearly, this arrangement requires a support mechanism in the language system. If an instance of a child class is sent a message for which it contains no protocol, but its parent (or ancestor) does, then the message must be sent "up the superclass chain" until the relevant method is discovered.

The second application is the basis of a powerful abstraction mechanism involving *polymorphic redefinition*.

11.4.1 Polymorphism

We recall that polymorphism in the programming language context means "possessing, or being able to deal with, many types". As we have seen, the levels within inheritance hierarchies are related, looking towards the root, by the "is a" relationship, and this provides the basis for a particular form of polymorphism.

The consequence of the "is a" relationship means that an entity within such a hierarchy will possess the attributes of all the ancestor entities up to the root of the hierarchy – it can "be" any one of them. This means that it is possible to write polymorphic code, i.e. to write code in terms of one level in a hierarchy, which will then be correct for all entities at lower levels. This is a very powerful abstraction mechanism, as illustrated in the following example.

Suppose it is required to write a program dealing with geometric shapes – perhaps in order to optimize the cutting of such shapes from a piece of material so as to minimize waste. A small fragment of code calculates the total area of the set of shapes defined for the particular program run. We might imagine a pseudo-code version of this fragment as follows:

```
for_each SHAPE in BAG_OF_SHAPES
loop
        TOTAL_AREA := TOTAL_AREA + AREA_OF(SHAPE);
end loop;
```

We understand that the **for_each** construct is a slightly more advanced version of the typical **for** construct, which combines an iterator with the loop so as to extract the members of the collection **BAG_OF_SHAPES** (a bag is a mathematical object like a set but which permits multiple instances of members) one at a time, the loop body being executed once for each member as the value of the loop variable **SHAPE**. We also assume that **BAG_OF_SHAPES** contains an arbitrary collection of different shapes: squares, polygons, ellipses, and so on.

This fragment of pseudo-code is a close approximation to an informal version expressed along the lines of "we take each shape in turn, find its area and add it to the total". The human mind has no difficulty in coping with the idea of a generalized calculation like "find the area of (any) geometrical shape", as represented by the **AREA_OF** operation, capable of determining the area of any kind of figure that has two-dimensional extension. It would be desirable, therefore, from the point-of-view of intelligibility, for an implementation of this design to exhibit a similar simplicity, deriving from the use of such an abstract operation.

In practice, it is rather difficult to realize this idea using a conventional language, even one as powerful as Ada, particularly if an object-based approach is used. One problem is that the different shapes that the program is required to accommodate would naturally be realized as different (abstract) types, and so there is the immediate difficulty of allowing **SHAPE** to assume different types during execution of the loop. A similar, and more serious, problem confronts the writer of the **AREA_OF** function, which is required to be invoked with actual parameters of different types. Ada's generic facility, as we saw in Chapter 9, is a compile-time mechanism and thus unable to cope with parameter types determined at run-time.

The only possible solution to these problems, within the Ada 83 context, is to implement the family of geometric shapes as a variant record type: a feature similar to the Pascal variant record feature, or C **union**. This provides for alternative structures to be defined for a record type, discriminated by a "tag" field in the record, known as a *discriminant* in its Ada version. This feature would allow the declaration of a record type, say **figure**, with a discriminant of an enumerated type containing literals such as **square, circle, rectangle,** etc. The declaration of **figure** would include variants corresponding to each value of the discriminant type: the **circle** variant would possess fields containing data defining centre and radius, for **polygon** vertices, and so on. Ada also permits the declaring of subtypes corresponding to the individual variants of such a type, and so it would be possible for **SHAPE** and the parameter of **AREA_OF** to be of type **figure**, while accepting objects of the variant subtypes corresponding to **circle**, etc.

There are, however, a number of drawbacks to this solution, some serious enough to invalidate it completely. The variant structure would be complex, containing the defining characteristics of the whole geometric figure hierarchy; where this included subclass relationships these would need to be represented by nested variant structures. Furthermore, this structure would be "hardwired" into the program, the **AREA_OF** function consisting of a large case statement mirroring the variant record structure, with corresponding nesting – a characteristically error-prone arrangement. The addition of a new geometric shape would require modification to both the variant record structure and the associated code. There would be no possibility of treating the various shapes as abstract data types, as subtypes do not possess sufficient independence to allow for the creation of separate interfaces.

The variant subtype idea does, however, suggest the kind of relationship between types that could support the abstraction we are trying to achieve. What is required is the recognition of the "shape subtypes", **circle, square,** etc, as being types in their own right, while retaining their "family resemblance" to the more general, higher-level type **figure**. In other words, to create an inheritance hierarchy with **figure** at its root, and the other shapes subclassed from it. This would permit the specification of generalized, abstract operations such as **AREA_OF** in terms of the correspondingly generalized type **figure**, *whilst applying to all the shape subtypes*. In this way, **AREA_OF** can be defined as a polymorphic operation, capable of accepting operands that are instances of any of the subclasses of **figure**. This is known as "inclusion" polymorphism, because it is dependent on the resemblance of classes "included" in a class hierarchy.

11.4.2 Specialization and redefinition

The effect of the inheritance mechanism is to make available to an object the set of methods contained both in its class and in all its ancestor classes. Each new subclass adds new methods, specializing the nature of the objects instantiated from it. Continuing the geometric figures example, the **polygon** class might well provide an iterator to allow the extraction of the vertices – the perimeter-defining points – for a polygon object. This would be an inappropriate operation for the more generalized **figure**, which might include curved perimeter segments. In the same way the class **square**, inheriting from and specializing **polygon**, might provide methods relating to to the diagonal of a square object – a feature not generally found in polygons.

The relationship between classes established by the inheritance of generalized attributes from superclass to subclass means that:

An instantiation of a class can always be used where an instantiation of one of its ancestor classes can be used.

This is simply an expression of the idea that if A "is a" B, then A can do anything that B can do. In implementation terms this results from the inheritance, by A, of all B's methods. The reverse is not generally true, because the "is a" relationship is not symmetrical.

This picture is slightly complicated by matters both practical and abstract. If we return to the **AREA_OF** operation, while we can imagine the inclusion of the function in the class **figure**, in practice the writing of such a function would be difficult. Also, it would be very inefficient to use such a general-purpose algorithm to calculate the areas of simple shapes such as circles or squares.

The avoidance of this sort of inefficiency (or even impossibility) is achieved by the *redefinition* of inherited methods within heirs, or subclasses, i.e. by supplying operations with the same name, thus preventing the promotion of the associated messages to high-level, generalized methods, which are then said to be *overridden*. In practice, a call to **AREA_OF** would invoke methods contained in the specific shape classes, such as circle and square, each redefining the high-level method contained in **figure**. In fact, there would be *no* algorithm for **AREA_OF** in **figure**. The method would simply produce an error message, as it should never be invoked. The existence of the method has a symbolic significance only, to ensure that such a method is provided by an appropriate redefinition, in all the descendants of the class. Classes containing symbolic, or abstract, methods like this are often known as *abstract super classes*, and are not intended to be instantiated but exist to impose interface commitments on their subclasses, in the form of methods to be redefined.

11.4.3 Late binding

Returning once again to the example:

```
for_each SHAPE in BAG_OF_SHAPES
loop
        TOTAL_AREA := TOTAL_AREA + AREA_OF(SHAPE);
end loop;
```

we have seen it is possible for **SHAPE** and **AREA_OF** to cope with the different classes of objects extracted from **BAG_OF_SHAPES**, provided these are all subclasses of a common superclass. We have also seen that the requirements of efficiency and practicality make it appropriate that **AREA_OF** is redefined in each of these subclasses, so that there will be a version for the **circle** subclass, one for **square**, and so on. The question then arises: how is the correct version of **AREA_OF** invoked in each case? The "correct version" is obviously determined by the class of the object that **SHAPE** denotes on each call to **AREA_OF**, but this determination is lost at the source program level.

In fact the "correct version" is selected by the operation of an OOPl mechanism called *late binding*. The "binding" is between the call to **AREA_OF** (in this case) and the code of the version of the function matching the class of the object that **SHAPE** currently denotes. In conventional languages this binding between textual call statement and code is performed at compile time, but of course in the example the sequence of classes of objects that **SHAPE** denotes is unknown at compile time, and, in any case, there is no single version of **AREA_OF** that is correct. Instead, the binding of call to code must be performed at run-time, in fact every time that the call to **AREA_OF** is made, hence the "late" in late binding.

Late binding is dependent on the ability of the program code to determine dynamically the (sub)class of an entity like **SHAPE**, and to invoke, or "despatch the call to", the appropriate code version. Perhaps surprisingly this feature can be provided with only a small overhead.

Inclusion polymorphism and late binding provide for a considerable raising of abstraction – to the level indeed of the initial description of the example algorithm. The details of the individual shape subclasses are abstracted away from the "program"; as a natural result of this a new shape subclass can be added without the need to modify either the remaining class hierarchy, or the various existing **AREA_OF** implementations. All that is required is that the new subclass "claims its inheritance", and supplies its own appropriate redefinition of **AREA_OF**.

194

11.4.4 Type and class hierarchies

Method overriding by redefinition gives rise to the possibility of "blanking out" inherited methods – by redefining them as null methods or error conditions. In some cases this may be difficult to avoid. Consider a queue class defined as a subclass of a linked list class, not unlike the Ada example given in Chapter 8. There is little problem in adding methods to respond to enqueue or dequeue messages, and a method for `is_empty` might well be included already in linked list. However, the conventional operations for linked lists include support for the ability to insert items *anywhere* into the sequential structure of the list, and methods for enabling this kind of insertion would be part of any useful linked list class. Their use would not, however, be appropriate for a queue – insertion into a queue at any point other than at its "end" would destroy the FIFO discipline. The queue class would therefore, presumably, override the offending methods so as to disable them. But in doing this we would have destroyed the "is a" relationship! We could no longer guarantee that an instance of any subclass of linked list could be used where any of *its* instances could be used, because such use might well depend on its "free insertion" properties.

This problem arises from the existence of two kinds of inheritance hierarchy, generally conflated in actual examples. These are *type hierarchies*, where the inheritance relationship is defined in terms of interface details only, and *class hierarchies*, where it is defined in terms of implementation detail. In the case of the queue/linked list relationship, it can be seen that the direction of inheritance will be opposed in the two alternative hierarchies. In a type hierarchy, the behaviour of a queue is clearly a generalization of the behaviour of a linked list, and so the latter will inherit from the former. In the case of a class hierarchy, the queue inherits naturally from the linked list. The distinction between the two types of hierarchy is only rarely recognized, with occasional anomalous results as in this case.

Clients and heirs

The nature of inheritance means that any class potentially has two kinds of "user": the *client* whose use is confined to the standard interface presented by the class to the world of external objects, and the *heir* who inherits from the class via the subclass relationship. The description above mentions operations, or methods, as the currency of inheritance and it is the case that this provides a realistic picture of the technique. It is also the case that a number of languages make accessible more than the methods of superclasses to their subclasses – some or all of the data structure defined in a class may also be made accessible: that is *directly* accessible via assignment. This, of course, destroys, or at least compromises, the encapsulation of a class in so far as its heirs are concerned.

There are two schools of thought on this matter. One holds that the tight coupling implied between a class and its heirs is unacceptable in a soft-

195

ware engineering environment. A change in the internal implementation of a class that changed the names or the use made of some of the instance variables would invalidate subclasses that accessed them. The other school holds that the relationship between a class and its heirs is, of necessity, an intimate one and that the implementor of a subclass must expect to be committed to the class involved, in the way that the implementor of a client would not.

The inheritance mechanism supports an approach to software reuse that differs considerably from the conventional model exemplified by the Ada library approach. In the conventional model software components are black boxes – their internal features hidden from users either completely or effectively. Even if a user can examine the code of an Ada library component it is completely inaccessible from the point of view of extension or modification. As we have seen, it is not always possible to build on an existing component to create a more powerful, specialized component, without resorting to inelegant measures. By contrast, the use of inheritance frequently necessitates the visibility of the implementation of the existing component, or class. This is obviously required in the case where access is made, by name, to instance variables.

11.5 Summary

In this chapter we have discussed the important characteristics of object-oriented languages. These have been discovered to be based on the essential feature of data abstraction, and its related concept, the abstract data type, realized in terms of objects – dynamic instantiations of classes – with their independence emphasized by the message-passing metaphor. To data abstraction is added the new dimension of inheritance, so that relationships between abstract data types may be recognized and exploited, both in the service of software reuse and in the raising of abstraction by the support of polymorphism. In the following chapters the way in which these concepts are realized in specific examples of OOPls will be discussed.

11.6 Further reading

Until recently, the literature available in respect of object-oriented languages and techniques was restricted to language-specific books – concerned with Smalltalk or Eiffel, for example – or the proceedings of the OOPSLA ("Object-oriented programming systems, languages and applications") conferences that took place in a variety of desirable locations in the USA in the late 1980s. This situation is changing, and a number of recent publications have started to fill this vacuum; for example G. Blair, J. Gallagher, D. Hutchinson, D. Shepherd, *Object-oriented languages, systems and applications* (London: UCL Press, 1993).

A discussion of the transformation of the traditional software development process effected by the characteristics of object-oriented environments is given in A. Goldberg, "Programmer as reader" in *Information Processing 86*, H. J. Kugler (ed.) (Amsterdam: North-Holland, 1986).

B. Meyer, *Object-oriented software construction* (Reading, Mass.: Addison-Wesley, 1988), is mainly concerned to provide an exposition of the Eiffel language, but it also contains an excellent introduction to object-oriented programming in general, and includes comparisons between Eiffel and other languages, including Ada. Perhaps not surprisingly, Meyer is slightly less than fair to Ada.

CHAPTER 12

Pure object-oriented languages

12.1 Introduction

In the last chapter the general characteristics of object-oriented languages were introduced in a manner generally non-specific to any particular language. In this chapter the way in which these characteristics are exhibited by two specific languages is explored, with the intention not so much of providing an exhaustive "manual" in each case, but of conveying the essential nature of each of the variations on the theme. The "theme" in question is that of a "pure" realization of the object-oriented paradigm – each of the languages discussed being designed specifically to support OOP, and essentially unusable in any other way. The next two chapters are devoted to "hybrid" languages, which support the paradigm, but with a "ring-fenced" set of features that may optionally be ignored by a user.

Despite the non-specific nature of the last chapter, much of its material applies directly to Smalltalk, as the result of the pervasive influence that Smalltalk has had on object-oriented culture, particularly in relation to terminology. The explosion of interest in object-oriented languages and environments that occurred during the 1980s was undoubtedly initiated by Smalltalk, and it still commands an important position within the object-oriented world. Because of this importance it is appropriate to give a reasonably complete picture of Smalltalk, in its most widely-distributed variant Smalltalk 80, which can also serve as a standard against which to compare other OOPls.

12.2 Smalltalk

12.2.1 Introduction

The first and important point to make about Smalltalk is that it is a *programming environment* that surrounds a language – the actual details of the language almost fade into insignificance against the other major features of the environment. These include a very highly developed interactive interface, characterized by the kind of window-driven facilities that have become identified with the term graphical user interface (GUI), and a very comprehensive *class hierarchy*, which is the result of years of accumulated development. Smalltalk exhibits all the characteristics identified previously as belonging to an object-oriented language: data abstraction, dynamic binding, inheritance, polymorphism and message-passing.

Many of Smalltalk's characteristics result from an overall aim to make program development a natural, free-flowing, incremental process, suited particularly to the rapid prototyping of software. The emphasis is on continuous, small-grained modification rather than the traditional coarse-grained, episodic life-cycle model. It is probably true to say that the object-oriented paradigm is seen as the means to achieve this overall aim rather than being the end in itself.

12.2.2 The Smalltalk system

In more specific terms, the Smalltalk system provides a "single-mode" environment in which code input, translation and testing are performed in a highly interleaved manner. Each input, translate and test cycle typically involves only a few lines of text, by virtue of the system's support for programming-by-difference – the specialization of existing classes in the hierarchy. The process is controlled by a unified interface to all the relevant system components, utilizing a "pointing" device such as a mouse.

Two major features of the system support this very dynamic environment:

- The code of the system is *interpreted* rather than compiled. The system contains a translator, which is known as the compiler, but its function is a "statement level" conversion of the source text into an intermediate format that can be executed by an interpreter. This means that "compilation" is fast but that the ensuing execution is relatively slow – the appropriate trade-off for the rapid incremental development of prototype software. The more semantic features of compilation in its conventional sense are not supported, particularly type checking. In the Smalltalk context this means that no attempt is made to check that a method exists in the class of an object, or one of its ancestor classes, capable of responding to a message specified as being sent to it. (Some implementations of Smalltalk now provide genuine compilation.)
- A fundamental feature of the Smalltalk system which might be seen as necessitated either by the application of the object-oriented paradigm in a rigorous way, or by the requirements of the highly dynamic environment, is the fact that *everything* in the system is an object, including every member of the class hierarchy. This feature both provides an elegant solution to the conundrum of how essentially static classes may take part in the dynamic creation of objects, and

contributes practically to the rapid response necessary for a system like Smalltalk to be usable.

As might be expected from the nature both of the object-oriented paradigm and these features of the Smalltalk system the language at the core of Smalltalk is somewhat unconventional.

12.2.3 The Smalltalk language

The language used to write Smalltalk programs has comparatively few large structures: each program, or program increment, typically consists of some messages organized into methods within a class definition.

Messages

There are three variants of the message format: *unary*, *binary* and *keyword*, which are distinguished by the number of parameters that they require. A unary message consists of a single identifier (the term being used much as in any language) and requires no parameters, e.g: **tree isEmpty**, where **tree** is the receiver object of the message, which requests a Boolean response as to whether **tree** is empty. (The style of identifier used here, where words are run together with their initial letters capitalized, apart from the first word, is a standard Smalltalk convention.) A binary message takes one parameter: the "other" parameter implied by *binary* is the receiver object. Characteristic binary messages are the equivalents of the arithmetic and relational operators in conventional languages, for example **total > 100**. Keyword messages permit several parameters to be defined, each introduced by an identifier known as the keyword for the parameter. Conventionally, keywords are suffixed by a colon. For example:

> **symbolTable at:next put:variable**

This is a characteristic form of message used to insert an item, in this case referenced by **variable**, into some kind of search structure object, here referenced by **symbolTable**, at a position indicated by **next**.

Assignments

One structure that is not a message is the assignment, which has a rather different role from that found in conventional languages. Essentially, assignment accomplishes the binding of a name – an identifier – to an object. We recall that the requirements for the handling of dynamic objects demand that such a binding is an indirect one, and that no copying of the object involved takes place, unlike assignment in a conventional language.

Assignment is frequently associated with object creation, either explicitly by the sending of a **new** message to the appropriate class (object), or implicitly, for example by the assignment of literal values. Examples:

symbolTable ← Dictionary new

where the name **symbolTable** is bound to the newly-created object of class **Dictionary**, a search structure providing keyed access.

vector ← #[65, 24, 26, 13]

which will create an array, referenced by the identifier **vector**, with the values shown in the square brackets.

As noted previously, there is no type-related variable declaration or type checking in Smalltalk, the class of the object referenced by an identifier is determined simply by the last assignment made to it. There is no restriction on the objects that an identifier may reference during execution.

Control structures
Control structures in Smalltalk, as in other languages, provide for the execution of alternative or iterated pathways through the the code, depending on the values of *conditions*. The Smalltalk versions of the standard control structures, as might be expected, conform to the message-passing metaphor. A condition is evaluated by the sending of an appropriate message, perhaps the binary message <, and responds with an object denoted by one of the pseudo-variables *true* or *false*. (Pseudo-variables resemble ordinary variables except that their denotations are fixed and may not be changed.) The objects to which *true* and *false* are bound respond, for example, to the message **ifTrue:**, which takes a parameter in the form of a *block*. A block is a piece of program code delimited by square brackets, which is evaluated on receipt of a message, rather than when the execution sequence reaches it. The **ifTrue:** method provides such a message and thus causes the evaluation of the block parameter. The Smalltalk equivalent of:

```
if a > b
then a := a - b;
end if;
```

is:

```
a > b ifTrue:[a ← a - b]
```

When the **ifTrue:** message is sent to *false* then the parameter is not evaluated. The equivalent of the "else" path of the conventional *if* statement is provided by the **ifFalse:** message, which causes its block parameter to be evaluated when it is sent to *false*.

A similar mechanism provides the Smalltalk equivalent of the *while* loop.

Classes
As remarked above, the standard way of "writing Smalltalk programs" is by writing new class definitions in the form of subclasses related to the

existing class hierarchy. The "hook" that attaches such a class onto the hierarchy is an expression that heads its definition and specifies the immediate superclass, or parent, of the new class. For example, a class **Queue** would be defined as a child class of **LinkedList** by the expression:

LinkedList subclass: #Queue

Note that class names are conventionally started by a capital letter, and also that **Queue** is defined to be a unique name in the system, as it must be, by making it a *symbol* as indicated by the "#".

The version of inheritance supported by the major versions of Smalltalk is that known as *single* inheritance in which, as its name suggests, any class may have only one superclass. Only one expression such as that shown above may appear in a class definition, therefore.

Smalltalk terminology has already been introduced in the last chapter; to summarize: class definitions include *instance methods*, each of which is an operation associated with one of the *messages* to which instances of the class respond. The data structure encapsulated by the class, at least in so far as its clients are concerned, comprises a set of *instance variables*, whose values survive the execution of individual methods. Individual methods may have *temporary* variables, the values of which are lost when control leaves the methods. The collection of methods and instance variables (and *class variables* (p. 205)) are known as the *protocol* for the class.

The format of a class definition is not unlike that of a Modula-2 implementation module or Ada package body, although with considerably less "syntactic sugar" in the form of reserved words. (Generally, the Smalltalk language cannot be highly recommended either for its readability or self-documenting qualities.) The protocol for each method is preceded by the selector(s) of the message that invokes it, with identifiers for the formal parameters in binary or keyword messages. The following shows the protocol for a **factorial** method that might be added to a subclass of **Integer**.

factorial
"answer the factorial of the receiver"
    self > 0
        ifTrue: [↑ self * (self - 1) factorial]
    self = 0
        ifTrue: [↑ 1]

This short example illustrates a number of Smalltalk features. Comments are enclosed in double quotes. The entity **self** is the Smalltalk name, actually a pseudo-variable, for the "receiver of the message", in this case an object that is an instance of **Integer**. If the value of the receiver object is greater than 0 then, because the priority of a unary message is greater than that of a binary, the **factorial** message is sent recursively to **(self - 1)** until this expression becomes 0, when the **Integer** object 1 is returned as the parameter to the first of the binary "*" messages that have been stacked up, causing the calculation of the factorial.

The ↑ symbol indicates the expression whose evaluation is returned as the response of the method. As can be seen, a method may contain several return expressions, the one that is executed being determined by the value of the condition and thus the path through the method.

In addition to the "executable" code of messages and assignments, class definitions include data items in the form of instance and temporary variables, both of which are classified as *private* in Smalltalk terminology, although the instance variables of a class are directly accessible to its subclasses. Instance variables and temporary variables are "declared" by being listed at the head, respectively, of the class and method definition to which they belong, between vertical bars in the case of temporary variables. Something of the flavour of a full class definition can be obtained from the (slightly amended and drastically truncated) protocol for class **Tree** shown in Figure 12.1.

No separate interface specification, along the lines of the definition module or package specification is required *as part of the language*, but is generated by the environment, which will produce a display of the messages to which each class responds.

Abstract classes
In the last chapter the concept of *inclusion polymorphism* was introduced as supporting the use of abstract operations, applicable to high-level classes and made available through polymorphic redefinition. This form of polymorphism is central to Smalltalk and is realized by the vehicle of abstract classes.

The classes in the regions of the hierarchy near to and including the root, the class *object*, naturally in view of the semantics of inheritance, are very generalized – to such an extent that they are not intended to support the creation of instances but to provide to, and impose on, their descendants a consistent set of methods. As we have seen, such classes are known as *abstract (super) classes*. A typical example of an abstract class is *magnitude*, which defines protocol for objects that can be compared or measured, including the relational operations, such as = and <, realized as binary messages. The descendants of *magnitude* include the numerical classes *integer* and *float* and also the class of ASCII characters *char*. An example of polymorphic redefinition that is frequently given is the `printOn` message, which causes a textual representation of the receiver object to be output. This message is included in the protocol for *object*, the most abstract of all classes, being the root of the class hierarchy, and so a commitment to respond to it is placed on every class in the hierarchy. Obviously, the operations involved in producing the output vary greatly according to the nature of the class in question, and so each class redefines the protocol for

Object subclass: #Tree
    instanceVariableNames 'root maxLevel avgLevel'
    classVariableNames "

    deleteLeft: aNode
      "Delete left offspring of aNode"
      |nodeToDelete|
      nodeToDelete ← aNode left.
      nodeToDelete left isNil ifTrue:[↑ aNode left: nodeToDelete right].
      nodeToDelete right isNil ifTrue:[↑ aNode left: nodeToDelete left].
      ↑aNode left: (self predecessorOf: nodeToDelete).

    predecessorOf: aNode
      "Replace aNode with its inorder predecessor"
      |predecessor|
      predecessor ← aNode predecessor.
      predecessor = aNode left ifFalse[
          aNode left right: predecessor left.
          predecessor left: aNode left].
      predecessor right: aNode right.
      ↑predecessor.

    insert: aNode
      "Insert based on key value in aNode subclass"
      |parent|
      self empty ifTrue: [↑self root: aNode].
      aNode key < parent key
          ifTrue:[parent left: aNode]
          ifFalse:[parent right: aNode].
      ↑self.

Figure 12.1   Part of the protocol for class **Tree**.

this message so that the particular characteristics of the class are accommodated.

The methods included in an abstract class are present only to place a commitment on its descendants, and are not intended to be executed but to be redefined in each descendant. If a message selecting such a method actually reaches it then the result will be an error message produced by the execution of the method **subclassResponsibility**, which is also one of the methods exported by the class *object* and therefore inherited by all classes.

The redefinition of methods in Smalltalk is quite unconstrained – there is nothing to prevent, say, the redefinition of the + operation as "minus", for example, foolish though this would be.

Classes as objects

As we have seen, the consistency of the application of the object-oriented paradigm is carried through, in Smalltalk, to the extent that classes themselves are objects. The conceptual distinction between objects and classes is not lost by this arrangement, although it does lead to the possibility of confusion.

Classes are objects and so may respond to messages, by means of what are known as *class methods*. The commonest example of a class method is **new**, which responds with a newly-created instance of the class. Class methods also characteristically provide information about the class; for example one might respond with the number of instances currently in existence.

A class may also declare *class variables*, which are accessible to all instances of the class. In a sense, class variables are global to instances, and represent a degradation of encapsulation. Their use is normally to hold constant data values with some fundamental relevance to the class and are obviously not *intended* to be used as global variables as such, although they are not protected by anything other than convention. A typical example of a class variable is **DaysInMonth** in the class **Date**, which defines protocol for the manipulation of dates. **DaysInMonth** is an array that contains the twelve values of the number of days in the months of the year.

Meta classes

The fact that *everything* in a Smalltalk system is an object, including each of its classes, leads to a rather complex conceptual structure involving a new kind of entity – the *meta class*. As objects, classes are themselves instances of classes, which are distinguished by the special name *meta class*. Every class in the hierarchy has a meta class, which is created when the class is created. In a characteristically consistent way, meta classes are themselves instances of only one class, so the threatened infinite regress in which a class is an instance of a class, which is an instance of a class, and so on, is short-circuited.

There seems little doubt that the existence of meta classes adds considerable complexity to the conceptual elegance of the basic class hierarchy model, which perhaps might have been avoided by abandoning the exclusive view of Smalltalk entities as being objects only. The insistence on regarding classes as objects certainly provides for consistency, specifically in the creation of instances where the create message is sent to the class in question. If classes were not objects then their ability to receive messages would require a special mechanism – but as there is a clear conceptual distinction between classes and objects this does not seem to present any great difficulty.

12.2.4 The Smalltalk class hierarchy

The Smalltalk class hierarchy is known as the *image*, because of the fact that classes exist as objects within the memory occupied by the run-time system. By mid 1990 the image contained over two hundred classes. The environment provides the *browser* tool to enable the user to become familiar with the structure of the image. Physically, the browser appears as a window within which the class hierarchy, or the code of individual classes, may be scrolled. In addition to the browser tool, the documentation of the image is highly structured as an aid to the accessibility of its details.

This is not the place to give an exhaustive description of the Smalltalk image but it will be useful to give a brief picture of its structure, together with some selected detail, particularly of how polymorphism is managed.

The structure of the image may be categorized as follows:

- **Magnitude classes** – These classes define objects that may be compared, measured, counted or arithmetically manipulated. They include numbers, characters, dates and times. They are the most commonly used classes.
- **Collection classes** – The data structures used in Smalltalk are the collection classes, or are developed from them. They include arrays and dictionaries: structures indexed by alphanumeric key.
- **Stream classes** – These classes are used in accessing external devices and files.
- **Windows** – Applications developed under Smalltalk are invariably window driven, and a number of related classes are provided to support this type of user interface.
- **Graphics** – The normal platform for Smalltalk is a workstation equipped with a high-resolution bit-mapped graphics display. The graphics classes enable the facilities of these displays to be exploited by Smalltalk users.
- **Kernel classes** – provide the protocol for the internal operations intrinsic to Smalltalk such as the creation of subclasses and the operation of the inheritance mechanism.
- **System classes** – encompass the operations involved in maintaining the Smalltalk image.
- **Interface classes** – provide facilities for communicating with the operating system, allowing "call-outs" to non-Smalltalk code.

Of these categories the first three, with the addition of the class **boolean**, which occupies a unique position in providing for alternative execution sequences, are the basis of what might be termed application programming in the conventional sense. The remaining classes are either concerned with the highly responsive Smalltalk user interface, replete with windows, pull-down menus, icons, and so on, which is transferable, suitably modified, to applications, or with low-level features of the Smalltalk environment and its (operating system) environment. In passing we might note

Collection
　Bag
　Set
　　Dictionary
　　　IdentityDictionary
　　SequenceableCollection
　　ArrayedCollection
　　　Array
　　　　LiteralArray
　　　String
　　　WordArray
　　Interval
　　LinkedList
　　OrderedCollection

Figure 12.2 The hierarchy subtree based on Collection.

the unusually open nature of the environment, where all the system functions such as "compilation" (actually interpretation) and the tools, such as
the system browser, are accessible by the user.

The collection category, which is a complete subtree of the hierarchy
rooted by the class **Collection**, is perhaps the most interesting from the
point of view of application development. As remarked above, it is the
repository for the data structure classes provided in the Image and, as
such, displays the richness of the hierarchy. An outline of the subtree is
shown in Figure 12.2, indicating the subclass relationship by indentation.
The major characteristics of the members of the subtree rooted on **Collection** are as follows:

1. **Collection** is an abstract superclass and thus does not have instances,
   but defines methods that are intended to be redefined in its subclasses. The essential nature of a collection is that it is a group of individuals, upon which structural relationships may be imposed. The
   main methods defined are **add:, remove:, includes:** and **do:** (the colon
   following the method selector means that a following parameter is
   required. In the first three cases the parameter specifies the object that
   is to be added to, removed from or whose presence is to be tested for
   in, the collection.) The method invoked by **do:** applies an operation to
   every member of a collection.

   Collection contains three class variables that define default max-
   ima for the number of members in a collection, and the sizes of
   general object members and strings.

2. **Set** and **Bag** are the most abstract of the subclasses of **Collection**, adding little additional protocol. They provide for *unordered* collections,

and differ in that a **Set**, in conformity with the corresponding mathematical entity, contains no repeated members, while a **Bag** may contain repeated members. **Bag** accordingly provides a method that responds with the count of instances of a repeated member. A typical application for a set is to provide a "coarse" recognizer for the reserved words of a language: the set is created containing the reserved words; as tokens are extracted they can be tested using the **includes:** method.

3. **Dictionary** is a subclass of **Set**, which specializes its superclass by restricting members to **Associations**. An association is a pair of objects, in which the first is used to reference the second, in the manner of a key. The dictionary provides, therefore, an indexed structure that can be used in many applications that require data retrieval by key. Retrieval is supported by the **at:** method, which takes an object that is the first member of an association pair and returns the second member. An association may be updated by the **at: put:** method: the first parameter identifies the association and the second provides the new value for the second member.

4. **SequenceableCollection** is an abstract superclass of classes that have members possessing a well defined order, in which it makes sense to refer to "the first member", "the next member" and so on.

5. **ArrayedCollection** is a subclass of **SequenceableCollection** but is still an abstract superclass of classes with external fixed-range integer keys. The subclasses **array** and **string** provide conventional, and highly comprehensive, support for these data structures. **ByteArray** is a specialized class whose members are defined as 8-bit fields and which is used in low-level applications involving machine code.

   WordArray also is used in low-level applications, particularly in accessing and changing bit maps used to store graphics display elements.

6. **LinkedList** provides protocol supporting an abstract form of the linked list: abstract in the sense that no data fields are included in the nodes of the list, and that insertions may be made only at the ends of the list. The intention is that appropriate additions will be made in subclasses. **OrderedCollection** is a class defining a structure whose members are ordered with reference to the sequence in which they are inserted or removed. Typical specializations of **OrderedCollection** are stacks and queues.

12.2.5 The MVC triad

As we saw in Chapter 8, the MVC triad is a standard architectural pattern for GUI-based applications. It was in fact developed within the Smalltalk environment, and is the basic structure for an application developed in

Smalltalk. A considerable portion of the Smalltalk image is taken up with the support of the MVC triad, which provides the user with the potential to create GUIs with a responsiveness and power matching that of the Smalltalk environment itself.

12.3 Statically and strongly-typed OOPls

Despite its very considerable dynamic power, and the richness of the mature class hierarchy, Smalltalk has never found favour in what might be termed "serious" software engineering. The reasons for this include the unavoidable inefficiency of interpreted systems, Smalltalk's nature as essentially a single-user system, but particularly the lack of strong typing reinforced by compiler checking. The possibility that a new operational circumstance might involve an untested message/object combination, resulting in nothing more constructive than an error message, is one that software engineering managers are commonly unwilling to contemplate. The major benefit of strong typing – the ability of the compiler to detect errors that, although syntactical in nature, frequently arise from errors in logic or design – is well understood and there is considerable reluctance to abandon it. In the object-oriented context it is appropriate that the normally implied qualification "statically" – meaning determined at compile time – is made explicit. In conventional languages, strong typing is invariably enforced statically. In object-oriented languages the dynamic nature of name-binding, and polymorphism, would appear to make static type checking at best difficult, at worst impossible. Before describing the approach adopted in several OOPls, it is as well to remind ourselves of what static type checking is intended to achieve in the object-oriented context. This may be stated as: it will never be the case, in a correctly compiled program, that a message will be sent to an object whose class, or whose ancestor classes, are incapable of responding to it.

The immediately obvious problem in achieving this intention is that if objects can be created and bound to names without constraint, there is no possibility that the compiler can check if the messages including such a name as the reference to the receiver object are appropriate. Clearly the possibility of static checking must depend on some form of restriction as to the nature of the objects that may be bound to each name. One approach would be to adopt strong typing in the manner of Pascal or Ada, and declare every name as being of a particular class; the compiler would then check that every object bound to a name was of the correct class. But this approach is too restrictive – it would preclude inclusion polymorphism because in, say, Ada 83 terms a subclass of a class is of a different type from its parent, and so the operations exported from its parent may not be applied to its instances. How can we avoid throwing out the polymorphism baby with the type clash bathwater?

12.3.1 Static typing and inheritance

The representative of statically typed OOPs that will be considered – Eiffel, from Interactive Software Engineering Inc. – extends the notion of *type compatibility* to reconcile inheritance and inclusion polymorphism with strong, static typing. Type compatibility, or *conformance* as it is known in this context, in OOPls is based on the principle of inheritance that a subclass may be used wherever its superclass may be used, but not vice versa. This is a consequence of the fact that the "is a" relationship existing between a class and its parent is not generally symmetrical. If we imagine a class hierarchy including the class "wheeled vehicle" with one of its many subclasses "wheelbarrow", it is clear that every wheelbarrow "is a" wheeled vehicle, but that not every wheeled vehicle "is a" wheelbarrow.

Following this idea, a class is considered to be compatible with its parent, and indeed with all its ancestors, and therefore its instances may be used wherever instances of its ancestors are required. As we have seen, if the objective of statically-checked strong typing is to be achieved, type conformance must be observed in the binding of names (*entities* in Eiffel) to objects. This conformance is enforced by a modified version of the conventional variable declaration mechanism. Every name is declared as being associated with a specific class, which remains unchanged throughout the execution of the program. During the execution of the program a name may be bound to, or used to denote, several objects as the result of dynamic binding. The type compatibility rule means, however, that the objects to which an entity is bound must be instances either of its declared class, *or of subclasses of its declared class*. In this way, the possibility of an inappropriate message being sent to an object is prevented, because the instance of a subclass can always respond to any message to which an instance of its parent class can respond. At the same time inclusion polymorphism is not precluded. (It should be noted that this type system is dependent on the avoidance of method restriction – no class should be permitted to "reject its inheritance".)

12.4 Eiffel

Eiffel, which is associated very much with its designer Bertrand Meyer, represents a comprehensive reconciliation of the object-oriented paradigm with software engineering. In scope, Eiffel rivals Ada, although it does not possess constructs designed explicitly to support concurrency. Like Ada it provides for static parametric polymorphism in the form of generics, and also an exception mechanism. The system exhibits a conventional approach to compilation, as might be envisaged from its commitment to static type checking.

Something of the difference in the flavour of Smalltalk and a strongly-typed language can be gleaned from considering the task of creating an array of objects of different classes. In Smalltalk arrays are simply indexed cell structures that are created without reference to the classes of the objects that will populate them. In Eiffel an array is created with a defined class for its elements. The rule of type conformance allows for objects of different classes to be inserted into such an array, provided these different classes are subclasses of the defined element class. The effect is to encourage more cohesion in the class hierarchy, and to impose considerably more discipline on the programmer.

12.4.1 Class definitions

The language provides much more syntactic sugar than Smalltalk and supports readability to a level approaching that of Ada. Eiffel code is written exclusively to define classes, which are unambiguously described by Meyer as "the implementations of abstract data types". There is no risk of confusion between classes and objects in Eiffel: classes are static code modules, objects exist only dynamically, at run-time. A class definition contains a number of *features*, some or all of which constitute the external interface of the class as indicated in an **export** list, much after the style of a Modula-2 internal module. Features may be either *attributes* or *routines*. Attributes are data items, whose existence in an instance is much like that of the fields of a record, i.e. they are directly accessible by other objects, but in read-only mode. Write access to attributes is provided only to operations internal to the class, preserving encapsulation of a modified sort. The inclusion of attributes seems to be an attempt at a compromise avoiding the need for "get" operations for each simple exported data item. Whether or not this justifies the complication necessarily incorporated into class interface designs is a moot point.

Routines are classified conventionally into procedures and functions, and they possess a conventional structure with a heading line containing the routine name and formal parameter list, followed by an executable body bracketed between **do** and **end**. As might be expected, formal parameters and function results have declared types and substitution is governed by type conformance as described above – an object supplied as an actual parameter must be an instance of the class specified for the corresponding formal, or of one of its subclasses.

The meaning of the term "type" is very close to that of "class". The difference between the two exists to permit generic classes to be distinguished from their instances, in the sense of generic instantiation, not object instantiation. When a class is created by compile-time substitution from a generic class, the result defines a type. Non-generic classes are indistinguishable from types.

Eiffel exhibits a standard message-passing format for calls "on" objects – "receiver_object.message(parameters)". This is modified in the case of a set of basic types, including **integer** and **boolean**; expressions including them, particularly control expressions, may be written in a style that is

```
          ——Linked list elements
class LINKABLE [T] export
     value, change_value, change_right, put_between
feature

     value : T;

     Create(Initial : T) is
          —— Initialize with value Initial
     do value := Initial
     end; – – Create

     change_value(new : T) is
          – Assign value new to current element
     do value := new
     end; – – change_value

     right :like Current – automatic declaration in subclass

     change_right(other : like Current) is
          —— Put other to right of current element
     do right := other
     end; – – change_right

     put_between(before, after : like Current) is
          —— Insert current element between before and after
     do
          if not before.Void then—— is before initialized?
               before.change_right(Current)
          end;
          change_right(after);
     end; – – put_between
end; – – class LINKABLE
```

Figure 12.3   The Eiffel class *LINKABLE*.

recognisably similar to conventional languages. Eiffel implements dynamic name binding in a way that is standard within the object-oriented paradigm – names, or *entities*, denote references to objects that have an uninitialized value of **void** when first declared, corresponding to **void** in C++. Objects are created by invoking the **Create** routine on the entity, rather than the class, in a way that is rather reminiscent of the creation of dynamic objects in Pascal or Modula-2. The result of **Create** is to make the entity denote a "reference", or pointer, to the newly created object.

An example of a simple class is shown in Figure 12.3 (note the Ada-like comments). The *LINKABLE* objects defined by the class are nodes for linking into lists. The class is generic, with a generic formal parameter T that specifies the type of the data field in each *LINKABLE* node. The example is taken from a standard library that forms part of the Eiffel environment, which, although not as imposing as the Smalltalk image, nevertheless is a rich and evolving one.

12.4.2 Declaration by association

Each *LINKABLE* object is a "cell" or "node" containing two fields: the attributes *value*, the data value held in the node, and *right*, a reference to the next node, which is on the "right" in a singly-linked list. The declaration of *right* illustrates an interesting Eiffel feature, that of *declaration by association*. A declaration by association takes the form *entity*: **like anchor**, where "anchor" is either the name of an entity, declared conventionally in the same class declaration, or *Current*. *Current* is the Eiffel name for the "current" or "receiver" object. The idea underlying declaration by association is that inheritance frequently involves a systematic substitution of the types involved in the declaration of subclasses, with that of the subclass, or types associated with the subclass, being substituted for that of the superclass, or types associated with it.

The Eiffel standard library contains another list element class *BI_LINKABLE*, which is intended to provide the building block for doubly-linked lists. It differs, therefore, from *LINKABLE* by having a "backwards" reference *left*, together with a *change_left* operation. The remainder of the code will be effectively identical to that of *LINKABLE*, and so it seems appropriate to make *BI_LINKABLE* a subclass of *LINKABLE*.

As we have seen, *LINKABLE* contains the *right* attribute to link to the next node, which will be a *LINKABLE* object. The immediately obvious type for *right*, therefore, would appear to be *LINKABLE*. (Recall that all Eiffel entities are references – pointers, in other words – and so the declaration *right* : *LINKABLE* would allow *right* to point to the next node.) When we consider the subclass *BI_LINKABLE*, however, for similar reasons *right*, and *left* will need to be of type *BI_LINKABLE*. Therefore rather than be inherited, *right* be redefined – and given a full new declaration. This is not

$$--Doubly-Linked\ list\ elements$$
class $BI\_LINKABLE\ [T]$ export
$$value, change\_value, change\_right, change\_left$$
inherit

$$LINKABLE[T]$$
redefine $right, change\_right$

feature

$left$: like $Current$

Figure 12.4 Part declaration of *BI_LINKABLE*.

the only instance of the need to substitute *BI_LINKABLE* for *LINKABLE* in the subclass, the parameter types of the routines *change_right* and *put_between* must be treated similarly. It would seem, therefore, that much of the point of inheriting *BI_LINKABLE* from *LINKABLE* is lost, as it would be necessary to reproduce much of the latter to accomplish the necessary redefinitions.

This effective duplication can be avoided by the use of declaration by association, in this particular case, as shown in Figure 12.3 by using the form **like** *Current*, for example for the declaration of *right*. In a *LINKABLE* object this has the equivalent effect of *right* : *LINKABLE*. Its significant effect, in the context of the problem of duplication, is that in any subclass of *LINKABLE*, if *right* is specified as being redefined, it will be automatically redeclared as possessing the subclass type. So that in *BI_LINKABLE*, *right* will effectively be inherited with the type *BI_LINKABLE*. Note that it, and any other systematically redeclared entity, such as the routine parameters mentioned above, is simply nominated in the **redefine** clause of the subclass declaration. No explicit redefinition is required. The initial part of the declaration of *BI_LINKABLE* is shown in Figure 12.4 including the **inherit** clause nominating *LINKABLE*, the **redefine** clause nominating *right*, and the use of declaration by association for *left*, for further subclassing.

Assertions
This imposition of cohesion within the class hierarchy is supported by another feature of Eiffel – the use of *assertions*. Assertions are logical expressions including program entities, that allow the programmer to define relationships between the values of the entities that must be true. Assertions are related to well defined program structures such as statements, subprograms or, indeed, programs. There are several kinds of assertion, of which two are recognized as being particularly important in the Eiffel context:

- *pre-conditions*, which precede their related program structure and define relationships between the input values that must be true if the execution of the structure is to be valid;
- *post-conditions*, which follow their related program structure and define the effect that the execution of the program structure has on program entities.

A simple example might be a square root function **sqroot**. The pre-condition restricts the values of the argument to positive values. The post-condition specifies that the result actually is the square root of the argument. In Eiffel the pre- and post-conditions are respectively introduced by the reserved words **require** and **ensure**, and so the code for the function might look as follows:

```
sqroot(I : integer): float;
require I >= 0
–
– code for (say) Newton Raphson root algorithm
– leaving the final value in result
ensure I = result**2
```

Additionally, a different type of assertion called an *invariant* may be included, which states a logical relation between program entities that must remain unchanged as the result of the program construct execution.

Assertions used in this way are effectively specifying the semantics of the piece of program with which they are associated. Indeed, one of the important formal specification techniques, VDM ("Vienna Development Method"), uses pre- and post-conditions and invariants to define the semantics of programs.

(The reader may well be questioning the apparent abandonment of the algebraic specification technique, about which considerable claims were made in Chapter 10. The point is that algebraic specifications are particularly appropriate to the specification of abstract data types viewed *externally*, but here we are concerned with the specification of the operations viewed *internally*, where they must be considered independently. As we have seen, algebraic specifications define the semantics of operations by equating their composition, and so are not appropriate for specifying operations considered in isolation.)

In the context of OOPls, assertions provide a means by which the designer of a class can prevent others from destroying or distorting the semantics of the class during the process of redefining operations. This is because Eiffel requires that any assertions associated with an operation are valid for any redefinition of that operation in a subclass. In this way we can prevent the kind of idiocy referred to previously where "plus" is redefined to mean "minus". This feature of Eiffel is an unusual one in any programming language – although, as we have seen, it is supported by some C++

```
       P : Polygon;
       R : Rectangle;
  do

       R.Create; -- create a rectangle object bound to R
       P := R; -- dynamic binding of rectangle object
               -- to entity P of static type polygon
       l := P.perimeter; -- Polymorphic choice available
```

Figure 12.5 An example of dynamic binding.

implementations – but its application to the problem of uncontrolled redefinition seems to be a particularly appropriate one. This is particularly
true in relation to abstract classes, defined to impose semantics on their
descendants; in Eiffel abstract classes are known as *deferred* classes – the
implementations of their features being deferred to their subclasses.

This is also an important point when (inclusion) polymorphism is taken
into account. The effect of polymorphism is to permit alternative implementations of an abstract operation, as created by redefinition, to be invoked according to the dynamic binding of the entity involved. To return
to the example from the last chapter: given a class called *polygon* we may
envisage a subclass *rectangle*. Polygon exports an operation *perimeter* that
returns the length of the perimeter of the polygon object. The implementation of this operation provides for the full generality of polygonal shapes,
with no effective limit on the number of sides, with a correspondingly
(relatively) complex algorithm. In comparison, the algorithm for determining the perimeter of a rectangle is simple, and so it is appropriate that the
perimeter operation is redefined in the rectangle subclass. The existence
of these alternative implementations would impact on the example of
dynamic binding shown in Figure 12.5. The effect of the dynamic binding
of a rectangle object to the entity P will be to cause the invocation of the
"rectangular" perimeter operation on the right-hand side of the assignment to 1, despite P's static type being polygon. It is, therefore, highly
desirable that the semantic properties of the perimeter operation are preserved in its redefinitions. (It should be noted that current versions of the
Eiffel compiler are not able to check that assertions and invariants are satisfied by the code; an optional run-time check may be imposed, however.)

12.5 Multiple inheritance

Multiple inheritance – the ability of a class to inherit from more than one
superclass – is a feature of a number of more recent OOPls, including Eiffel
and, as we shall see, C++. Given multiple inheritance, the class hierarchy
takes the form of an acyclic directed graph rather than a tree.

The additional power that multiple inheritance bestows is qualitative rather than quantitative – the design of new classes is largely identified with the *combination* of the properties of several parents, rather than with the *specialization* of one, although of course the latter technique is always available within an environment supporting multiple inheritance.

The characteristic example often given to illustrate multiple inheritance is the window – as found in many workstation user interface systems. A window possesses the attributes both of an output stream – textual and graphical data is written to it for display to the user – and of a geometric figure, normally rectangular. With multiple inheritance, a window class may be defined by inheriting from appropriate parents; an output stream class and a rectangular figure class. The actual amount of additional code requiring to be written would be negligible. The corresponding implementation using only single inheritance would require the window class to inherit from either the output stream class or the rectangular figure class. Whichever is chosen, the operations of the other will have to be reimplemented as part of the window class.

The proponents of multiple inheritance maintain, with some justification, that it is "true" inheritance and that single inheritance is too constraining to allow the full power of the technique to be deployed. The question might therefore reasonably be asked, why do not all OOPls support multiple inheritance?

The answer is that multiple inheritance involves a number of conceptual problems perceived by some – namely the supporters of single inheritance – to have been sufficiently intractable to necessitate its rejection, albeit with reluctance. The supporters of multiple inheritance, on the other hand, declare that these problems are largely illusory. As might be expected, the truth seems to lie somewhere between these poles: the problems are not so great as to invalidate multiple inheritance, but they do introduce a certain unavoidable level of complexity.

The most obvious problem arises from the possibility that two (or more) of the parents of a class may have operations with the same name. Apart from the difficulty of unambiguously invoking one of the operations from within the descendant class, if the name is used by a client of the class, up which superclass chain does the inheritance mechanism go? Eiffel adopts a practically-oriented approach and recognizes that it would be unreasonable to expect the parent classes of some projected new class to be rewritten because they possess a common operation name. Instead, Eiffel provides a renaming facility that allows such operations to be given new names for use both within the descendant class, and by its clients.

A more complex problem arises when the superclass chains form a class join – in other words, when the parents of a class have a common ancestor. The question arises as to whether an operation that has such a *repeated inheritance* is singular. This means that, the fact that it is derived from two inheritance chains is ignored, or replicated, i.e. both inherited versions are invoked. This is irrelevant for an idempotent operation but not if the operation is affected by some internal state. In fact both possibilities are applicable, depending on the circumstances, and Eiffel recognizes this fact. If such an operation, obtained by repeated inheritance from a common ancestor, is renamed in any of its inheritance chains, then it is treated as replicated; if it is not so renamed then it is treated as shared.

12.6 Summary

In this chapter we have described the salient features of two representative pure object-oriented languages, distinguished by their approach to typing, and the program development process. These are the archetypal OOP1, Smalltalk, intended for rapid, incremental prototyping, and Eiffel, possessing a software engineering orientation evidenced by its support for static strong typing, together with the advanced feature of multiple inheritance. In the next two chapters we turn to two hybrid languages, C++ and Ada 95, which have been created by the "retro-fitting" of support for the object-oriented paradigm to existing, non-OOP languages.

12.7 Further reading

Smalltalk is well served by a number of books written by members of its design team, notably A. Goldberg & D. Robson, *Smalltalk 80, the language and its implementation* (Reading, Mass.: Addison Wesley, 1983) and A. Goldberg, *Smalltalk 80, the interactive programming environment* (Reading, Mass.: Addison Wesley, 1983). A good introduction is provided in L. J. Pinson & R. S. Wiener, *An introduction to object-oriented programming and smalltalk* (Reading, Mass.: Addison Wesley, 1988).

CHAPTER 13

C++ as an OOPl

13.1 Introduction

C++ has already been introduced, in Chapter 6, as an example of a language that supports data abstraction – indeed, as providing a very natural and powerful support for abstract data types. This support is, of course, a typical feature of an object-oriented language, and it is true to say that C++ is generally seen as an OOPl, rather than an object-based language. It should be remembered, however, that C++ is a *hybrid* language, in that the remaining features of the object-oriented paradigm – particularly inheritance and polymorphism – are provided as options, which may be ignored by the user in a way that would not be possible with, say, Smalltalk. Despite their optional nature, the elements of the paradigm are comprehensively supported in C++, including the "message-passing" format resulting from the way in which the "methods" – the function members – of a class-instance are invoked by selecting on its name.

Given this, and the all-pervasiveness of the "C culture", it is hardly surprising that C++ has become easily the most popular object-oriented language. In comparison with Smalltalk, still significant as the pioneer in the paradigm, C++, of necessity in view of its hybrid status, is a more conventional language. This is the appropriate term rather than "environment". It does not, currently at least, possess a large, standard class hierarchy, although the standard template library mentioned in Chapter 9 is perhaps indicative of a move in this direction, and it is typically compiled and linked using the underlying C language processor on whatever platform it is found. It should be noted, however, that environments supporting incremental compilation, with large dedicated class libraries, are becoming widely available, and that this tendency might be expected to grow strongly. It is already the case that C++ is the *lingua franca* of object-oriented research and related activities.

As we have seen, the C++ class construct provides, as might be expected, a faithful realization of the class concept, which is central to the object-oriented paradigm. As in Eiffel, and other compiled languages, the

C++ class is essentially a static, source program entity, not an object existing dynamically during program execution.

The additional features that qualify C++ as a true OOPl are concerned with inheritance and (inclusion) polymorphism, and these are discussed in the remainder of this chapter.

13.2 Inheritance in C++

The support for inheritance in C++ is comprehensive and more sophisticated, particularly in its treatment of the visibility of instance variables, than Smalltalk or Ada 95. C++ also supports multiple inheritance.

The declaration of a new class that is intended to inherit from an existing class "claims the inheritance" by nominating the (super) class in its heading. For example, a class **polygon**, intended to inherit from class **shape** might indicate this as follows:

```
class polygon: public shape{
```

The expression introduced by the colon and terminated by " **{** " indicates that **polygon** inherits, or in C++ terminology *is derived*, from **shape**. **Polygon** is referred to as the *derived* class, **shape** as the *base* class, of the derivation. The expression is known as a *derivation list*, and it is the only syntactical difference between a derived and a non-derived class. Classes may be derived from more than one base class, and thus exhibit multiple inheritance, in which case the base class names are separated by commas in the derivation list.

13.2.1 Access levels

The appearance of the keyword **public** in the derivation list indicates that the base class **shape** has a public access level *within* **polygon**. This means that the public members of **shape** are also public members of **polygon**, and so may be accessed via a **polygon** object.

Alternatively, a base class may be declared as having a private access level in a derived class, either by the appearance of the keyword **private** immediately before it in the derivation list, or by the absence of any access level specification – **private** is the default. Note that the scope of an access level specification extends only for one base class name, thus a derivation list such as:

```
class edit_window: public window, text{
```

will confer a private access level on **text** within **edit_window**.

The effect of specifying a base class as having a private access level within a derived class is to make the public members of the base class private in the derived class, i.e. they may be accessed within the class, but not from outside. Given the following declarations:

```
class shape{
        public:
           shape();
           int get_x();
           // etc etc
        private:
           int x, y;
        };
```

```
class polygon: public shape{
```

then **shape::get_x()** may be called on a **polygon** object:

```
                polygon p;
                int xpos;
* * *
                // assign x position of p to xpos
                xpos = p.get_x();
```

If, however, **polygon**'s declaration includes:

```
class polygon: private shape{
```

shape::get_x() is not available to a *user* of a **polygon** object, but it is available within the **polygon** class definition, and so may be used to provide the value indirectly:

```
int polygon::get_x()
               {
                  return shape::get_x();
               }
```

In either case, of course, **shape**'s private members are not available either to a user of **polygon** or to **polygon** itself.

The protected access level

So far we have come across two access levels: public and private. These reflect the binary divide in the world of data abstraction – that between the interface, which is public and available to users, and the implementation, which is private, and known only to the implementor of the abstract data type (class).

Inheritance creates a three-way divide in which the third category is that of the "inheritors" – in effect another type of "user", whose use, however, is *reuse* of the textual code of a class rather than its executable operations. This distinction has been made in terms of *clients*, who are external users of a class, and *heirs*, who inherit from it.

221

OOP languages differ in their view of how privileged an heir should be in being able to access the internal details of its superclass(es). Smalltalk provides complete visibility of the internal structure of a class to its subclasses, and this is one reason why a body of opinion holds that Smalltalk cannot be considered seriously as a software engineering language. The point is that the visibility of a class implementation to its subclasses implies a commitment to maintaining the details of this implementation; otherwise subclasses may become invalidated by changes introduced into the class.

C++ does not provide privileged access to the private members of a class (the equivalents of Smalltalk instance variables and method protocol) to classes derived from it. On the face of it this would seem to be a considerable limitation, in that it precludes access to the underlying data structure of the base class, and thus restricts derived class methods to the same range of possibilities provided for clients of the superclass. There are, so far, two possibilities for overcoming this problem:

1. The entire internal structure of such a base class is made **public**, so that derived classes can access the data structure. In which case encapsulation is thrown away.
2. Encapsulation is maintained, but then derived classes have no special access to the implementation and the possibilities of "programming by difference" are reduced to what is available via the public interface – a restriction that would generally be considered to fall outside what is meant by object-oriented programming.

This limitation is confronted by the introduction of a third access level, *protected*, which is specifically related to inheritance in that protected members are hidden as far as clients are concerned, but visible to heirs. In other words, the protected members of a base class may be accessed from derived classes, but may not be accessed by users of the base class or users of any of its derived classes. If the **shape** class is modified as follows:

```
class shape{
        public:
          shape();
        protected:
          int get_x();
          int get_y();
        private:
          int x, y;
        };
```

the get_x() and get_y functions will not be accesssible to an external user, or client, but will be accessible to a derived class such as **polygon**, and so the version of **polygon::get_x()** shown previously will still work.

The existence of the protected access level is a very powerful feature of

C++ in that it permits the creation of an "internal" interface, for the use of heirs. The implementation of a base class containing such an interface may then be modified without prejudice to classes derived from it, provided the interface is preserved.

13.2.2 Features of inheritance

Under public inheritance, an instance of a derived class provides the public interface of its base class, and the latter's base class, and so on, with only the following exceptions:
- constructors;
- destructors;
- overloadings of the assignment operator.

It should also be noted that inheritance is not overloading, i.e. a member function of a derived class declared with the same name as a member of one of the ancestor classes will hide the inherited function *even though its parameter profile is different*.

Constructors under inheritance

As we saw in Chapter 6 a class constructor is invoked whenever an instance of the class is created. When the class in question is a derived class, an instance of it is also an instance of the base class(es), and so the base class constructor is also invoked. If the class is the result of a number of derivations, then the constructors for all the classes in the "superclass chain" are invoked.

The sequence in which the constructors are invoked is determined by the rule that the constructor for the base class in a derivation is invoked before that for the derived class. Where the base class is itself derived, then the same rule applies, and so the sequence of invocation starts at the highest level in an inheritance hierarchy. If, therefore, a class `quadrilateral` is derived from `polygon`, the sequence of constructor invocations on the creation of a `quadrilateral` object will be:

```
shape
polygon
quadrilateral
```

Parameter passing   In many cases it will be necessary to pass parameter values to the base class constructor invoked at the creation of a derived class object. The only cases where this will not be so are where a default constructor exists *and* the initialization provided by the default constructor is appropriate. The mechanism for passing parameter values to the base class constructor(s), as might be expected, is the member initialization list, with the "function call" comprising of the tag name of the base class followed by the parameter values in parentheses. Where there are several overloadings of the base class constructor, the appropriate one is selected by the particular parameter profile.

As an example, we assume that the **shape** class contains only a pair of data members, interpreted as xy coordinates that in some way define a position for a **shape** object. A **polygon** object contains two vectors of values, **x_offsets** and **y_offsets** containing, respectively, offsets in the x and y directions in relation to the **shape** position, that define the positions of the vertices of the polygon, together with an **int** constant **vrts** holding the number of vertices. The parameters of the **polygon** constructor, accordingly, comprise the xy coordinate values, which are to be passed to the **shape** constructor, the two offset vectors and and a value giving the length of the vectors. The relevant part of the **polygon** constructor might appear as follows:

```
polygon::polygon
  (int rx, int ry, int *vx, int *vy, int vl):
        shape(rx, ry), // pass to superclass
        vrts(vl), // initialize polygon
        x_offsets(new int[vl]), // data
        y_offsets(new int[vl])// members
{
    // etc., etc.
```

An important point to note is that *there is no way of passing parameter values more than one level up* using this mechanism – member initialization lists may contain only class member names or base class names, and the term "base class" means "parent" rather than "ancestor". This means that some care must be taken in ensuring an appropriate pathway exists, from successive derived classes to base classes, to allow for the initialization of classes near the root of the hierarchy. (It might also be added that there is an exception to this rule, discussed in a later section.)

Destructors under inheritance

The order of invocation of destructors when an object of a derived class is destroyed is the reverse of that for constructors – the derived class destructor is invoked, followed by the base class destructor. Where there is a chain of derivations this ordering is preserved up the chain, with the destructor for the root class being invoked last. The invocation of destructors is affected, given appropriate declarations, by polymorphic late binding, but a discussion of this must be postponed briefly to deal generally with polymorphism in C++.

13.3 Polymorphism in C++

We have met polymorphism already in Chapter 11. To recapitulate briefly, polymorphism refers to the ability of an object apparently to possess several types; inclusion polymorphism results from the inheritance of behaviour from a common ancestor class, which is accordingly exhibited by all the descendents of the class. Instances of any of these descendents will exhibit the behaviour, or respond to function calls, defined for the ancestor.

For the same reason, it is valid to pass, say, a **polygon** object to a function that requires a **shape** object, or to allow a variable declared as of the class **polygon** to denote a **quadrilateral** object. Thus it is possible to write polymorphic code.

Returning to the example presented in Chapter 11, a C++ version of the piece of code that accumulates the total area of a collection of shapes is shown below. The **while** loop extracts a sequence of shapes, in the form of pointers to objects that are instances of classes derived from **shape**, from a **collection** class object **bag**.

```
shape *ns;
collection bag;
// etc.
while (ns = bag.next())
    total += ns->area()
```

The function **area()**, which is declared in the **shape** class interface, is inherited by any class derived from **shape**, and so can be called on any of its subclass instances, in this case via the pointer to **shape ns** taking the value returned by the iterator **collection::next()**.

13.3.1 Redefinition and overriding

As we have seen, it is possible to redefine a member function in a derived class, which has the effect of hiding the original declaration. Thus if the declaration of **polygon** is made to include **get_x**, the original version from **shape** will be unavailable on **polygon** or **quadrilateral** objects – in standard OOP terminology it is said to be *overridden*.

Overriding is frequently desirable, in order to take into account the specialization of the subclasses towards the leaves of the inheritance tree. In the case of the shapes hierarchy, it is clear that the **area()** function appropriate to a **square** object can be simplified considerably as compared with that for a **polygon** object. It would be appropriate, therefore, for **area()** to be redefined, at each level in the hierarchy in fact. This is also a practical requirement, as the writing of a general version of **area()** for any geometrical shape is hardly feasible, and we might imagine that the version implemented for **shape** would simply output an error message.

13.3.2 Polymorphic redefinition – virtual functions

We know that variable **ns** may, on any particular iteration of the loop, point to an object that is an instance of any of the classes derived from **shape**. We have now (conceptually) redefined the **area()** function in all the subclasses of **shape**, and we recall from Chapter 11 that late binding, which is fully supported by C++, automatically selects the appropriate version of **area()** for each denotation of **ns**. So that when **ns** is pointing at a **square** object the code for a square area calculation is called, and so on.

Polymorphic redefinition in C++ is achieved by the use of *virtual* functions. A virtual function is declared with the reserved word **virtual** in its first declaration (i.e. at the highest point in the class hierarchy that it appears). Redefinitions *must* exhibit exactly the same parameter profile, but need not repeat the **virtual** keyword, in order to partake in late binding. An appropriate declaration of **area()** would be, therefore:

```
virtual int area();
```

Late binding invocation

An important point to note is that late binding will occur only if the polymorphically redefined function is called via a *pointer* or a *reference*; if the ordinary class selection operator is used "." static binding, i.e. to the version associated with the declared type of the variable, will be carried out. Thus the previous code fragment which invoked area via a pointer would not have worked correctly if the assignment had been written:

```
total += ns.area()
```

This restriction is intended to allow the programmer to avoid polymorphic invocation, with its perceived inefficiency. As the use of pointers is very widespread in C++, it would be entirely natural that the iterator in the example *would* return a pointer to the successive shapes in the collection, and the choice is easy to overlook.

13.3.3 Abstract super classes

It was noted above that the feasibility of writing a "real" version of **area()** for the **shape** class is such as to make it highly impractical. The appearance of the function in **shape** is symbolic only – it is there to ensure that all the classes derived from **shape** provide redefinitions. As such there is no value in providing an implementation, and so it should be declared as being a *pure virtual* function, with no implementation, by extending its declaration as follows.

```
virtual int area() = 0;
```

A pure virtual function *must* be redefined in any class derived from the class in which it appears. If the first declaration of a virtual function is *not* pure, then it must provide an implementation (i.e. a body).

A class declaration that contains a pure virtual function is known as an *abstract super* class. Any attempt to create an instance of an abstract super class is an error – it is intended to define an abstract interface, to which its derived classes will be obliged to conform.

13.3.4 Virtual destructors

The typical use of a destructor is to release heap memory allocated to the object in question by its constructor. The configuration of this memory usage may well be quite distinct in different subclasses derived from a common ancestor. It is important therefore that when **delete** is applied to a pointer variable, ostensibly addressing an ancestor class instance but actually addressing an instance of a derived class, the appropriate destructor is invoked.

This could be arranged by a switch statement with a case for each derived type in the hierarchy, invoking the appropriate destructor either directly or indirectly, assuming that each derived class exports a function member **isA** that returns the name of the class:

```
shape *ps;
* * *
switch (ps->isA())
      {
      case square:
      // direct call to destructor
          ((square*)ps -> square::~square();
          break;
      case polygon:
      // indirect call via delete
          delete (polygon*) ps;
          break;
      // etc.
```

Apart from the rather less than intuitive type casting, this "solution" destroys all the benefits of polymorphic late binding, in "hard-wiring" the particular version of the class hierarchy. Fortunately an alternative is available in the form of virtual destructors, i.e. by the declaration of the destructor of the root class,

```
~shape()
```

in this case, to be virtual. The recognition of the destructors of the derived classes to be correspondingly virtual requires a slight "bending of the rules" because, of course, the names of the destructors of the derived classes are different from **~shape()**. However, the singular nature of destructors allows this to be readily accommodated, and thus they may be invoked polymorphically. In the example this would be achieved by:

delete ps;

provided

shape::~shape()

was declared as

virtual ~shape();

– the effect of late binding being to dispatch the call to the destructor for the class of the object currently addressed by **ps**.

13.4 Multiple inheritance

Following the later "pure" OOPls C++ supports multiple inheritance; any number of base classes may appear in the derivation list of a derived class. The existence of access levels in C++, and their appearance, implicit or otherwise, in derivation lists means that some interesting effects can be achieved. As noted in a previous chapter, multiple inheritance can be used to mix the properties of two or more superclasses, either to produce a common subclass supporting their combined interfaces, or, in a technique that depends on features specific to C++, to separate interface from implementation, in a way that possesses the potential for more flexibility than conventional data abstraction. The technique achieves this by defining a class that inherits its external interface from one superclass, and its implementation from another. If we consider a queue example, the interface can be derived from an abstract class declaring the classical queue interface:

```
class superQ{
            public:
                virtual void enQueue(element) = 0;
                virtual element deQueue() = 0;
                virtual short contains()= 0;
            };
```

The implementation might be essentially array based, but avoid some of the problems arising from a fixed-length structure by using a "circular buffer", i.e. an array with **put** and **get** operations that both auto-increment and "wrap-around". An appropriate class declaration, together with an indication of the implementation is shown in Figure 13.1.

```
class cirBuff{
        public:
            cirBuff(short);
            void put(element);
            element get();
            short contains();
        private:
            element* array;
            element* index;
            element* outdex;
            short length;
            short count;
        };
cirBuff::cirBuff(short len): array(new element[len]), length
            {
                index = outdex = array;
                count = 0;
            }
void cirBuff::put(element val)
            {
                if (index == array + length)
                        index = array;
                *index++ = val;
                count++;
            }
element cirBuff::get()
            {
                element val;
                if (outdex == array + length)
                outdex = array;
                count--;
                val = *outdex++;
                return val;
            }
short cirBuff::contains()
            {
                return count;
            }
```

Figure 13.1 Circular buffer class.

```
// pass parameter up to superclass constructor
queue::queue(short len): cirBuff(len){}

void queue::enQueue(element val)
        {
  put(val);
        }

element queue::deQueue()
{
  return get();
}
short queue::contains()
{
  return cirBuff::contains();
}
```

Figure 13.2   Implementation of queue class.

A concrete queue class might then inherit from both of these, redefining the virtual function members of **superQ**, with a straightforward mapping to the members of **cirBuff**, as shown in Figure 13.2.

If the declaration of **queue** indicates **public** inheritance from the two superclasses, by the derivation list:

```
class queue: public superQ, public cirBuff{
```

the class will possess the unwelcome property of providing the **cirBuff** interface, albeit inherited only, to external clients; this could be used to subvert the FIFO discipline **queue** is intended to support. However, the **cirBuff** interface can be hidden from clients by making the derivation *private*, with a declaration as follows:

```
class queue: public superQ, private cirBuff{
```

The effect of this is to make public members of **cirBuff** private to **queue** – available within the class, but not to its clients – which fits very well the requirements of a distinct and encapsulated implementation. (It might be noted that the following declaration

```
class queue: public superQ, cirbuff{
```

has the same effect, because the default derivation is private. This may not always be what is required.)

The inheritance that **queue** claims from **cirBuff** is the latter's public interface. If it was necessary for **queue** to access the hidden data members of `cirBuff`, say `count`, for example if the `contains()` public member did not exist, then `count` would have to be given a `protected` access level in the declaration of `cirBuff`.

It might be remarked that the use of multiple inheritance to separate interface and implementation in this way avoids the kind of problems mentioned in the last chapter concerned with opposed class and type hierarchies. It also gives a foretaste of the topics of Chapter 15.

13.4.1 Virtual base classes

As we saw in Chapter 11, the use of multiple inheritance can throw up some ambiguities when two (or more) parents of a class themselves possess a common ancestor. In such cases:

- Does the derived class have two copies of the data members of the common ancestor?
- Where redefinitions of function members of the common ancestor occur in more than one subclass chain, which version does the derived class inherit?

C++ provides a clear answer to both these questions.

Multiple copies

In the default case the derived class will possess multiple copies of the data members of the common ancestor – one for each parent involved in the multiple derivation. In some cases this may be what is required, but normally it might be expected that only a single copy would be appropriate. Perhaps rather surprisingly, this requires a special form of derivation, by which the common ancestor is defined as a *virtual* base class by its children. The effect of this is that these child classes contain a pointer to the data members of the ancestor, rather than a copy, so that only one set exists.

Consider a class hierarchy, or rather DAG (Directed Acyclic Graph), with the superclass `vehicle`, from which are derived the subclasses `wheeledVehicle` and `boat`. As amphibious vehicles possess the attributes of both wheeled vehicles and boats the corresponding class might reasonably inherit from both `vehicle`'s subclasses. The avoidance of incorporating two copies of `vehicle`'s data members into instances of `amphibiousVehicle` is achieved by making `vehicle` a virtual base class in each of the derivations of its child classes:

```
class wheeledVehicle: public virtual vehicle{
class boat: virtual public vehicle{
```

(Note that the order of `public` and `virtual` is immaterial.) Although this achieves the desired result, the mechanism possesses the disadvantage of requiring classes such as `boat` to "be aware" of subclasses that may be derived from them, or to require modification with consequent recompiling if such prescience is not available.

Initialization

As we have seen, virtual derivation results in a single set of data members for the ancestor class, which need to be initialized when an instance of one of its descendents is created. When an instance of a derived class is initialized, the components that it inherits are initialized in reverse order, i.e. starting at the remotest ancestor. In each case, under non-virtual derivation, any parameter values required by the parent class constructor are supplied from the initialization list of the child class. In the case of virtual derivation, however, the common ancestor class will have two or more child classes, but only one set of data members, and so the question arises as to which is allowed to supply the initializing values, or is the initialization repeated? In fact, neither is the case – the possibility of ambiguity is avoided by inverting the normal rule, so that initializing values are supplied by the *most derived* class, i.e. the one with the most levels of derivation between it and the common ancestor, rather than an immediate child. In the example, the initialization of **vehicle** would be performed in the initialization list of **amphibiousVehicle::amphibiousVehicle()**.

Alternative overridings

In general, ambiguous references to members of a common ancestor class can be disambiguated by using the scope operator. This is the case both where function members have been given alternative redefinitions by subclasses of the common (virtual) ancestor, and under non-virtual derivation, where two sets of ancestor class data members exist. For example, if **vehicle** was defined as a non-virtual base class, then one set of its data members would be accessible by prefixing them with **wheeledVehicle::**, the other with **boat::**.

The only case where this is unnecessary is when derivation paths of unequal length exist under virtual derivation. If, for example, **boat** and **vehicle** were separated by an intermediate class **nonWheeledVehicle**, then a **vehicle** function member could be called on an instance of **amphibiousVehicle**, unambiguously without the use of the scope operator, following the rule that the most derived version is selected, i.e.

nonWheeledVehicle::*function_name*

13.5 Summary

In this chapter we have discussed the support that C++ provides for the object-oriented paradigm. What is remarkable about the language is that the addition of a comparatively small number of features to an existing, and perhaps rather unpromising, language has resulted in in a comprehensive and, particularly, natural realization of the paradigm. That this should be done in a manner compatible with static (reasonably) strong typing is a great achievement, and a tribute to the ingenuity of the designer of C++, Bjarne Stroustrup.

13.6 Further reading

S. Lippman's and B. Stroustrup's books also cover C++ as an OOPl. We should also mention Stroustrup, *History and design of* C++ (Reading, Mass.: Addison-Wesley, 1993), which explains the way in which C++ was developed, and how its features have attained their current form, complete with examples of where this has not produced an ideal result.

CHAPTER 14

Ada 95

14.1 Introduction

In Chapter 5 Ada was discussed in terms of its very comprehensive support for data abstraction. Ada has recently undergone its first major revision since 1983. The new version is known as Ada 95, in line with a fairly well respected convention using the year of the official recognition (an international standard – ANSI/ISO/IEC-8652:1995 – in this case) a distinguishing mark.

Ada 95, as is to be expected, is almost totally compatible with the earlier version, now known as Ada 83. Certainly the strong support for data abstraction remains unchanged, and all the examples given in Chapter 5 (and Chapter 9) are compatible with both standards. The major external development that has overtaken the Ada 83 standard is undoubtedly the widespread penetration of object-oriented programming and a significant part of the changes in Ada 95 are devoted to retro-fitting aspects of OOP, particularly inheritance and polymorphism, into the language. The style of the retro-fit is oriented towards a practical approach to OOP, specifically intended to support code reuse – programming-by-difference.

14.2 Derived types

Ada 83 provides an embryo version of inheritance – the term is used frequently in the original Ada language reference manual – dependent on *derived types*. In Ada 83 a type may be derived from another, by a declaration of the form:

```
type derived_type is new parent_type;
```

In the Ada 83 language definition a type is defined very clearly, in a manner familiar from Chapter 10, in terms of a set of values together with a set of *applicable operations*. This is a set of values from which a variable or expression of the type may possess one at any particular time, together with a set of procedures and functions possessing one or more formal parameters, or returned expression in the case of a function, of the type concerned. The applicable operations may be *predefined* – supplied by the system, as in the case, for example of "+" for numeric types like **integer** – or they may be user-defined, often within a package exporting the declaration of the type. All types, with the exception of limited private types, are provided with predefined assignment and the test for equality by default.

The effect of the derived type declaration above is to create a new type **derived_type** with a copy of the set of values of **parent_type** and a set of operations *inherited* from it. To give a rather artificial example, the following shows a package exporting type **parent_type**:

```
package parent is
        type parent_type
            record
                field : integer;
            end record;
        procedure set (b : in out parent_type;
                    elem :integer);
end parent;

package body parent is
        procedure set (b : in out parent_type;
                    elem : integer) is
        begin
            b.field := elem;
        end set;
end parent;
```

We may now derive a type from **parent_type**, and add to the applicable operations available to it, as follows:

```
with parent; use parent;
package derived is
        type derived_type is new parent_type;
        function get(d : derived_type) return integer;
end derived;

package body derived is
        function get(d : derived_type) return integer is
        begin
            return d.field;
        end get;
end derived;
```

235

The result is that objects of type **derived** have two applicable operations (in addition to assignment and "**=**"), the function **get** and the procedure **set**, which is inherited from type **parent_type**. On the face of it then this appears to provide the basis for inheritance hierarchies, and thus full object-oriented programming. There are, however, two important limitations affecting derived types in the Ada 83 version:

1. A derived type declaration may not modify the data declaration of the parent type, i.e. no further "instance variables" can be added.
2. If the data structure of the parent of a derived type is protected, for example, the record type that underlies **parent_type** is made private, then this applies to the implementation of the derived type as to any other program unit – a derived type has no privileged access to its parent's private part. If **parent_type** was made private the use of **d.field** in function **get** would not be permitted. Thus the encapsulation of data within objects cannot be combined with inheritance in the Ada 83 model of type derivation.

These shortcomings prevented Ada 83 from being accepted as an object-oriented language. However, the existence of derived types and the limited version of inheritance in the 1983 standard provided a basis for the introduction of the much more complete realization of the object-oriented paradigm that has been incorporated into Ada 95.

14.3 Inheritance in Ada 95 – tagged types

The model of inheritance built into Ada 95 is very clearly implementation orientated, with the main new features of the language being concerned with permitting the *extension* of the underlying data structure in a derived type, while preserving encapsulation. The model assumes a parent type based on a record data structure, which may then have additional fields appended to it, in a derived type, so providing the basis for specialization. No new features are required for operation inheritance, which was already provided for derived types as described above, except to provide access to data structures of the parent types where these are private.

The core of the inheritance model is the *tagged* type. Syntactically, a tagged type is a record type (or a private type implemented as a record type) that contains the reserved word **tagged** in its declaration. Once a type has been declared as tagged, it may be *extended*, or in other words types may be derived from it by adding fields to the original. A type derived from a tagged type is itself tagged, automatically.

For example, a tagged type **figure**, with a very minimal data structure allowing for the specification of the *xy* coordinates of a reference point, might be declared as follows:

```
type figure is tagged
     record
           x_ref : integer;
           y_ref : integer;
     end record;
```

A type `circle` can then be derived from it, extending the data structure to include a radius, as follows:

```
type circle is new figure with
     record
           rad : integer;
     end record;
```

Such a derived type is known as an *extension* of its parent, the term applying to the whole structure, rather than just the new components such as `rad` in the extension `circle`. The new components are referred to as the "record extension part".

The "tagged" terminology derives from the Pascal/Modula-2 variant record usage, where a *tag* field is used to distinguish between variants. In the Ada 95 tagged type model it is envisaged that a number of types may be derived, or inherit, from a tagged root type, creating an inheritance hierarchy, or tree, in a way familiar from, say, Smalltalk. (For example, a `square` type might also be derived from `figure`.) The types within such a hierarchy possess a "family resemblance", which, of course, provides the basis for polymorphism, but the objects declared as instances of the types need to be distinguishable so that late binding can operate. The purpose of the tag in the Ada 95 context is to allow the specific type of an object to be determined at run-time in situations where the object might possess any one of a hierarchy of types. `circle` objects, then, would be distinguished from `square` objects by the possession of different tags. It should be emphasized that the tags are created by the system, rather than the programmer, unlike the case of variant records.

14.3.1 Operation inheritance

As we have seen, every type has a set of operations associated with it, which are either predefined operations or subprograms that *operate on* the type – they are procedure or function subprograms, each of which has at least one formal parameter or returns a value of the type in question. In Ada 95 the set of operations associated with a type includes its *primitive operations* – essentially those "most closely" associated with the type. The primitive operations of a type include those declared in the same declarative region as it (typically in a package specification). The type `figure` might have the following primitive operations:

```
-- set XY reference point values
procedure set_X_ref(X_val : integer; shape : figure);
procedure set_Y_ref(Y_val : integer ; shape : figure);
-- get XY coords of ref point
function X_ref(shape : figure ) return integer;
function Y_ref(shape : figure ) return integer;
-- get area of figure
function area_of(shape : figure) return integer;
```

In the context of inheritance the significance of primitive operations is that the primitive operations of a tagged type are inherited by a type derived from it. In other words, the declaration of a type derived from a tagged type is accompanied by implicit declarations of the tagged type primitive operations, with the derived type substituted for the tagged type. These implicitly declared, inherited operations are then included in the set of primitive operations of the derived type, unless overridden by explicit declarations, so that inheritance may operate through indefinitely many levels of derivation.

Thus, the function **x_ref**, which is a primitive operation of type **figure**, is inherited by the derived type **circle** as:

```
function X_ref(shape : circle) return integer;
```

Further primitive operations may, of course, be declared for the derived type.

14.3.2 Encapsulation

Both tagged types and their extensions may be declared as private (or limited private) so protecting their implementations from client access except through their primitive operations. In each case, the full declaration of the type is given after the **private** heading:

```
package figure_p is

  type figure is tagged private;
  -- set XY reference point values
  procedure set_X_ref
    (X_val : integer; shape : figure);
  procedure set_Y_ref
    (Y_val : integer; shape : figure);
  -- get XY coords of ref point
  function X_ref(shape : figure ) return integer;
  function Y_ref(shape : figure ) return integer;
  -- get area of figure
  function area_of(shape : figure) return integer;
```

```
private
   type figure is tagged
        record
                x_ref : integer;
                y_ref : integer;
           end record;
   end figure_p;

package circle_p is
   type circle is new figure with private;
   procedure set_rad(disc : in out circle);
private
   type circle is new figure with
        record
                rad : integer;
           end record;
```

There are, however, still problems in accessing the private data of the parent. Consider a **square** type derived from **figure**, with an additional point defining the "other end of the diagonal" from the reference point possessed by all **figure**s. The corresponding package specification might look as follows:

```
with figure_p; use figure_p;
package square_p is
   type square is new figure with private;
   procedure set_X_diag
     (shape : square; x_val : integer);
   procedure set_Y_diag
     (shape : square; y_val : integer);
   function area_of(shape : square) return float;
private
   type square is new figure with
     record
             x_diag, y_diag : integer;
         end record;
   end square_p;
```

The primitive operations for type **square** include subprograms to set the value of the "other point", and to read it out. The implementations of these operations require only access to the extension part. The primitive operations also include a redefinition of **area_of**, which will override the function inherited from **figure** – a natural thing to do in view of the simplicity of the square-specific area calculation. This calculation requires access to both specified points – the point defining the end of the diagonal of the square, and the reference point set using the inherited **figure** operations. The latter is hidden from direct access by "client" users, i.e. other program units using the interface defined in the public part of the specification. The coordinates of the reference point are also hidden from any type derived from **figure**. In other words, although an object of type **square** contains **x_ref** and **y_ref** fields, they cannot be accessed directly by an expression of the form **shape.x_ref**. The inherited operations from **figure** are available, however, and so the **x_ref** value can be obtained by **x_ref(shape)**.

As we have seen, it is conventional in object-oriented languages to provide encapsulation for the data structure of an object – its instance variables, as far as clients are concerned – but to allow direct access for subclasses. This is not without problems in so far as maintenance is concerned – the so-called "inheritance breaks encapsulation" problem – but certainly many applications require the operations of a subclass to have access to their superclass data structure. In Ada terms, encapsulation is achieved by the use of private types and yet derived type extensions possess no privileged access to the private structures of their ancestors. It would seem therefore that the derived type mechanism, even with the significant augmentation of tagged types, still provides only a restricted version of inheritance – sufficiently restricted indeed as to be precluded from general use. Specifically, only applications where subclasses can work adequately with the standard client interface can be supported.

If this was the end of the features introduced into Ada 95 to support programming by extension there might well be some question whether the considerable ingenuity expended had been worth the effort. However, a separate but associated new feature – *child* packages – can be combined with tagged type derivation to support fully the conventional object-oriented paradigm.

14.4 Child packages

Ada was designed above all to provide for the writing of secure libraries of software components. Secure in the sense that the syntactical and semantic checking of a program composed from a collection of library units would be as rigorous as if the original sources had been compiled together at the same time; also, because of Ada's powerful support for data abstraction, in being capable of being protected from misuse. In the latter consideration it can be seen that the absolute protection afforded by the package construct, particularly with the use of private types, has been over restrictive, in preventing reuse by programming by difference, or extension.

For this reason the designers of Ada 95 have introduced a means whereby a package can be declared as a "child" of an existing package, with the important result that the private part of the parent is accessible to the child, permitting an alternative version of programming by extension. Syntactically, the declaration of a child package is distinguished by the fact that its name is prefixed by that of its parent, with the usual dot separator, i.e. *parent.child*. For example, if we imagine that the `figure_p` package did not provide operations to read out the reference point coordinates, these could be supplied by a child package, as follows:

```
package figure_p.ex_figure_p is
    function x_ref(shape : figure) return integer;
    function y_ref(shape : figure) return integer;
end figure_p.ex_figure_p;
```

The effect of such a declaration is *as if* the body of the child, `ex_figure_p`, had been declared at the beginning of the body of `figure_p`, and so the contents of the private part of `figure_p` are accessible to it, as can be seen in the following:

```
package body figure_p.ex_figure_p is

    function x_ref(shape : figure) return integer is
    begin
        return shape.x_ref;
    end;
    function y_ref(shape : figure) return integer is
    begin
        return shape.y_ref;
    end;

end figure_p.ex_figure_p;
```

If the child possesses a private part then the parent's private part is accessible within this also.

14.5 Child packages and tagged types

Child packages provide a different form of programming by extension from that of tagged types, essentially concerned with the extension of an existing program structure – a package – rather than a type. The possibility of this different form reflects the looser relationship between the Ada package and types as compared with the C++ class. A package may contain the declarations of a number of types (possibly none), whereas a C++ class defines a type, and thus a child class must define a subtype.

On the other hand, the child package and tagged type mechanisms integrate together in a very natural way, and in such a way as to resolve the apparent restriction referred to above. If the **square_p** package is made a child of **figure_p** then the reference point coordinates contained within the encapsulated details of type **figure** will be accessible to **square_p**'s body, permitting the following implementation of **area_of**:

```
package body figure_p.square_p is
-- type square is new figure with private;

          function area_of(shape : square) return integer
             is
          begin
            return ((shape.x_diag - shape.x_ref) ** 2 +
                    (shape.y_diag - shape.y_ref) ** 2) / 2;
          end area_of;
       end figure_p.square_p;
```

Therefore the combination of tagged types and child packages allows Ada 95 to provide support for the conventional "client/heir" dichotomy of accessibilities in a manner similar to Smalltalk or C++. Perhaps surprisingly Ada 95 does not provide a means to allow the package designer to protect encapsulated entities absolutely, in the manner of the C++ private access level.

14.6 Abstract types and operations

The appearance of the **area_of** function in the specification of **figure_p** means that a corresponding function body must appear in the body of **figure_p**; this is an invariable rule in Ada, which is designed to prevent the calling of non-existent subprograms. The data structure provided for the type **figure** is, of course, inadequate to define anything possessing an area, and so the implementation of **area_of** could return some "impossible" value, perhaps 0. This is rather unsatisfactory, however, as the intention in declaring the tagged type **figure** is not to enable the creation of objects, but to provided a root type for a collection of derived types. In particular, the appearance of **area_of** is intended to impose a commitment on each of these derived types – to provided a redefinition of the function that will provide the area of the "real" shape in each case – not to provide an operation to be called for an object of type **figure**.

These intentions can be more appropriately implemented by making **area_of** an *abstract* operation, by a specification of the form:

```
function area_of
   (shape : figure) return integer is abstract;
```

This indicates that the specification possesses no corresponding body, and is there purely in order to require redefinition in derived types. The non-existence of any implementation for the function means that under no circumstances may an object of type **figure**, of which **area_of** is a primitive function, be created. This must be explicitly specified by making **figure**, in turn, an *abstract type*, resulting in a declaration consisting of a somewhat intimidating string of reserved words:

```
type figure is abstract tagged private
```

Abstract types are, of course, the Ada 95 equivalents of abstract classes in Smalltalk or C++.

As can be seen, it is possible for abstract types to have non-abstract operations, like those concerned with the reference point in **figure**; indeed, they may have no abstract operations at all. The rule still applies, however, that no object of an abstract type may be created.

14.7 Polymorphism – class-wide types

The existence, as a central feature of the object-oriented paradigm, of inheritance hierarchies, brings with it the possibility of (using Wegner's terminology) *inclusion polymorphism*. As we have seen, polymorphism generally refers to the creation of structures or entities capable of dealing with several types. These might be, for example, subprograms capable of handling actual parameters of different types, or program variables capable of denoting values of different types. Inclusion polymorphism depends on the inheritance relationship whereby every descendent of a class possesses at least its characteristics, and so is compatible with it.

At first sight the idea of introducing polymorphism into Ada seems problematic, to say the least. Ada is very strongly typed, to such an extent that the following declarations:

```
ar1 : array (1..10) of integer;
ar2 : array (1..10) of integer;
```

involve two different array types, so that;

```
ar1 := ar2;
```

is illegal. It is also the case that there are very few situations in which type conversions may be applied; interestingly, one of these is between a derived type and its parent. Ada type conversions take the form, of a "function call" like the C++ equivalent, where the "function name" is the target type and the "actual parameter" is the expression to be converted. So given a type **derived** derived from type **parent**, an expression **devex** of type **derived** can be converted to type **parent** by **parent(devex)**.

The primitive operations of a tagged type are, of course, effectively polymorphic, in so far as their parameters of the type are concerned. An object of any of the types within the derived type tree rooted at the tagged type may be supplied as the actual parameter to substitute such a parameter. In our running example a **square** or a **circle** may be substituted for the **figure** parameter of **figure_p.x_ref**, for example. Strictly speaking (hence the use of "effectively" above), this is not polymorphism, as inherited operations are implicitly declared as primitive operations for the derived types, with the tagged type systematically replaced by the derived type in each case.

A more interesting question concerns the possibility of writing a polymorphic non-primitive operation – a procedure or a function, with a parameter of the tagged type, which is not declared within the package where the type is declared. In a language with an approach to typing at the same sort of strength as C++ it would be natural to assume that an object of any type derived from the tagged type could be supplied as an actual parameter to such an operation, by virtue of the "is a" relationship mentioned above. But this is to reckon without Ada's strong typing, and the requirements of compatibility between the Ada 83 and Ada 95 standards.

The motivation underlying the inclusion of derived types in Ada 83 was precisely to allow apparently identical types to be recognized as distinct, so that erroneous mixing of values is flagged by the compiler. To borrow an example from Barnes, given the declarations:

```
type apples is new integer;
type oranges is new integer;
no_of_apples : apples;
no_of_oranges : oranges;
```

the compiler will not allow us to write:

```
no_of_apples = no_of_oranges;
```

Even though the types of the expressions are apparently identical, they are based on separate *copies* of the values of integer.

As a major objective of the Ada 95 revision was to maintain virtually complete compatibility with the Ada 83 standard it was necessary to preserve the distinct nature of derived types. Thus even though a tagged type is based on a record structure that is copied into any of the structures underlying its derived types, it is still a *separate* type, and so the substitution of a derived type object for a tagged type parameter needs an explicit conversion. If we imagine a procedure that outputs the coordinates of the reference point of a **figure**, as follows:

```
procedure print_ref_pt(shape : figure) is
begin
        put("X_ref is ");
        int_io.put( shape.x_ref);
        put(" Y_ref is ");
        int_io.put(shape.y_ref);
        new_line;
end print_ref_pt;
```

(**int_io** is an input/output package for integers.)
   An attempt to call the procedure as follows:

```
disc : circle;
begin
      . . .
        print_ref_pt(disc);
```

would not compile. An explicit type conversion must be used:

```
disc : circle;
begin
      . . .
print_ref_pt(figure(disc));
```

This, of course, is not polymorphism in the sense of having written a procedure capable of handling different types. We are required to convert them
before actually calling the subprogram. It should also be noticed that type
conversions may be carried out only *towards the root* of a tree based on a
tagged type. For example **circle** may be converted to **figure**, but not
vice versa. This is because the ancestors in such a tree do not possess the
extension parts of their descendents, and cannot be converted into them.

   It would seem therefore that Ada's strong typing presents a major
stumbling block to the general use of polymorphism – a significant disadvantage. Once again a new feature of the language is called into play.

14.7.1 Class-wide types

The final component in Ada 95's support for the object-oriented paradigm
is the *class-wide type*. In the Ada context the term "class" is used quite
differently from conventional OOP usage – as used in C++ say – meaning
"the implementation of an abstract data type". In Ada the term is used to
apply to a set of types possessing certain common characteristics. In Ada
83 the idea of the class is not strongly emphasized, being used only with
reference to the distinction between scalar (e.g. integer), composite (e.g.
array), access and private types, etc. The idea is much more strongly developed in Ada 95, with the significant extension, in the context of OOP, that
the tree of types derived from a single root type constitutes a class.

The idea is then developed further with the introduction of a new kind of type altogether – the class-wide type. Like any other type a class-wide type is characterized by a set of values and a set of primitive operations, although the latter, for reasons which will become obvious, is always empty. The set of values of a class-wide type is the discriminated union[1] of all the sets of values of a class of types – specifically of the class consisting of the tree of types derived from a tagged type. In other words, the values of a class-wide type *include* all the values within a tagged type derivation tree, providing the basis for *inclusion* polymorphism.

Class-wide types are not declared as such. Therefore there is no declarative region within which primitive operations may be declared for a class-wide type. Instead, every tagged type automatically has a class-wide type associated with it, the name of which involves the use of the **class** attribute, in conjunction with the name of the tagged type. For example:

```
figure'class
```

This name may then be used like any other type name in declarations of other entities. We may rewrite the profile of the print function, therefore, as:

```
procedure print_ref_pt(shape : figure'class)
```

Because of inclusion polymorphism **figure'class** is compatible with any of the types derived from **figure**, so the following is now correct:

```
disk : circle;
rect : square;
begin
      . . .
      print_ref_pt(disk);
      print_ref_pt(rect);
```

14.7.2 Class-wide objects

Class-wide types represent a new kind of type concept in Ada. (For the sake of completeness it should be noted that Ada 83 possessed *universal* numeric types, which have some features in common with class-wide types.) As we have seen the class-wide type includes the values of a complete class of "conventional" types, which are known as *specific* types. The terminology suggests that class-wide types are in some sense "non-specific". What is being referred to is the fact that at any particular time a class-wide object may possess a value from any one of the value-sets of the specific types "covered" by the class-wide type. The Ada term for this

---

1. In a discriminated union of a number of sets the values retain the identity of the sets from which they originate.

"non-specificity" is *unconstrained* (we met it in Ch. 5 in relation to un-constrained arrays).

The fact that a type is unconstrained affects the freedom with which it may be used to declare entities. There is nothing mysterious about this, the rules simply ensure that the compiler is able to allocate memory in the particular circumstance. A formal parameter may be declared using an unconstrained type because the memory may be allocated for it dynamically – when the call is executed – and the size of the actual parameter is known. On the other hand, the memory for a static object such as a program variable is allocated at compile time, from information given in the object's declaration. Unconstrained types, such as class-wide types, are too non-specific to provide this information. There are two ways of dealing with this:

1. The object declaration may be *initialized* with a value that must be of a specific type, and thus constrains the class-wide object. For example:

```
disk : circle;
. . .
shape : figure'class := disk;
-- shape is now constrained to circle values
```

2. The object may be declared as a pointer to a class-wide object, rather than such an object itself. Pointers, or "access values" in Ada, have a standard size, and present no problem for the allocation of memory.

```
type figure_ptr is access figure'class;
shape_ptr : figure_ptr;
```

Of these alternatives the second is potentially more powerful, allowing as it does, the possibility of an object (indirectly) denoting values from any one of the specific types within a derivation tree – supporting possibilities of abstract, or "class-wide" programming.

14.7.3 Late binding

We have come across late binding in Chapter 11, as an important feature of the object-oriented paradigm. The Ada 95 implementation of late binding is known as *dispatching*, which is, perhaps, slightly more suggestive than the conventional term. Although the dispatching mechanism is not restricted to primitive operations of abstract tagged types it is possibly more straightforward to describe in that context.

If we consider the primitive operations of an abstract tagged type, such as **figure**, each possesses at least one formal parameter, or returned expression in the case of a function, of the type itself. Such a parameter is known as a *controlling* parameter (or controlling result). The question arises as to the nature of the actual parameters or returned expressions that can be supplied when a primitive operation is actually invoked. Clearly, in the case of the primitive operations of **figure**, they cannot be objects of type **figure**, because the abstract nature of the type precludes the creation of **figure** objects. Of course, they must be objects of types within the derivation tree rooted at **figure** – of any of these (non abstract) types in fact. Again, the subprogram body invoked for **area_of** must be from a package other than **figure_p**, because the latter contains no body for the function.

We recollect that the motivation underlying the incorporation of polymorphic late binding into object-oriented languages is essentially to raise the level of abstraction at which programs may be written. So we can write routines in terms of abstractions like **figure**, rather than having to test laboriously, typically in large case statements, for each concrete possibility: **square, circle**, and so on. The set of primitive operations for an abstract tagged type like **figure** provides an abstract interface to be used to manipulate concrete objects that are instances of the types derived from **figure** – it cannot be used to manipulate objects of type **figure** as the abstract nature of the type precludes the creation of such objects. The question then arises as to how objects of specific, concrete types such as **circle** can be manipulated by the abstract interface provided for **figure**.

The answer is via the mediation of the class-wide type, which, as we have seen, characterizes or "covers" the entire derivation tree of the tagged type with which it is associated, *and with which it is compatible for parameter substitution*. An object of a class-wide type may denote a value from any one of the specific types within the derivation tree covered by the type, and may be supplied as an actual parameter for a controlling parameter of a primitive operation of the associated tagged type. As noted previously, the values of a class-wide type comprise the *discriminated* union of the values of all the types within the associated derivation tree, in other words, each value retains the identity of the specific type that possessed it. This identity is referred to as the *tag* of the value – hence the nomenclature of tagged types, which are types whose values are tagged to retain their identification when "submerged" within an associated class-wide type. The purpose of tagging is to support dispatching – the invocation of the appropriate redefinition of a primitive operation of a tagged type, i.e. the redefinition for the derived type identified as the original source of the value of the class-wide object.

In terms of **figure** this means that the **area_of** function, which has a formal parameter of type **figure**, can accept an actual parameter of type **figure'class**, which may "actually" be a **circle**. The effect of dispatching will be to invoke the version of **area_of** declared in **circle_p**. We may use the flexibility of dispatching to extend the **print_ref_pt** procedure to output the area of its parameter, without the need to test for the specific type of the parameter, as follows:

```
procedure print_ref_pt(shape : figure'class) is
begin
        put("X_ref is ");
        int_io.put( shape.x_ref);
        put(" Y_ref is ");
        int_io.put(shape.y_ref);
        put(" area is ");
        int_io.put(area_of(shape));
        new_line;
  end print_ref_pt;
```

This example shows the two quite distinct applications of class-wide types:
1. *for writing class-wide operations*, i.e. by using **figure'class** as the formal parameter type, thus allowing substitution by any type derived from **figure**;
2. *for invoking dispatching* by passing the class-wide object **shape** to the controlling parameter of the primitive operation **area_of** of **figure**.

Late binding, or dispatching, is *only* implemented when the call involved possesses this latter configuration, when the call is to a primitive operation of a tagged type, and the actual parameter supplied for the controlling parameter(s) of the operation is an object of a class-wide type. Other combinations do not invoke dispatching, and therefore may be used to avoid the (relatively small) overheads involved.

14.8 Controlled types

In Chapter 6 Ada's provision for the initialization of abstract data type objects was compared unfavourably with those of the C++ constructor mechanism. Ada, in the 1983 version, does provide discriminants, which can be used to supply size information for the declaration of such an object. But there is no way in which initialization involving the execution of statements, for example to create an initial linked list structure, can be effected by discriminants.

Ada 95 has gone some way towards resolving this shortcoming, although in a manner that requires the use of inheritance, and thus is, strictly speaking, not relevant to purely object-based programming. The basis of the mechanism is a standard library package **ada.finalization**, which exports two abstract tagged private types, **controlled** and **limited_controlled**. As its name suggests, **limited_controlled** is a limited private type. Both types have the primitive operations **initialize** and **finalize** (Ada is still an American language despite its intellectual provenance, hence the spelling). Redefinitions of these procedures are called automatically when an object of a type derived from **controlled/ limited_controlled** is declared, or created by an allocator, or destroyed, and thus perform a function analogous to that of constructors and destructors in C++. Figure 14.1 shows the use of **limited_controlled** to permit the specification of an appropriate initialization, supplied as a redefinition of **initialization**, for a doubly-linked list.

In addition to **initialize** and **finalize, ada.finalization** exports a procedure called **adjust**, with the same parameter profile as the other two. **Adjust** is called automatically in conjunction with an assignment to a variable of a **controlled** subtype. (As assignment is not permitted for variables that are **limited, adjust** is provided only for **controlled** variables.) When an assignment is made to such a variable, **finalize** is called first to allow for the tidying up of the object that is to be overwritten – and thus undergoes deletion – the source object is copied across to the target of the assignment, and then **adjust** is called to perform any rectification of the target that may be required. In the case of a pointer-connected structure such as **list** in Figure 14.1 the copy operation would apply only to the **anchor** pointer, and so **adjust** would need to construct a list structure with the same configuration as the source object, and copy across the node data values. **Adjust** performs a function similar to that of the copy constructor in C++.

The inclusion of controlled types in Ada 95 represents a significant raising of the level of abstraction supported by the language. It is no longer necessary to rely on the user to remember to call operations to deal with the life-cycle events of objects, or their assignment. It may be objected that the mechanism is slightly cumbersome, requiring the use of inheritance where it may not otherwise be involved. However, the obligation to inherit from **ada.finalization** may be compared with the similar obligation to inherit from *Object* in Smalltalk.

14.9 Summary

The retro-fitting of the major elements of the object-oriented paradigm into Ada represents a considerable achievement, particularly in that the strong typing of the original language has been preserved. It would be difficult to argue that the resulting implementation of the paradigm possesses the intuitive appeal of that supported by its main rival, C++. However, the proponents of Ada assert, with some justification, that this appeal is based on foundations that are less than secure, in areas such as the default activities the C++ system performs "under the surface", and the lack of a secure library system.

It is also the case that the objectives of Ada development are very clearly aimed at the provision of a facility for reuse, through programming by

```
with ada.finalization;  use ada.finalization;
generic
type element is private;
package list_p is
    type list is new controlled with private;
    procedure insert(this : element);
--
-- other list operations
--
-- redefine initialize
    procedure initialize(nulist: in out list);
private
    type node;
    type node_ptr is access node;
    type list is new controlled with
            record
                anchor: node_ptr;
            end record;
end list_p;

package body list_p is
    type node is record
                    left, right : node_ptr;
                        data : element;
                    end record;
    procedure initialize(nulist: in out list) is
-- redefinition of finalization.initialize
        begin -- create new node and anchor it
            nulist.anchor := new node;
            -- left and right point to self
            nulist.anchor.left := nulist.anchor;
            nulist.anchor.right:= nulist.anchor;
        end initialize;
        -- rest of implementation
```

Figure 14.1 Use of a controlled type to permit initialization.

difference, and compatibility between the two language standards – Ada
83 and Ada 95 – which has been achieved to a very high degree, was of
great importance.

14.10 Further reading

Ada 95 is documented in the International Standard ANSI/ISO/IEC-8652:1995 *Ada 95 reference manual* (the "ARM"), together with the less formal *Ada 95 rationale*, which contains introductory and explanatory material. Both are published by Intermetrics Inc. and are available from Ada Language (UK) Ltd. One of the major contributors to the *rationale*, and to the design of Ada 95, was J. G. P. Barnes, who has updated his *Programming in Ada*, retitled as *Programming in Ada 95* (London: Addison Wesley, 1996) to cover the revised language.

CHAPTER 15

Inheritance as an abstraction mechanism

15.1 Introduction

In the development and exploitation of the object-oriented paradigm a number of quite distinct views or motivations have become apparent. Roughly speaking these are alternative answers to the question "why use object-oriented techniques, particularly object-oriented programming?" They may be characterized as follows:

- because it is the natural way of implementing designs produced by a sequence of object-oriented analysis and design (OOA – OOD);
- because it provides for software reuse in a natural, flexible yet disciplined way;
- because it provides an extremely powerful tool for abstraction in the construction of programs.

Of these, the third is perhaps the most recent to have emerged. Accordingly, it has received less exposition than the other two, and yet it is arguably as important. For this reason, and because it provides a structural recapitulation of one of the major themes of this book – abstraction – it forms the subject of this final chapter.

The essential basis of the use of inheritance as an abstraction mechanism lies in the substitutability of subclass instances for variables or parameters of the superclass, and also the interchangeability of different subclasses of a common superclass. This provides for a higher level of abstraction than that supported by data abstraction, where a class may provide an abstract interface to a whole hierarchy of subclasses, with the correct association of operation invocation and implementation ensured by polymorphic overriding. This allows the separation of implementation from interface to be developed to the extent, for example, of having alternative implementations for a particular interface installed dynamically during program execution.

The flexibility and power that this kind of approach gives to the program design process has led to the development of a new area of research, that of *design patterns*. Briefly, a design pattern is a structure of class placeholders linked together – either by inheritance or reference where one class contains, as an instance variable, a pointer to the other class – in order to provide the solution to a characteristic program design problem. Note that the nodes in such a structure are class place-holders, which are replaced by specific classes determined by the domain of each application in which the pattern is used. A recent book by Gamma et al. provides a description of 23 such patterns, to some extent following the work of Coplien. We will not attempt to provide an exhaustive survey here, but rather give some significant examples together with a discussion of the principles involved. Generally, the examples are illustrated with C++ code, following the convention found in the growing body of literature on this subject. In some instances Ada 95 alternatives are also given.

15.2 Alternative implementations

As the possibility of providing alternative implementations for an abstract data type has been mentioned, the first example will consider such an arrangement. Again the ubiquitous stack provides a tolerably realistic example, where there are two clear alternative data structures on which to base an implementation – the array and the linked list. Apart from the way in which their elements are physically connected together, these structures differ in their mode of memory occupancy – the array being of a fixed, or *bounded*[1] size, while the linked list is of a variable and indefinite size, or *unbounded*. In particular applications these characteristics may be significant, and so the provision of both implementations, perhaps within a class library, would be reasonable.

The interface supported by both implementations would, of course, be identical: the standard "classical" stack interface. This is enshrined within a class declaration, specifically of an *abstract* class intended purely to define this standard interface. The two alternative implementations are then defined as subclasses of this abstract class. Three appropriate C++ declarations are shown in Figure 15.1. At the risk of stating the obvious, this simple arrangement decouples the alternative implementations from the standard interface so that the remainder of the program need be entirely unaware of which particular subclass is installed. Of course yet another implementation could be added, by declaring a new subclass, without the need to modify the existing program, or even recompile it.

15.2.1 Builders

This arrangement requires the user to "know about" the implementations of the two concrete subclasses of **stack**, which are visible, to a certain

---

1. The bounded/unbounded categorization is a significant feature in Booch's *Software components*.

```
class stack{
        public:
        virtual void push(element) = 0;
        virtual element pop() = 0;
        virtual int isempty() = 0;
        };
class arrayStack : public stack{
        public:
        arrayStack(unsigned size);
        void push(element);
        element pop();
        int isempty();
        private:
        element* store;
        element* TOS;
        };
class listStack : public stack{
        public:
        listStack();
        void push(element);
        element pop();
        int isempty();
        private:
        struct node{
                    element val;
                    node* next;
                    };
        node* head;
        );
```

Figure 15.1 Stack class hierarchy.

extent at least, in their respective declarations. For example, in an application where the required stack size is well known to be less than 10 elements, something along the following lines would be required:

```
stack * stptr = new arrayStack(10);
```

In fact a knowledge of the existence of the implementation subclasses should be unnecessary – the user should need to know only the standard interface and the existence of the bounded/unbounded variants. This can be provided for by encapsulating the details of the hierarchy within another class, known as a *builder*. Such a class provides a `createStack` function, which returns a pointer to the required kind of stack, as determined by the user selecting a bounded or unbounded stack – perhaps providing a non-zero size for bounded, 0 otherwise.

```
class stackBuilder{
                public:
                   stack* createStack(unsigned size);
                };
stack* stackBuilder::createStack(unsigned size)
                {
                   if (size == 0)
                        return new listStack;
                   else return new arrayStack(size);
                }
```

The existence of the common superclass `stack` permits `createStack()` to return a pointer to either `listStack` or `arrayStack`.

15.2.2 Separate implementation hierarchies – the bridge

A further development in abstracting away implementation details, with important possibilities that can only be hinted at in this simple example, is to separate the implementation into a parallel hierarchy. To change the example slightly, we may imagine a queue class (first in first out list). Once again we have the possibility of implementations based on an array or a linked list. Using the so-called *bridge* design pattern the implementation subclasses inherit from an abstract implementation class, `Q_imp`, rather than from `queue` – the class that serves to define the client interface. The `queue` class possesses a pointer to a `Q_imp` object, converting calls to its member functions to calls on the `Q_imp` object. The `Q_imp` interface must obviously provide sufficient functionality to support `queue`, but need not be identical. It might well provide for a general "end-access" structure, as follows:

```
class Q_imp{
            public:
                virtual void addAtLeft(element) = 0;
                virtual void addAtRight(element) = 0;
                virtual element getLeft() = 0;
                virtual element getRight() = 0;
                virtual unsigned contains() = 0;
            };
```

This abstract class possesses (at least) two subclasses `listQimp` and `arrayQimp` providing, respectively, list and array based implementations.

The `queue` class interface is standard, as follows:

```
class queue{
        public:
          queue(unsigned size);
          void insert(element);
          element take();
          int isEmpty();
        private:
          Q_imp* imp;
        };
```

Note that the visible data structure is now, rather in the manner of a Modula-2 opaque type, reduced to a pointer. The implementation of the class is shown, incompletely, below:

```
queue::queue(unsigned size)
          {
          if (size == 0)
          imp = new listQimp;
          else imp = new arrayQimp(size);
          }
void queue::insert(element val)
          {
          imp->addRight(val);
          return 0;
          }
int queue::isEmpty()
          {
          return (imp->contains() == 0);
          }
```

This implementation requires the interface class **queue** to "know about" the implementation hierarchy, so as to be able to choose between the concrete implementation subclasses **listQimp** and **arrayQimp**. We could have avoided this by the use of a separate builder class as in the previous example.

The separation of the client interface from the implementation hierarchy permits the independent development of either. For example, we might introduce a subclass of **queue** to provide the functionality of a *dequeue*, that is a queue permitting elements to be extracted from both ends – a combined stack and queue in fact. This is a straightforward extension of the standard **queue** interface, with a declaration as follows:

```
class dequeue : public queue
          {
          public:
            element pop()
          };
```

Of course the implementation of this additional function depends on the corresponding functionality of the `Q_imp` class:

```
element dequeue::pop()
            {
            return imp->getRight();
            }
```

The separation of the interface from the implementation hierarchies avoids the combinatorial multiplicity of subclasses that would otherwise be needed – **dequeue** would require its own list and array subclasses, as would any further extension of the queue interface. The avoidance of "subclass explosions", which create significant problems in OOP applications, is also a feature of the next pattern.

15.3 Dynamically extending interfaces – object composition

A standard characterization of type inheritance is that of extension – of the interface defining the type – by the addition of operations in the subtype interface. In some applications, however, the number of interface extensions is relatively large, and they are not obviously related by the inheritance relationship. A common example is the window, characteristic of GUI systems. Such systems invariably support many different kinds of window – with alternative borders, scrolling, editing, etc. Importantly, these "kinds" behave more like attributes of a basic window type, rather than distinct subtypes, particularly in that there is generally a requirement to compose several of these attributes (to "mix and match" them) on an *ad hoc* basis in different window instances.

This requirement can be met, using a conventional approach to inheritance, only by providing alternative subclass chains to allow for all the possible combinations – leading to an unacceptable explosion of classes. An alternative approach employs *object composition* in order to add dynamically the interface extensions corresponding to each attribute, which are "wrapped around" an existing object. Accordingly, the associated design pattern is known as a *wrapper* or *decorator*.

The technique relies on an inheritance hierarchy, but a relatively simple one consisting, in this example, of the abstract window superclass, together with two subclasses derived directly from this superclass. One of these provides the interface and implementation for the "plain vanilla" window; the other is the common parent of a set of "attribute" child classes – one each for bordered window, scrolling window, etc. The relationships are shown by the skeleton declarations in Figure 15.2, which shows some implementation details in the form of inline functions, for the sake of compactness.

```
class window{ // abstract superclass
          public:
              virtual void display() = 0;
              *    *    *

class plainWindow : public window
          { // plain ''vanilla'' window
          public:
              void display();
              *    *    *

class attribute : public window
          { // parent for 'attribute' subclasses
          public:
              attribute(window* wptr){winp = wptr;}
              void display(){winp->display;}
              *    *    *
          private:
              window* winp;
          };
class borderWin : public attribute
          {
              borderWin(window* wptr) : attribute(wptr){}
              void display(){attribute::display();
                           // then draw border
              *    *    *
```

Figure 15.2   Wrapper pattern hierarchy.

The **attribute** class supports the functionality inherited from **window** by possessing a pointer-to-**window** instance variable. **Attribute**'s constructor requires a pointer-to-**window** parameter to initialize this variable, which will in practice take the form of a pointer to **plainWindow**, being the only class capable of instantiating "real" stand-alone window objects. **Attribute** *forwards* all calls to the standard window interface to this embedded **plainWindow**, as shown in the implementation of **attribute:** **:display**. In this way, **attribute** maintains a transparent interface – any code making calls to a **plainWindow** object will work equally well with an **attribute** object. In fact, **attribute** objects are never called directly by clients, but indirectly via the attribute subclasses, such as **borderWin**. As can be seen, **borderWin**'s constructor also takes a pointer-to-**window** parameter, but this is used to initialize the **attribute** object on which a **borderWin** object is based. This is used to support the standard interface via inheritance, as calls are made on the **borderWin** object wrapped around the **attribute** object with its embedded **window**. For example, **borderWin::display()** invokes **attribute::display()**, before displaying the "border".

Object composition might perhaps be more specifically called "constructor composition", in that a composite object is created by supplying the appropriate constructor with a pointer to an object on which it is to be based. For example, given a **plainWindow** declaration:

```
plainWin* pwptr = new plainWin;
```

the **plainWindow** object pointed at by **pwptr** can be dynamically enhanced into a scrolling window by the following:

```
scrollWin * swptr = new scrollWin(pwptr);
```

which wraps a scrolling interface "skin", around the original **plainWindow**. **Swptr** could then be used wherever a **plainWindow** pointer is required, but can also support scrolling.

A further composition could then be applied to produce a bordered window:

```
borderWin* bswptr = new borderWin(swptr);
```

it should be noted, however, despite the example given in Gamma, that the scrolling interface will not be available via **bswptr** – inevitably, because **bswptr** points to a **borderWin** object, which does not support such an interface. The scrolling interface associated with the composite object can, however, still be accessed via **swptr**. In other words, it is necessary to retain a named object (pointer) to provide a "view" of each of the skins wrapped around a composite object – composition is not inheritance, and does not "compose" interfaces.

An equivalent Ada 95 implementation uses discriminants to allow for the parameterization of one object by another, or rather a pointer to another object, to effect composition. In appearance, this results in code looking not too dissimilar from the C++ version.

The implementation provides for the same type hierarchy, but realized as a tagged type class declared over a corresponding structure of packages. The basis of the pattern – the use of a pointer to an instance of one of the subtypes of **attribute**, to act as the "onion core" around which the skin of another attribute subtype can be wrapped – is clearly dependent on the class-wide type **window'class**, or more specifically, an access (pointer) type with **window'class** as its designated type. This type is given to the discriminant declared for all the members of the derived type tree rooted on **attribute**, effectively as a "parameter" to the type declaration in each case. It can be specified as a named type, or as an "access discriminant", i.e.

an expression of the form *name*: **access window'class** in which case any access type with the designated type **window'class** can be supplied. This has the advantage that the wrapper pattern structure can be added to an existing hierarchy without the need to include a declaration of a named access type, which would have to be declared at the root of the hierarchy, e.g. at **window**, thus requiring its modification and recompilation (unless the package designer was unusually percipient). The use of an access discriminant requires that **window** is a limited type, i.e. not provided with assignment by default, but this might be expected to be standard for the majority of tagged types.

The root of the hierarchy is the abstract type **window**, which both provides the standard interface, inherited by the "real" and "attribute" subtrees, and, by its class-wide type, the link between them.

```
package win_p is
-- root of window tree
--
    type window is abstract tagged limited private;
    procedure display(win : window) is abstract;
--
--       other subprogram declarations
--
private -- declare null data structure
    type window is abstract tagged limited null record;
end win_p;
```

Window possesses two type extensions, or child subtypes, **plain_win** and **attribute**. **Plain_win** provides a concrete type, which can be instantiated to produce "real" windows.

```
package win_p.plain_win_p is
--
    type plain_win is new window with private;
    procedure display(win : plain_win);
private
    type plain_win is new window with
        record
            -- implementation details
    * * *
```

Type **attribute** is the parent of the various "attribute" subtypes for bordered, scrollable, etc., windows. Its access discriminant **disc** provides it with a pointer to a **plain_win** object, to which calls on the standard interface are forwarded:

```
package win_p.att_p is
--
    type attribute(disc : access window'class) is
                    new window with private;
    procedure display(comp : attribute);
private
    type a_window_class is access all window'class;
    type attribute(disc : access window'class)
        is new window with
        record
            win_ptr : a_window_class := disc;
            -- other components
        end record;
end win_p.att_p;
```

Note that a named access type designating **window'class** is necessary to declare the pointer **win_ptr**; also the form **access all**, which is an Ada 95 development, allowing pointers to objects declared conventionally, i.e. not created by an allocator. This pointer is used to forward calls to the standard interface; for example the body of **display** might contain the following:

```
procedure display(win : attribute} is
begin
    display(win.win_ptr.all);
end display;
```

The expression **win_ptr.all** denotes an object of the class-wide type **window'class**, and thus the call to the procedure **display** is dispatching, invoking the corresponding operation on the underlying **plain_win** object pointed at by **win.win_ptr**.

The subtypes of **attribute** are similarly declared with an access discriminant, which is used to elaborate the underlying **attribute** object:

```
package win_p.attribute_p.border_win_p is
    type border_win(disc : access window'class) is
            new attribute(disc) with private;
    procedure display(win: border_win);
    -- other operations
private
    -- implementation details
    * * *
```

The body of **display** for **border_win** calls the **attribute** version to invoke the standard operation, before drawing the border:

```
procedure display(win : border_win) is
begin
        win_p.att_p.display(attribute(win));
        -- draw border
        --
end display;
```

Note that that the **border_win** parameter must be converted to an **attribute** by specific type conversion before being passed to the version of **display** for **attribute**.

As remarked above, the code using this pattern to create dynamically the decorated objects resembles the C++ equivalent quite closely:

```
type a_window_class is access window'class;
type a_plain_win is access plain_win;
type a_border_win is access border_win;
type a_scroll_win is access scroll_win;
wptr : a_window_class := new plain_win;
bwptr : a_border_win;
swptr : a_scroll_win;
begin
        * * *
        display(wptr.all); -- plain window
        -- wrap it with a border
        bwptr := new border_win(wptr);
        display(bwptr.all);
        -- wrap with scrolling interface
        swptr := new scroll_win(bwptr);
        -- standard interface still operative
        display(swptr.all);
        * * *
```

15.4 Recursive data structures – composites

Many applications require the modeling of structures that are assemblies of substructures, each of which is a structure in its own right and is an assembly of substructures . . . and so on, until an "atomic" or "primitive" level is reached. There are many diverse examples, from mechanical assemblies such as automobile engines, to constructs in programming languages. From the standpoint of programming methodology the techniques for modeling these kinds of structures are well known, invariably involving the use of tree data structures. Trees provide a natural way of maintaining the relationships between elements within hierarchies; there are, however, some problems in obtaining an appropriate level of abstraction in providing for general operations capable of being applied to an arbitrary subtree, because of the possibility that such a subtree may be a *leaf*, i.e. have no descendants.

To borrow an example from Gamma, graphics application domains frequently exhibit the kind of recursive structure described above. Graphics entities may be composed, often by user interaction, of fairly arbitrary collections of shapes and text, and may themselves be combined into higher level entities. A natural requirement is for the entities at any level to provide a uniform interface, for example to draw (themselves) or to be moved. A "uniform interface" suggests immediately a suitable subject for inheritance – an abstract class supporting such an interface can be defined, from which entity subclasses may be derived, each obliged to redefine the abstract operations, ensuring the uniformity of the interface.

The problem with this arrangement is that it is a static hierarchy – as are all inheritance hierarchies defined in a statically typed language such as Eiffel, C++ or Ada 95. Yet the hierarchical structures generated in our graphics application are generally dynamic – created during program execution in response to user interaction – and so the straightforward use of an inheritance hierarchy is of comparatively little use. The problem is rather reminiscent of that which led to the devising of wrapper classes, and its solution, unsurprisingly, possesses similarities to them.

The essential feature of the solution, a pattern known as a *composite*, is, as usual, an abstract general interface-defining superclass, from which is derived a number of subclasses for "standard" entities – text items, geometrical shapes, etc., which will be leaves on the dynamically created tree, *plus* a general "graphics aggregate" subclass. The latter allows for the dynamic construction of aggregate entities by supporting an interface permitting the addition of "child" entities to the aggregate, and allowing the children to be extracted individually, for example to be removed. The instance variables that record the children of an aggregate, which are maintained within an appropriate structure such as a list, are pointers to the superclass so that child entities may either be aggregates themselves, or primitive "standard" items. Thus the recursive definition within the inheritance hierarchy provides for the dynamic generation of recursive structures. Importantly, the superclass interface contains both the "standard" subclass interfaces and the "aggregate" interface, providing for the desired uniformity. The salient features of such an interface, for a graphics application, are shown below:

```
class grafItem{ // composite superclass
        public:
            // standard component interface
            virtual void draw() = 0;
            virtual void move(int dx, dy) = 0;
            // * * *
```

```
    // aggregate -- child management interface
    // addChild incorporates child object into
  // aggregate returns unsigned identifier
  // for child passed as pointer to graphicsItem
    virtual unsigned addChild(grafItem* kidPtr);
    // return number of children
    virtual unsigned childCount();
    // remove child
    virtual void removeChild(unsigned kidno);
    * * *
```

The aggregate class **grafAggregate** will provide redefinitions of the complete interface, the **grafAggregate::draw()** function implementation, for example, calling the **draw()** functions of its children, recursively in the case of child aggregates. Pointers to the children are held in a list structure.

```
class grafAggregate: public grafItem
    {
    public:
      grafAggregate();
      // standard component interface
      void draw();
      void move(int dx, dy);
      // * * *
      // child management interface
      unsigned addChild(grafItem* kidPtr);
      unsigned childCount();
      void removeChild(unsigned kidno);
    private: // list data structure to hold
            // children
      struct node{
                node* next;
                grafItem* chptr;
                };
      node* kids;
      unsigned count;
    };
```

By contrast, the subclasses for the "standard" items will not redefine the **graphicsItem** functions, such as **addChild()**, that are concerned specifically with aggregates. Instead they are allowed to inherit the versions from **grafItem**, which provide default "null behaviour", or possibly raise an error status, because the standard items cannot possess child entities. Hence these member functions are not declared as abstract in the declaration of **grafItem**.

If we assume standard leaf classes such as **textItem** and **lineItem**, an arbitrarily complex display could be built up dynamically and displayed by code such as the following:

```
grafItem* txp = new textItem;
grafItem* lip = new lineItem;
grafItem* agp1 = new grafAggregate;
grafItem* agp2;
* * *
agp1 -> addChild(txp);
agp1 -> addChild(lip);
agp2 = new grafAggregate;
agp2 -> addChild(agp1);
agp2 -> addChild(txp);
agp2 -> draw();
```

An Ada 95 version of this composite is sketched below.

```
package graf_item_p is

type graf_item is abstract tagged limited private;
type a_graf_item_class is access graf_item'class;

-- standard graphics item interface
procedure draw(this : access graf_item) is abstract;
procedure move(this : access graf_item;
               dx, dy : integer) is abstract;

-- child management interface
procedure add_child(to : access graf_item;
                    kid: a_graf_item_class);
-- etc.
```

This implementation uses the Ada 95 feature of *access parameters*, which can be substituted by any access type with the specified designated type (**graf_item** in the above example) in a way reminiscent of access discriminants. Significantly, subprograms declared within the same region as a type, with access parameters that designate the type (such as **draw**) are primitive operations for the type and the access parameters are dispatching. This is convenient in this type of application, where the dynamic nature of the structures make the use of allocators, and therefore pointers, natural.

The specification of the package declaring the aggregate type is shown in Figure 15.3. It will be seen that both the wrapper and composite patterns utilize the inheritance relationship in the inverse direction to that conventionally used – in order to construct an artificial abstract superclass,

```
package graf_item_p.aggregate_p is

    type graf_aggregate is new graf_item with private;

    procedure draw(this : access graf_aggregate) ;
    -- etc.
    procedure add_child(to : access graf_aggregate;
                        kid: a_graf_item_class);

    -- etc.
private
    type node;
    type node_ptr is access node;
    type node is record
                      child_ptr : a_graf_item_class;
                             next: node_ptr;
                 end record;
    type graf_aggregate  is  new graf_item with
                 record
                      count : natural := 0;
                      kids : node_ptr;
                 end record;
end graf_item_p.aggregate_p;
```

Figure 15.3 Package specification including aggregate type.

amalgamating dissimilar classes, rather than producing extensions, or specializations, as subclasses of an existing class.

15.5 Summary

In this chapter we have seen a number of examples of design patterns. All involve significant features of the object-oriented paradigm, particularly inheritance and its associated form of polymorphism, together with the late binding that the latter confers. As mentioned at the start of the chapter, these patterns represent a new area of application for the paradigm. They are not inspired by the universality of the "specialization" relationship, which, it is claimed, is a fundamental and natural way of categorizing real-world entities – they are largely concerned with "program objects", and such specialization that they do involve is extended over quite shallow hierarchies. Again, they are not generally related to "programming by difference", seen as a process essentially occurring over a sequence of events in time. Most of the patterns might be expected to be installed as a complete structure, although the extensibility characteristic of the use of late binding certainly supports incremental development.

The essential commonality in the design patterns is the use of polymorphism – inclusion polymorphism – together with the polymorphic overriding and late binding that is enabled by it. This introduces another level of abstraction, or, another dimension for decoupling, which reduces the problems of software development, particularly those arising from the continuing enhancement/modification characteristic of all non-trivial software systems. OOP provides another, or extended, tool in the quest for abstracting away commitments impacting on new or changed requirements, and causing cost/time overruns with depressing regularity.

There is the glimmering here of a new "hiding" methodology, to be compared with the "information hiding" that led to the recognition of data abstraction, following functional abstraction, as a significant technique. Data abstraction emphasizes the separation of interface from implementation and, indeed, the primacy of the former in terms of significance to programming in the large. However it says little about the nature of interfaces, other than that they should be as uncommitted as possible to their underlying implementations. The new methodology, depending on inheritance and polymorphism, we might term "interface abstraction". It is concerned with the construction of abstract interfaces, permitting the derivation of multiple compatible concrete interfaces from them. As such it represents a further level of decoupling of interface and implementation. Such abstract interfaces provide the possibility of enabling non-disruptive change by virtue of the fact that they permit the abstracting away of precisely those areas where change can be predicted. The "pluggability" of components supporting concrete interfaces, identified as a desirable objective in Chapter 1, is then greatly enhanced by the operation of polymorphic overriding, selecting dynamically the correct concrete instance matching a particular abstract interface.

We see then, that despite the apparently esoteric nature of the object-oriented paradigm, it represents the latest, and as yet most powerful, stage on a path leading directly from considerations of software design quality, via modularity, data abstraction and object-based programming.

15.6 Further reading

The main influence on this chapter is E. Gamma, R. Helm, R. Johnson, J. Vlissides, *Design patterns: elements of reusable object-oriented software* (Reading, Mass.: Addison-Wesley, 1995). A more detailed treatment of some of the issues raised is contained in J. Coplien, *Advanced C++ : programming styles and idioms* (Reading, Mass.: Addison-Wesley, 1992).

Index